Vivian by Maria Edgeworth

Maria Edgeworth was born at Black Bourton, Oxfordshire on January 1st 1768. Her early years were with her mother's family in England. Sadly, her mother died when Maria was five.

Maria was educated at Mrs Lattafière's school in Derby in 1775. There she studied dancing, French and other subjects. Maria transferred to Mrs Devis's school in Upper Wimpole Street, London. Her father began to focus more attention on Maria in 1781 when she nearly lost her sight to an eye infection.

She returned home to Ireland at 14 and took charge of her younger siblings. She herself was home-tutored by her father in Irish economics and politics, science, literature and law. Despite her youth literature was in her blood. Maria also became her father's assistant in managing the family's large Edgeworthstown estate.

Maria first published 1795 with 'Letters for Literary Ladies'. That same year 'An Essay on the Noble Science of Self-Justification', written for a female audience, advised women on how to obtain better rights in general and specifically from their husbands.

'Practical Education' (1798) is a progressive work on education. Maria's ambition was to create an independent thinker who understands the consequences of his or her actions.

Her first novel, 'Castle Rackrent' was published anonymously in 1800 without her father's knowledge. It was an immediate success and firmly established Maria's appeal to the public.

Her father married four times and the last of these to Frances, a year younger and a confidante of Maria, who pushed them to travel more widely: London, Britain and Europe were all now visited.

The second series of 'Tales of Fashionable Life' (1812) did so well that she was now the most commercially successful novelist of her age.

She particularly worked hard to improve the living standards of the poor in Edgeworthstown and to provide schools for the local children of all and any denomination.

After a visit to see her relations Maria had severe chest pains and died suddenly of a heart attack in Edgeworthstown on 22nd May 1849. She was 81.

Index of Contents

PREFACE TO THE FIRST EDITION

Vivian exposes one of the most common defects of mankind. To be "infirm of purpose" is to be at the mercy of the artful or at the disposal of accident. Look round, and count the numbers who have, within your own knowledge, failed from want of firmness.

An excellent and wise mother gave the following advice with her dying breath: "My son, learn early how to say, No!"—This precept gave the first idea of the story of Vivian.

Great sacrifices and great benefits cannot frequently be made or conferred by private individuals; but, every day, kindness and attention to the common feelings of others is within the power, and may be the practice, of every age, and sex, and station. Common faults are reproved by all writers on morality; but there are errors and defects that require to be treated in a lighter manner, and that come, with propriety, within the province of essayists and of writers for the stage.

R. L. EDGEWORTH. May, 1812.

CHAPTER I

"To see the best, and yet the worse pursue."

"Is it possible," exclaimed Vivian, "that you, Russell, my friend, my best friend, can tell me that this line is the motto of my character!—' To see the best, and yet the worse pursue.—Then you must think me either a villain or a madman."

"No," replied Russell, calmly; "I think you only weak."

"Weak—but you must think me an absolute fool."

"No, not a fool; the weakness of which I accuse you is not a weakness of the understanding. I find no fault either with the logical or the mathematical part of your understanding. It is not erroneous in either of the two great points in which Bacon says that most men's minds be deficient in—the power of judging of consequences, or in the power of estimating the comparative value of objects."

"Well," cried Vivian, impatiently, "but I don't want to hear just now what Bacon says—but what you think. Tell me all the faults of my character."

"All!—unconscionable!—after the fatigue of this long day's journey," said Russell, laughing.

These two friends were, at this time, travelling from Oxford to Vivian Hall (in —shire), the superb seat of the Vivian family, to which Vivian was heir. Mr. Russell, though he was but a few years older than Vivian, had been his tutor at college; and by an uncommon transition, had, from his tutor, become his intimate friend.

After a pause, Vivian resumed, "Now I think of it, Russell, you are to blame, if I have any faults. Don't you say, that every thing is to be done by education? And are not you—though by much too young, and infinitely too handsome, for a philosopher—are not you my guide, philosopher, and friend?"

"But I have had the honour to be your guide, philosopher, and friend, only for these three years," said Russell. "I believe in the rational, but not in the magical, power of education. How could I do, or undo, in three years, the work of the preceding seventeen?"

"Then, if you won't let me blame you, I must blame my mother."

"Your mother!—I had always understood that she had paid particular attention to your early education, and all the world says that Lady Mary Vivian, though a woman of fashion, is remarkably well-informed and domestic; and, judging from those of her letters which you have shown me, I should think that, for once, what all the world says is right."

"What all the world says is right, and yet I am not wrong:—my mother is a very clever woman, and most affectionate, and she certainly paid particular attention to my early education; but her attention was too particular, her care was too great. You know I was an only son—then I lost my father when I was an infant; and a woman, let her be ever so sensible, cannot well educate an only son, without some manly assistance; the fonder she is of the son the worse, even if her fondness is not foolish fondness—it makes her over-anxious—it makes her do too much. My mother took too much, a great deal too much, care of me; she over-educated, over-instructed, over-dosed me with premature lessons of prudence: she was so afraid that I should ever do a foolish thing, or not say a wise one, that she prompted my every word, and guided my every action. So I grew up, seeing with her eyes, hearing with her ears, and judging with her understanding, till, at length, it was found out that I had not eyes, ears, or understanding of my own. When I was between twelve and thirteen, my mother began to think that I was not sufficiently manly for my age, and that there was something too yielding and undecided in my character. Seized with a panic, my mother, to make a man of me at once, sent me to — school. There I was, with all convenient expedition, made ashamed of every thing good I had learned at home; and there I learned every thing bad, and nothing good, that could be learned at school. I was inferior in Latin and Greek; and this was a deficiency I could not make up without more labour than I had courage to undertake. I was superior in general literature, but this was of little value amongst my competitors, and therefore I despised it; and, overpowered by numbers and by ridicule, I was, of course, led into all sorts of folly, by mere mauvaise honte. Had I been in the habit of exercising my own judgment, or had my resolution been strengthened by degrees; had I, in short, been prepared for a school, I might, perhaps, have acquired, by a public education, a manly, independent spirit. If I had even been wholly bred up in a public school, I might have been forced, as others were, by early and fair competition, to exercise my own powers, and by my own experience in that microcosm, as it has been called, I might have formed some rules of conduct, some manliness of character, and might have made, at least, a good schoolboy. Half home-bred, and half school-bred, from want of proper preparation, one half of my education totally destroyed the other. From school, of course, I went to college, and at college, of course, I should have become one of the worst species of college lads, and should have had no chance, in my whole future life, of being any thing but a dissipated fool of fashion, one of the Four-in-Hand Club, or the Barouche Club, or the Tandem Club, or the Defiance Club, had not I, by the greatest good fortune, met with such a friend as you, and, by still greater good fortune, found you out for myself; for if my mother had recommended you to me, I should have considered you only as a college tutor; I should never have discovered half your real merit; I doubt whether I should have even seen that you are young and handsome: so prejudiced should I have been with the preconceived notion of a college tutor, that I am not certain whether I should have found out that you are a gentleman as well born and well bred as myself; but, be that as it may, I am positive that I never should have made you my companion and friend; I should never have thrown open my whole soul to you, as I have done; nor could you ever have obtained such wondrous power as you possess over my mind, if you had been recommended to me by my mother."

"I am sorry," said Russell, smiling, "that, after so many wise reflections, and so many fine compliments, you end by proving to me that my wondrous power is founded on your wondrous weakness. I am mortified to find that your esteem and friendship for me depended so much upon my not having had the honour of your mother's recommendation; and have not I reason to fear, that now, when I have a chance of becoming acquainted with Lady Mary Vivian, and, perhaps, a chance of her thinking me a fit companion and friend for her son, I must lose his regard and confidence, because I shall labour under the insuperable objection of an affectionate mother's approbation?"

"No, no," said Vivian; "my wilful folly does not go quite so far as that. So that I maintain the privilege of choosing my friends for myself, I shall always be pleased and proud to find my mother approve my choice."

After a few moments' pause, Vivian added, "You misunderstand, quite misunderstand me, if you think that I am not fond of my mother. I respect and love her with all my soul:—I should be a most ungrateful wretch if I did not. I did very wrong to speak as I did just now, of any little errors she may have made in my education; but, believe me, I would not have said so much to any one living but yourself, nor to you, but in strict confidence; and, after all, I don't know whether I ought not to lay the blame of my faults on my masters more than on my poor mother."

"Lay the blame where we will," said Russell, "remember, that the punishment will rest on ourselves. We may, with as much philosophic justice as possible, throw the blame of our faults on our parents and preceptors, and on the early mismanagement of our minds; yet, after we have made out our case in the abstract, to the perfect satisfaction of a jury of metaphysicians, when we come to overt actions, all our judges, learned and unlearned, are so awed, by the ancient precedents and practice of society, and by the obsolete law of common sense, that they finish by pronouncing against us the barbarous sentence, that every man must suffer for his own faults."

"'I hope I shall be able to bear it, my lord,' as the English sailor said when the judge—But look out there! Let down that glass on your side of the carriage!" cried Vivian, starting forward. "There's Vivian Hall!"

"That fine old castle?" said Russell, looking out of the window.

"No; but farther off to the left, don't you see amongst the trees that house with wings?"

"Ha! quite a new, modern house: I had always fancied that Vivian Hall was an old pile of building."

"So it was, till my father threw down the old hall, and built this new house."

"And a very handsome one it is.—Is it as good within as without?"

"Quite, I think; but I'll leave you to judge for yourself.—Are not those fine old trees in the park?"

From this time till the travellers arrived at Vivian Hall, their conversation turned upon trees, and avenues, and serpentine approaches, and alterations that Vivian intended to make, when he should be of age, and master of this fine place; and he now wanted but a twelvemonth of being at legal years of discretion. When they arrived at the hall, Lady Mary Vivian showed much affectionate joy at the sight of her son, and received Mr. Russell with such easy politeness that he was prepossessed at first in her favour. To this charm of well-bred manners was united the appearance of sincerity and warmth of feeling. In her conversation there was a mixture of excellent sense and general literature with the frivolities of the fashionable world, and the anecdotes of the day in certain high circles, of which she seemed to talk more from habit than taste, and to annex importance more from the compulsion of external circumstances than from choice. But her son,—her son was the great object of all her thoughts, serious or frivolous. She was delighted by the improvements she saw in his understanding and character; by the taste and talents he displayed, both for fine literature and for solid information: this flattered her hope that he would both shine as a polished gentleman and make a figure in public life. To his friend Russell she attributed these happy improvements; and, though he was not a tutor of her own original selection, yet her pride, on this occasion, yielded to gratitude, and she graciously declared, that she could not feel jealous of the pre-eminent power he had obtained over her son, when she saw the admirable use he made of this influence. Vivian, like all candid and generous persons, being peculiarly touched by candour and generosity in others, felt his affection for his mother rapidly increased by this conduct; nor did his enthusiasm for his friend in the least abate, in consequence of the high approbation with which she honoured him, nor even in consequence of her ladyship's frequent and rather injudicious expressions of her hopes, that her son would always preserve and show himself worthy of such a friend.

He joined in his mother's entreaties to Russell to prolong his visit; and as her ladyship declared she thought it of essential consequence to her son's interest and future happiness, that he should, at this turn of his life, have such a companion, Russell consented to remain with him some time longer. All parties were thus pleased with each other, and remained united by one common interest about the same objects, during several weeks of a delightful summer. But, alas! this family harmony, and this accord of reason and will, between the mother and son, were not of longer duration. As usual, there were faults on both sides.

Lady Mary Vivian, whose hopes of her son's distinguishing himself by his abilities had been much exalted since his last return from Oxford, had indulged herself in pleasing anticipations of the time when he should make his appearance in the fashionable and in the political world. She foresaw the respect that would be paid to her, on his account, both by senators and by matrons; by ministers, who might want to gain a rising orator's vote, and by mothers, who might wish to make an excellent match for their daughters: not only by all mothers who had daughters to marry, but by all daughters who had hearts or hands to dispose of, Lady Mary felt secure of having her society courted. Now, she had rather extravagant expectations for her son: she expected him to marry, so as to secure domestic happiness, and, at the same time, to have fashion, and beauty, and rank, and high connexions, and every amiable quality in a wife. This vision of a future daughter-in-law continually occupied her ladyship's imagination. Already, with maternal Alnascharism, she had, in her reveries, thrown back her head with disdain, as she repulsed the family advances of some wealthy but low-born heiress, or as she rejected the alliance of some of the new nobility. Already she had arranged the very words of her answers to these, and determined the degrees and shades of her intimacies with those; already had she settled

"To whom to nod, whom take into her coach, Whom honour with her hand;"

when one morning, as she sat at work, absorbed in one of these reveries, she was so far "rapt into future times," that, without perceiving that any body was present, she began to speak her thoughts, and said aloud to herself, "As if my son could possibly think of her!"

Her son, who was opposite to her, lying on a sofa, reading, or seeming to read, started up, and putting down his book, exclaimed, in a voice which showed at once that he was conscious of thinking of some particular person, and determined to persist in the thought, "As if your son could possibly think of her!—Of whom, ma'am?"

"What's the matter, child? Are you mad?"

"Not in the least, ma'am; but you said—"

"What!" cried Lady Mary, looking round; "What did I say, that has occasioned so much disturbance?—I was not conscious of saying any thing. My dear Selina," continued her ladyship, appealing to a young lady, who sat very intent upon some drawing beside her, "my dear Selina, you must have heard; what did I say?"

The young lady looked embarrassed; and the colour which spread over her face, brought a sudden suspicion into Lady Mary's mind: her eye darted back upon her son—the suspicion, the fear was confirmed; and she grew instantly pale, silent, and breathless, in the attitude in which she was struck with this panic. The young lady's blush and embarrassment had a very different effect on Vivian; joy suddenly sparkled in his eyes, and illumined his whole countenance, for this was the first instant he had ever felt any hope of having obtained an interest in her heart. He was too much transported at this moment to think either of prudence or of his mother; and, when he recollected himself, he was too little practised in dissimulation to repair his indiscretion. Something he did attempt to say, and blundered, and laughed at his blunder; and when his mother looked up at him, in serious silence, he only begged pardon for his folly, confessed he believed he was mad, and, turning away abruptly, left the room, exclaiming that he wondered where Russell had been all the morning, and that he must go and look for him. A long silence ensued between Vivian's mother and the young lady, who were left alone together. Lady Mary first broke the silence, and, in a constrained tone, asked, as she took up the newspaper, "Whether Miss Sidney had found any news?"

"I don't know, ma'am," answered Miss Sidney, in a voice scarcely articulate.

"I should have imagined there must be some news from the continent: but you did not find any, I think you say, Miss Sidney;" continued Lady Mary, with haughty, averted eyes. After turning over the pages of the paper, without knowing one word it contained, she laid it down, and rose to leave the room. Miss Sidney rose at the same time.

"Lady Mary, one instant; my dear Lady Mary."

Lady Mary turned, and saw Selina's supplicating eyes full of tears; but her ladyship, still retaining her severity of manner, coldly said, "Does Miss Sidney desire that I should stay?—Does Miss Sidney wish to speak to me?"

"I do—as soon as I can," said Selina in a faltering voice; but, raising her eyes, and perceiving the contemptuous expression of Lady Mary's countenance, her own instantly changed. With the firm tone of conscious innocence, she repeated, "I do wish to speak to your ladyship, if you will hear me with your usual candour; I do not expect or solicit your usual indulgence."

"Miss Sidney," replied Lady Mary, "before you say more, it becomes me to point out to you, that the moment is past for confidence between us two; and that in no moment could I wish to hear from any person, much less from one whom I had considered as my friend, confessions, extorted by circumstances, degrading and unavailing."

"Your ladyship need not be apprehensive of hearing from me any degrading confessions," said Miss Sidney; "I have none to make: and since, without any just cause, without any cause for suspicion, but what a blush, perhaps, or a moment's embarrassment of manner may have created, you think it becomes you to point out to me that the moment for confidence between us is past, I can only lament my mistake in having believed that it ever existed."

Lady Mary's countenance and manner totally changed. The pride of rank yielded before the pride of virtue; and perhaps the hope that she had really no cause for suspicion at once restored her affection for her young friend. "Let us understand one another, my dear Selina," said she; "if I said a hasty or a harsh word, forgive it. You know my affection for you, and my real confidence; in actions, not in words, I have shown it.—In thought, as well as in actions, my confidence in you has been entire; for, upon my word, and you know this is not an asseveration I lightly use, upon my word, till that unfortunate moment, a suspicion of you never crossed my imagination. The proof—if there could need any proof to you of what I assert—the proof is, the delight I take in your society, the urgent manner in which I have so frequently, this summer, begged your company from your mother. You know this would have not only been the height of insincerity, but of folly and madness, if I had not felt a reliance upon you that made me consider it as an absolute impossibility that you could ever disappoint my friendship."

"I thank your ladyship," said Selina, softened by the kind tone in which Lady Mary now spoke, yet still retaining some reserve of manner; "I thank your ladyship for all your kindness—it has flattered me much—touched me deeply—commanded my gratitude, and influenced my conduct uniformly—I can and do entirely forgive the injustice of a moment; and I now bid you adieu, my dear Lady Mary, with the conviction that, if we were never to meet again, I should always hold that place in your esteem and affection with which you have honoured me, and which, if it be not too proud an expression, I hope I have deserved—Won't you bid me farewell?"

The tears gushed from Lady Mary's eyes. "My dear, charming, and prudent Selina, I understand you perfectly—and I thank you: it grieves me to part with you—but I believe you are right—I believe there is no other safety—no other remedy. How, indeed, could I expect that my son could see and hear you—

live in the house with you, and become intimately acquainted with such a character as yours, without danger! I have been very imprudent, unaccountably imprudent, to expose him to such a temptation; but I hope, I trust, that your prudence will repair, in time, the effects of my rashness—and again and again I thank you, my dear young friend—but, perhaps it might be still better that you should not leave us abruptly. Still better than your absence, I think, would be the conviction you might impress on his mind of the impossibility of his hopes: if you were to stay a day or two, and convince him by your indifference that—" "Excuse me, that is what I cannot undertake," said Selina, blushing, and conscious of blushing. Lady Mary was too polite and too delicate to seem to observe her confusion, but, embracing her, said— "If we must part, then take with you my highest esteem, affection, and gratitude; and this much let me add, that my most sanguine expectations for my son's happiness would be realized, if amongst the women to whom family interests must restrict his choice, he could meet with one of half your merit, and half your attractions."

"Amongst the women to whom family interests must restrict his choice," repeated Selina to herself many times, as she journeyed homewards; and she pondered much upon the meaning of this phrase. Vivian was sole heir to a very large property, without encumbrances of any kind; what, therefore, was the necessity that restricted his choice? The imaginary necessity of ambition, which confined him to a certain circle of fashionable, or highly connected people. Selina Sidney, though she was not rich, was of a very good gentleman's family; her father had been a colonel in the British army: during his life, Mrs. Sidney had been in the habit of living a great deal in what is called the world, and in the best company; and though, since his death, she had lived in retirement, Miss Sidney had received an education which put her upon a footing with young ladies of the highest accomplishments and refinement in the kingdom. With every solid and amiable quality, she had all those external advantages of appearance and manner which Lady Mary Vivian valued most highly. Selina, who was convinced that Lady Mary appreciated her character, and was peculiarly fond of her company and conversation, could not but feel surprise, mixed with some indignation, perhaps with a little resentment, when she perceived that her ladyship's prejudices and ambition made her act so completely in contradiction to her better judgment, to her professions, and to her feelings of affection. Whatever Miss Sidney thought upon this subject, however, she determined to continue to avoid seeing Vivian any more—an excellent resolution, in which we leave her, and return to her lover.

A walk with Russell had brought him back in the full determination of avowing his attachment sincerely to his mother, and of speaking to her ladyship in the most respectful manner; but, when he found that Miss Sidney was gone, anger and disappointment made him at once forget his prudence, and his intended respect; he declared, in the most passionate terms, his love for Selina Sidney, and his irrevocable determination to pursue her, to the end of time and space, in spite of all opposition whatsoever from any person whatever. His mother, who was prepared for a scene of this sort, though not for one of this violence, had sufficient command of temper to sustain it properly; her command of temper was, indeed, a little assisted by the hope that this passion would be transitory in proportion to its vehemence, much by the confidence she had in Miss Sidney's honour, and in her absence: Lady Mary, therefore, calmly disclaimed having had any part in persuading Miss Sidney to that measure which had so much enraged her lover; but her ladyship avowed, that though it had not been necessary for her to suggest the measure, she highly approved of it, and admired now, as she had ever admired, that young lady's prudent and noble conduct.

Softened by the only thing that could, at this moment, soften him—praise of his mistress—Vivian, in a most affectionate manner, assured his mother that it was her warm eulogiums of Miss Sidney which had first turned his attention to the perfections of her character; and he now inquired what possible objections she could make to his choice. With the generous enthusiasm of his disposition, heightened by all the eloquence of love, he pleaded, that his fortune was surely sufficient to put him above mercenary considerations in the choice of a wife; that in every point, except this one of money, Selina Sidney was, in his own mother's opinion, superior to every other woman she could name, or wish for, as a daughter-in-law.

"But my tastes are not to blind me to your interests," said Lady Mary; "you are entitled to look for rank and high connexion. You are the representative of an ancient family, have talents to make a figure in public; and, in short, prejudice or not, I confess it is one of the first wishes of my heart that you should marry into a noble family, or at least into one that shall strengthen your political interest, as well as secure your domestic happiness."

Vivian, of course, cursed ambition, as all men do whilst they are in love. His arguments and his eloquence in favour of a private station, and of the joys of learned leisure, a competence, and domestic bliss, were worthy of the most renowned of ancient or modern philosophers. Russell was appealed to with much eagerness, both by mother and son, during their debates. He frankly declared to Lady Mary, that he thought her son perfectly right in all he now urged, and especially in his opinion of Miss Sidney; "but at the same time," added Russell, "I apprehend that he speaks, at this moment, more from passion than from reason; and I fear that, in the course of a few months, he might, perhaps, entirely change his mind: therefore, I think your ladyship is prudent in refusing, during the minority of your son, your consent to a hasty union, of which he might afterwards repent, and thus render both himself and a most amiable woman miserable."

Russell, after having given his opinion with the utmost freedom, when it was required by Lady Mary, assured her that he should no farther interfere; and he trusted his present sincerity would be the best pledge to her of his future discretion and honour. This equitable judgment and sincerity of Russell's at first displeased both parties, but in time operated upon the reason of both; not, however, before contests had gone on long and loud between the mother and son—not before a great deal of nonsense had been talked on both sides. People of the best abilities often talk the most nonsense where their passions are concerned, because then the whole of their ingenuity is exercised to find arguments in favour of their folly. They are not, like fools, content to say, This is my will; but they pique themselves on giving reasons for their will; and their reasons are the reasons of madmen, excellent upon false premises. It happened here, as in most family quarrels, that the disputants did not allow sufficiently for the prejudices and errors incident to their different ages. The mother would not allow for the romantic notions of the son, nor could the son endure the worldly views of the mother. The son, who had as yet no experience of the transitory nature of the passion of love, thought his mother unfeeling and barbarous, for opposing him on the point where the whole happiness of his life was concerned; the mother, who had seen the decline and fall of so many everlasting loves, considered him only as a person in a fever; and thought she prevented him, by her calmness, from doing that which he would repent when he should regain his sober senses. Without detailing the daily disputes which now arose, it will be sufficient to mark the result.

Vivian's love had been silent, tranquil, and not seemingly of any great consequence, till it was opposed; but, from the instant that an obstacle intervened, it gathered strength and force, and it presently rose rapidly, with prodigious uproar, threatening to burst all bounds, and to destroy every thing that stopped its course. Lady Mary was now inclined to try what effect lessening the opposition might produce. To do her justice, she was also moved to this by some nobler motives than fear; or, at least, her fears were not of a selfish kind: she dreaded that her son's health and permanent happiness might be injured by this violent passion; she was apprehensive of becoming an object of his aversion; of utterly losing his confidence, and all power over his mind; but, chiefly, her generous temper was moved and won by Selina Sidney's admirable conduct. During the whole time that Vivian used every means to see her, to write to her, and to convince her of the fervour of his love, though he won all her friends over to his interests, though she heard his praises from morning till night from all who surrounded her, and though her own heart, perhaps, pleaded more powerfully than all the rest in his favour; yet she never, for one instant, gave him the slightest encouragement. Lady Mary's esteem and affection were so much increased by these strong proofs of friendship and honour, that her prejudices yielded; and she at length declared, that if her son continued, till he was of age, to feel the same attachment for this amiable girl, she would give her consent to their union. But this, she added, she promised only on one condition—that her son should abstain from all attempts, in the interval, to see or correspond with Miss Sidney, and that he should set out immediately to travel with Mr. Russell. Transported with love, and joy, and victory, Vivian promised every thing that was required of him, embraced his mother, and set out upon his travels.

"Allow," said he triumphantly to Russell, as the chaise drove from the door, "allow, my good friend, that you were mistaken, in your fears of the weakness of my character, and of the yielding facility of my temper. You see how firm I have been—you see what battle I have made—you see how I have stood out."

"I never doubted," said Russell, "your love of your own free will—I never doubted your fear of being governed, especially by your mother; but you do not expect that I should allow this to be a proof of strength of character."

"What! do you suppose I act from love of my own free will merely?—Do you call my love for Selina Sidney weakness?—Oh! take care, Russell; for if once I find you pleading my mother's cause against your conscience—"

"You will never find me pleading any cause against my conscience. I have told your mother, as I have told you, my opinion of Miss Sidney—my firm opinion—that she is peculiarly calculated to make the happiness of your life, provided you continue to love her."

"Provided!—Oh!" cried Vivian, laughing, "spare your musty provisoes, my dear philosopher! Would not any one think, now, you were an old man of ninety? If this is all you have to fear, I am happy indeed."

"At present," said Russell, calmly, "I have no fear, as I have just told your mother, but that you should change your mind before you are of age."

Vivian grew quite indignant at this suggestion. "You are angry with me," said Russell, "and so was your mother: she was angry because I said, I feared, instead of I hoped, you would change your mind. Both parties are angry with me for my sincerity."

"Sincerity!—no; but I am angry with you for your absurd suspicions of my constancy."

"If they are absurd, you need not be angry," said Russell; "I shall be well pleased to see their absurdity demonstrated."

"Then I can demonstrate it this moment."

"Pardon me; not this moment; you must take time into the account. I make no doubt but that, at this moment, you are heartily in love with Miss Sidney; but the thing to be proved is, that your passion will not decline in force, in proportion as it meets with less resistance. If it does, you will acknowledge that it was more a love of your own free will than a love of your mistress that has actuated you, which was the thing to be proved."

"Hateful Q.E.D.!" cried Vivian; "you shall see the contrary, and, at least, I will triumph over you."

If Russell had ever used art in his management of Vivian's mind, he might have been suspected of using it in favour of Miss Sidney at this instant; for this prophecy of Vivian's inconstancy was the most likely means to prevent its accomplishment. Frequently, in the course of their tour, when Vivian was in any situation where his constancy was tempted, he recollected Russell's prediction, and was proud to remind him how much he had been mistaken. In short, the destined time for their return home arrived—Vivian presented himself before his mother, and claimed her promise. She was somewhat surprised, and a little disappointed, by our hero's constancy; but she could not retract her word; and, since her compliance was now unavoidable, she was determined that it should be gracious. She wrote to Selina, therefore, with great kindness, saying, that whatever views of other connexions she might formerly have had for her son, she had now relinquished them, convinced, by the constancy of her son's attachment, and by the merit of its object, that his own choice would most effectually ensure his happiness, and that of all his friends. Her ladyship added expressions of her regard and esteem, and of the pleasure she felt in the thoughts of finding in her daughter-in-law a friend and companion, whose society was peculiarly agreeable to her taste and suited to her character. This letter entirely dissipated Selina's scruples of conscience; Vivian's love and merit, all his good and all his agreeable qualities, had now full and unreproved power to work upon her tender heart. His generous, open temper, his candour, his warm attachment to his friends, his cultivated understanding, his brilliant talents, his easy, well-bred, agreeable manners, all heightened in their power to please by the charm of love, justified, even in the eyes of the aged and prudent, the passion he inspired. Selina became extremely attached to him; and she loved with the delightful belief that there was not, in the mind of her lover, the seed of a single vice which threatened danger to his virtues or to their mutual happiness. With his usual candour, he had laid open his whole character to her, as far as he knew it himself; and had warned her of that vacillation of temper, that easiness to be led, which Russell had pointed out as a dangerous fault in his disposition. But of this propensity Selina had seen no symptoms; on the contrary, the steadiness of her lover in his attachment to her—the only point on which she had yet seen him tried—decided her to trust to the persuasive voice of love and hope, and to believe that Russell's friendship had in this instance, been too harsh or too timorous in its forebodings.

Nothing now delayed the marriage of Vivian and Selina but certain legal rites, which were to be performed on his coming of age, and before marriage settlements could be drawn;—and the parties were doomed to wait for the arrival of some trustee who was with his regiment abroad. All these delays Vivian of course cursed: but, upon the whole, they were borne by him with heroic patience, and by Selina with all the tranquillity of confiding love, happy in the present, and not too anxious for the future.

CHAPTER II

"My dear Russell," said Vivian, "love shall not make me forget friendship; before I marry, I must see you provided for. Believe me, this was the first—one of the first pleasures I promised myself, in becoming master of a good fortune. Other thoughts, I confess, have put it out of my head; so now let me tell you at once. I hate paltry surprises with my friends: I have, you know—or rather, probably, you do not know, for you are the most disinterested fellow upon earth—I have an excellent living in my gift; it shall be yours; consider it as such from this moment. If I knew a more deserving man, I would give it to him, upon my honour; so you can't refuse me. The incumbent can't live long; he is an old, very old, infirm man; you'll have the living in a year or two, and, in the mean time, stay with me. I ask it as a favour from a friend, and you see how much I want a friend of your firm character; and I hope you see, also, how much I can value, in others, the qualities in which I am myself deficient."

Russell was much pleased and touched by Vivian's generous gratitude, and by the delicacy, as well as kindness of the manner in which he made this offer; but Russell could not consistently with his feelings or his principles live in a state of dependent idleness, waiting for a rich living and the death of an old incumbent. He told Vivian that he had too much affection for him, and too much respect for himself, ever to run the hazard of sinking from the rank of an independent friend. After rallying him, without effect, on his pride, Vivian acknowledged that he was forced to admire him the more for his spirit. Lady Mary, too, who was a great and sincere admirer of independence of character, warmly applauded Mr. Russell, and recommended him, in the highest terms, to a nobleman in the neighbourhood, who happened to be in want of a preceptor for his only son. This nobleman was Lord Glistonbury: his lordship was eager to engage a person of Russell's reputation for talents; so the affair was quickly arranged, and Lady Mary Vivian and her son went to pay a morning visit at Glistonbury Castle, on purpose to accompany Russell on his first introduction to the family. As they approached the castle, Vivian was struck with its venerable Gothic appearance; he had not had a near view of it for some years, and he looked at it with new eyes. Formerly he had seen it only as a picturesque ornament to the country; but now that he was himself possessor of an estate in the vicinity, he considered Glistonbury Castle as a point of comparison which rendered him dissatisfied with his own mansion. As he drove up the avenue, and beheld the towers, turrets, battlements, and massive entrance, his mother, who was a woman of taste, strengthened, by her exclamations on the beauty of Gothic architecture, the wish that was rising in his mind to convert his modern house into an ancient castle: she could not help sighing whilst she reflected that, if her son's affections had not been engaged, he might perhaps have obtained the heart and hand of one of the fair daughters of this castle. Lady Mary went no farther, even in her inmost thoughts. Incapable of double-dealing, she resolved never even to let her son know what her wishes had been with respect to a connexion with the Glistonbury family. But the very reserve and discretion with which her ladyship spoke—a reserve unusual with her, and unsuited to the natural warmth of her manner and temper—might have betrayed her to an acute and cool observer. Vivian, however, at this instant, was too much intent upon castle-building to admit any other ideas.

When the carriage drove under the great gateway and stopped, Vivian exclaimed, "What a fine old castle! how surprised Selina Sidney would be, how delighted, to see my house metamorphosed into such a castle!"

"It is a magnificent castle, indeed!" said Lady Mary, with a sigh: "I think there are the Lady Lidhursts on the terrace; and here comes my Lord Glistonbury with his son."

"My pupil?" said Russell; "I hope the youth is such as I can become attached to. Life would be wretched indeed without attachment—of some sort or other. But I must not expect," added he, "to find a second time a friend in a pupil; and such a friend!"

Sentiment, or the expression of the tenderness he felt for his friends, was so unusual from Russell, that it had double effect; and Vivian was so much struck by it, that he could scarcely collect his thoughts in time to speak to Lord Glistonbury, who came to receive his guests, attended by three hangers on of the family—a chaplain, a captain, and a young lawyer. His lordship was scarcely past the meridian of life; yet, in spite of his gay and debonair manner, he looked old, as if he were paying for the libertinism of his youth by premature decrepitude. His countenance announced pretensions to ability; his easy and affable address, and the facility with which he expressed himself, gained him credit at first for much more understanding than he really possessed. There was a plausibility in all he said; but, if it were examined, there was nothing in it but nonsense. Some of his expressions appeared brilliant; some of his sentiments just; but there was a want of consistency, a want of a pervading mind in his conversation, which to good judges betrayed the truth, that all his opinions were adopted, not formed; all his maxims commonplace; his wit mere repetition; his sense merely tact. After proper thanks and compliments to Lady Mary and Mr. Vivian, for securing for him such a treasure as Mr. Russell, he introduced Lord Lidhurst, a sickly, bashful boy of fourteen, to his new governor, with polite expressions of unbounded confidence, and a rapid enunciation of undefined and contradictory expectations.

"Mr. Russell will, I am perfectly persuaded, make Lidhurst every thing we can desire," said his lordship; "an honour to his country, an ornament to his family. It is my decided opinion that man is but a bundle of habits; and it's my maxim, that education is second nature—first, indeed, in many cases. For, except that I am staggered about original genius, I own I conceive with Hartley, that early impressions and associations are all in all: his vibrations and vibratiuncles are quite satisfactory. But what I particularly wish for Lidhurst, sir, is, that he should be trained as soon as possible into a statesman. Mr. Vivian, I presume you mean to follow up public business, and no doubt will make a figure. So I prophesy; and I am used to these things. And from Lidhurst, too, under similar tuition, I may with reason expect miracles—'hope to hear him thundering in the house of commons in a few years—'confess 'am not quite so impatient to have the young dog in the house of incurables; for you know he could not be there without being in my shoes, which I have not done with yet—ha! ha! ha!—Each in his turn, my boy! In the mean time, Lady Mary, shall we join the ladies yonder, on the terrace? Lady Glistonbury walks so slow, that she will be seven hours in coming to us; so we had best go to her ladyship: if the mountain won't go to Mahomet—you know, of course, what follows."

On their way to the terrace, Lord Glistonbury, who always heard himself speak with singular complacency, continued to give his ideas on education; sometimes appealing to Mr. Russell, sometimes happy to catch the eye of Lady Mary.

"Now, my idea for Lidhurst is simply this:—that he should know every thing that is in all the best books in the library, but yet that he should be the farthest possible from a book-worm—that he should never, except in a set speech in the house, have the air of having opened a book in his life—mother-wit for me!—in most cases—and that easy style of originality, which shows the true gentleman. As to morals—Lidhurst, walk on, my boy—as to morals, I confess I couldn't bear to see any thing of the Joseph Surface about him. A youth of spirit must, you know, Mr. Vivian—excuse me, Lady Mary, this is—an aside—be something of a latitudinarian to keep in the fashion: not that I mean to say so exactly to Lidhurst—no, no—on the contrary, Mr. Russell, it is our cue, as well as this reverend gentleman's," looking back at the chaplain, who bowed assent before he knew to what, "it is our cue, as well as this reverend gentleman's, to preach prudence, and temperance, and all the cardinal virtues."

"Cardinal virtues! very good, faith! my lord," said the lawyer, looking at the clergyman.

"Temperance!" repeated the chaplain, winking at the officer; "upon my soul, my lord, that's too bad."

"Prudence!" repeated the captain; "that's too clean a cut at poor Wicksted, my lord."

Before his lordship had time to preach any more prudence, they arrived within bowing distance of the ladies, who had, indeed, advanced at a very slow rate. Vivian was not acquainted with any of the ladies of the Glistonbury family; for they had, till this summer, resided at another of their country seats, in a distant county. His mother had often met them at parties in town.

Lady Glistonbury was a thin, stiffened, flattened figure—she was accompanied by two other female forms, one old, the other young; not each a different grace, but alike all three in angularity, and in a cold haughtiness of mien. After reconnoitring with their glasses the party of gentlemen, these ladies quickened their step; and Lady Glistonbury, making her countenance as affable as it was in its nature to be, exclaimed, "My dear Lady Mary Vivian! have I the pleasure to see your ladyship?—They told me it was only visitors to my lord."

Mr. Vivian had then the honour of being introduced to her ladyship, to her eldest daughter, Lady Sarah Lidhurst, and to Miss Strictland, the governess. By all of these ladies he was most graciously received; but poor Russell was not so fortunate; nothing could be more cold and repulsive than their reception of him. This did not make Lady Sarah appear very agreeable to Vivian; he thought her, at this first view, one of the least attractive young women he had ever beheld.

"Where is my Julia?" inquired Lord Glistonbury. "Ah! there she goes yonder, all life and spirits."

Vivian looked as his lordship directed his eye, and saw, at the farthest end of the terrace, a young girl of about fifteen, running very fast, with a hoop, which she was keeping up with great dexterity for the amusement of a little boy who was with her. The governess no sooner saw this than she went in pursuit of her young ladyship, calling after her, in various tones and phrases of reprehension, in French, Italian, and English; and asking whether this was a becoming employment for a young lady of her age and rank. Heedless of these reproaches, Lady Julia still ran on, away from her governess, "to chase the rolling circle's speed," down the slope of the terrace; thither Miss Strictland dared not pursue, but contented herself with standing on the brink, reiterating her remonstrances. At length the hoop fell, and the young lady returned, not to her governess, but, running lightly up the slope of the terrace, to her surprise, she came full in view of the company before she was aware that any strangers were there. Her straw hat being at the back of her head, Lady Glistonbury, with an indignant look, pulled it forwards.

"What a beautiful colour! what a sweet countenance Lady Julia has!" whispered Lady Mary Vivian to Lord Glistonbury: at the same time she could not refrain from glancing her eyes towards her son, to see what effect was produced upon him. Vivian's eyes met hers; and this single look of his mother's revealed to him all that she had, in her great prudence, resolved to conceal. He smiled at her, and then at Russell, as much as to say, "Surely there can be no comparison between such a child as this and Selina Sidney!"

A few minutes afterwards, in consequence of a sign from Lady Glistonbury, Julia disappeared with her governess; and the moment was unnoticed by Vivian, who was then, as his mother observed, looking up at one of the turrets of the old castle. All its inhabitants were at this time uninteresting to him, except so far as they regarded his friend Russell; but the castle itself absorbed his attention. Lord Glistonbury, charmed to see how he was struck by it, offered to show him over every part of the edifice; an offer which he and Lady Mary gladly accepted. Lady Glistonbury excused herself, professing to be unable to sustain the fatigue: she deputed her eldest daughter to attend Lady Mary in her stead; and this was the only circumstance which diminished the pleasure to Vivian, for he was obliged to show due courtesy to this stiff taciturn damsel at every turn, whilst he was intent upon seeing the architecture of the castle, and the views from the windows of the towers and loop-holes of the galleries; all which Lady Sarah pointed out with a cold, ceremonious civility, and a formal exactness of proceeding, which enraged Vivian's enthusiastic temper. The visit ended: he railed half the time he was going home against their fair, or, as he called her, their petrified guide; then, full of the Gothic beauties of Glistonbury, he determined, as soon as possible, to turn his own modern house into a castle. The very next morning he had an architect to view it, and to examine its capabilities. It happened that, about this time, several of the noblemen and gentry, in the county in which Vivian resided, had been seized with this rage for turning comfortable houses into uninhabitable castles. And, however perverse or impracticable this retrograde movement in architecture might seem, there were always at hand professional projectors, to convince gentlemen that nothing was so feasible. Provided always that gentlemen approve their estimates as well as their plans, they undertake to carry buildings back, in a trice, two, or three, or half a dozen centuries, as may be required, to make them Gothic or Saracenic, and to "add every grace that time alone can give." A few days after Vivian had been at Glistonbury Castle, when Lord Glistonbury came to return the visit, Russell, who accompanied his lordship, found his friend encompassed with plans and elevations.

"Surely, my dear Vivian," said he, seizing the first moment he could speak to him, "you are not going to spoil this excellent house? It is completely finished, in handsome modern architecture, perfectly comfortable and convenient, light, airy, large enough, warm rooms, well distributed, with ample means of getting at each apartment; and if you set about to new-model and transform it into a castle, you must, I see, by your plan, alter the proportions of almost every room, and spoil the comfort of the whole; turn square to round, and round again to square; and, worse than all, turn light to darkness— only for the sake of having what is called a castle, but what has not, in fact, any thing of the grandeur or solid magnificence of a real ancient edifice. These modern baby-house miniatures of castles, which gentlemen ruin themselves to build, are, after all, the most paltry, absurd things imaginable."

To this Vivian was, after some dispute, forced to agree; but he said, "that his should not be a baby-house; that he would go to any expense to make it really magnificent."

"As magnificent, I suppose, as Glistonbury Castle?"

"If possible:—that is, I confess, the object of my emulation."

"Ah!" said Russell, shaking his head, "these are the objects of emulation, for which country gentlemen often ruin themselves; barter their independence and real respectability; reduce themselves to distress and disgrace: these are the objects for which they sell either their estates or their country; become placemen or beggars; and end either in the liberties of the King's Bench, or the slaveries of St. James's."

"Impossible for me! you know my public principles," said Vivian: "and you know that I think the life of an independent country gentleman the most respectable of all others—you know my principles."

"I know your facility," said Russell: "if you begin by sacrificing thus to your taste, do you think you will not end by sacrificing to your interest?"

"Never! never!" cried Vivian.

"Then you imagine that a strong temptation will not act where a weak one has been found irresistible."

"Of this I am certain," said Vivian: "I could never be brought to sell my country, or to forfeit my honour."

"Perhaps not," said Russell: "you might, in your utmost need, have another alternative; you might forfeit your love; you might give up Selina Sidney, and marry for money—all for the sake of a castle!"

Struck by this speech, Vivian exclaimed, "I would give up a thousand castles rather than run such a hazard!"

"Let us then coolly calculate," said Russell. "What would the castle cost you?"

The expense, even by the estimates of the architects, which, in the execution, are usually doubled, was enormous, such as Vivian acknowledged was unsuited even to his ample fortune. His fortune, though considerable, was so entailed, that he would, if he exceeded his income, be soon reduced to difficulties for ready money. But then his mother had several thousands in the stocks, which she was ready to lend him to forward this castle-building. It was a project which pleased her taste, and gratified her aristocratic notions.

Vivian assured his friend at parting, that his reason was convinced: that he would not yield to the whims of taste, and that he would prudently give up his folly. So he determined; and he abided by his determination till he heard numbers speak on the other side of the question. With Vivian, those who spoke last frequently seemed to speak best; and, in general, the number of voices overpowered the weight of argument. By the persuasions of his mother, the example of his neighbours, and the urgency of architects and men of taste who got about him soon afterwards, he was convinced that there was no living without a castle, and that the expense would be next to nothing at all. Convinced, we should not say; for he yielded, against his conviction, from mere want of power to resist reiterated solicitations. He had no other motive; for the enthusiasm raised by the view of Glistonbury Castle had passed away: he plainly saw, what Russell had pointed out to him, that he should spoil the inside of his house for the sake of the outside; and, for his own part, he preferred comfort to show. It was not, therefore, to please his own taste that he ran into this imprudent expense, but merely to gratify the taste of others.

Now the bustle of building began, and workmen swarmed round his house; the foundations sank, the scaffolds rose; and many times did Vivian sigh and repent, when he saw how much was to be undone before any thing could be done; when he found his house dismantled, saw the good ceilings and elegant cornices knocked to pieces, saw the light domes and modern sashes give way; all taken out to be replaced, at profuse expense, by a clumsy imitation of Gothic; how often did be sigh and calculate, when he saw the tribes of workmen file off as their dinner bell rang! how often did he bless himself, when he beheld the huge beams of timber dragged into his yards, and the solid masses of stone brought from a quarry at an enormous distance!—Vivian perceived that the expense would be treble the estimate; and said, that if the thing were to be done again, he would never consent to it; but now, as Lady Mary observed, it was too late to repent; and it was, at any rate, best to go on and finish it with spirit—since it was impossible (nobody knew why) to stop. He hurried on the workmen with impatience; for he was anxious to have the roof and some apartments in his castle finished before his marriage. The dilatoriness of the lawyers, and the want of the trustee, who had not yet arrived in England, were no longer complained of so grievously by the lover. Russell, one day, as he saw Vivian overlooking his workmen, and urging them to expedition, smiled, and asked whether the impatience of an architect or of a lover was now predominant in his mind. Vivian, rather offended by the question, replied, that his eagerness to finish this part of his castle arose from his desire to give an agreeable surprise to his bride; and he declared that his passion for Selina was as ardent, at this moment, as it had ever been; but that it was impossible to make lawyers move faster than their accustomed pace; and that Miss Sidney was too secure of his affection, and he too well convinced of hers, to feel that sort of anxiety, which persons who had less confidence in each other might experience in similar circumstances. This was all very true, and very reasonable; but Russell could not help perceiving that Vivian's language and tone were somewhat altered since the time when he was ready to brave heaven and earth to marry his mistress, without license or consent of friends, without the possibility of waiting a few months till he was of age. In fact, though Vivian would not allow it, this consent of friends, this ceasing of opposition, this security and tranquillity of happiness, had considerably changed the appearance, at least, of his love. Lady Mary perceived it, with a resolution to say nothing, and see how it would end. Selina did not perceive it for some time; for she was of a most unsuspicious temper; and her confidence in Vivian was equal to the fondness of her love. She began to think, indeed, that the lawyers were provokingly slow; and when Vivian did not blame them as much as he used to do, she only thought that he understood business better than she did—besides, the necessary trustee was not come—and, in short, the last thing that occurred to her mind was to blame Vivian.

The trustee at length arrived, and the castle was almost in the wished-for state of forwardness, when a new cause of delay arose—a county election: but how this election was brought on, and how it was conducted, it is necessary to record. It happened that a relation of Vivian's was appointed to a new seventy-four gun ship, of which he came to take the command at Yarmouth, which was within a few miles of him. Vivian recollected that Russell had often expressed a desire to go on board a man-of-war. Vivian, therefore, after having appointed a day for their going, went to Glistonbury to invite Russell: his pupil, Lord Lidhurst, begged to be permitted to accompany them: and Lady Julia, the moment she heard of this new seventy-four gun ship, was, as her governess expressed it, wild to be of the party. Indeed, any thing that had the name of a party of pleasure, and that promised a transient relief from the tedious monotony in which her days passed; any thing that gave a chance of even a few hours' release from the bondage in which she was held between the restraints of the most rigid of governesses and the proudest of mothers, appeared delightful to this lively and childish girl. She persecuted her governess with entreaties, till at last she made Miss Strictland go with her petition to Lady Glistonbury; whilst, in the mean time, Lady Julia overwhelmed her father with caresses, till he consented; and with much difficulty, prevailed upon Lady Glistonbury to give her permission for the young ladies to go with their governess, their brother, their father, and Lady Mary Vivian, on this excursion. The invitation was now extended to all the company then at the castle; including the representative of the county, who, being just threatened with a fit of the gout, brought on by hard drinking at the last election, expressed some reluctance to going with this party on the water. But this gentleman was now paying his humble devoirs to the Lady Sarah Lidhurst; and it was represented to him, by all who understood the ground, that he would give mortal offence if he did not go; so it was ruled, that, hot or cold, gout or no gout, he must appear in the Lady Sarah's train: he submitted to this perilous necessity in the most gallant manner. The day proved tolerably fine—Vivian had an elegant entertainment provided for the company, under a marquee pitched on the shore—they embarked in a pleasure-boat—Lady Sarah was very sick, and her admirer very cold; but Lady Julia was in extasies at every thing she saw and felt—she feared nothing, found nothing inconvenient—was charmed to be drawn so easily from the boat up the high side of the ship—charmed to find herself on deck—charmed to see the sails, the ropes, the rigging, the waves, the sea, the sun, the clouds, the sailors, the cook dressing dinner—all, all indiscriminately charmed her; and, like a school-girl broke loose, she ran about, wild with spirits, asking questions, some sensible, some silly; laughing at her own folly, flying from this side to that, from one end of the ship to the other, down the ladders and up again; whilst Mr. Russell, who was deputed to take care of her, could scarcely keep up with her: Lord Glistonbury stood by, holding his sides and laughing aloud: Miss Strictland, quite disabled by the smell of the ship, was lying on a bed in the state cabin; and Lady Sarah, all the time shaded by an umbrella held by her shivering admirer, sat, as if chained upright in her chair of state, upon deck, scorning her sister's childish levity, and proving herself, with all due propriety, incapable of being moved to surprise or admiration by any object on land or sea.

Lady Mary Vivian, while she observed with a quick eye all that passed, and read her son's thoughts, was fully persuaded that neither of the Lady Lidhursts would be likely to suit his taste, even if his affections were disengaged: the one was too childish, the other too stiff. "Yet their birth and connexions, and their consequence in the county," thought Lady Mary, "would have made their alliance highly desirable." Every body seemed weary at the close of this day's entertainment, except Lady Julia, who kept it up with indefatigable gaiety, and could hardly believe that it was time to go home, when the boat was announced to row them to shore: heedless, and absolutely dizzy with talking and laughing, her ladyship, escaping from the assistance of sailors and gentlemen, made a false step in getting into the boat, and, falling over, would have sunk for ever, but for Mr. Russell's presence of mind. He seized her with a strong grasp, and saved her. The fright sobered her completely; and she sat wrapped in great-coats, as silent, as tractable, and as wet as possible, during the remainder of the way to shore. The screams, the ejaculations, the reprimands from Miss Strictland; the questions, the reflections, to which this incident led, may possibly be conceived, but cannot be enumerated.

This event, however alarming at the moment, had no serious consequence; for Lady Julia caught neither fever nor cold, though Miss Strictland was morally certain her ladyship would have one or the other; indeed she insinuated, that her ladyship deserved to have both. Lady Sarah's poor shivering knight of the shire, however, did not escape so well. Obliged to row home, in a damp evening, without his great-coat, which he had been forced to offer to Lady Julia, in a pleasure-boat, when he should have been in flannels or in bed, he had "cause to rue the boating of that day." His usual panacea of the gout did not come as expected, to set him up again. The cold he caught this day killed him. Lady Sarah Lidhurst was precisely as sorry as decorum required. But the bustle of a new election was soon to obliterate the memory of the old member, in the minds of his numerous friends. Lord Glistonbury, and several other voices in the county, called upon Vivian to stand on the independent interest. There was to be a contest: for a government candidate declared himself at the same moment that application was made to Vivian. The expense of a contested election alarmed both Vivian and his mother. Gratified as she was by the honour of this offer, yet she had the prudence to advise her son rather to go into parliament as representative for a borough than to hazard the expense of a contest for the county. Miss Sidney, also, whom he consulted upon this occasion, supported his mother's prudent advice, in the most earnest manner; and Vivian was inclined to follow this counsel, till Lord Glistonbury came one morning to plead the contrary side of the question: he assured Vivian, that from his experience of the county, he was morally certain they should carry it without trouble, and with no expense worth mentioning. These were only general phrases, to be sure, not arguments; but these, joined to her ambition to see her son member for the county, at length overpowered Lady Mary's better judgment: her urgent entreaties were now joined to those of Lord Glistonbury, and of many loud-tongued electioneerers, who proved to Vivian, by every thing but calculation, that he must be returned if he would but stand—if he would only declare himself. Russell and his own prudence strongly counselled him to resist these clamorous importunities; the two preceding candidates, whose fortunes had been nearly as good as his, had been ruined by the contests. Vivian was very young, but just of age; and Russell observed, "that it would be better for him to see something more of the world, before he should embark in politics, and plunge into public business." "True," said Vivian; "but Mr. Pitt was only three-and-twenty when he was minister of England. I am not ambitious; but I should certainly like to distinguish myself, if I could; and whilst I feel in youth the glow of patriotism, why should I not serve my country?"

"Serve it and welcome," said Russell: "but don't begin by ruining yourself by a contested election; or else, whatever glow of patriotism you may feel, it will be out of your power to be an honest member of parliament. If you must go into parliament immediately for the good of your country, go in as member for some borough, which will not ruin you."

"But the committee of our friends will be so disappointed if I decline; and my mother, who has now set her heart upon it, and Lord Glistonbury, and Mr. C—, and Mr. G—, and Mr. D—, who are such zealous friends, and who urge me so much—"

"Judge for yourself," said Russell, "and don't let any persons who happen to be near you persuade you to see with their eyes, and decide with their wishes. Zealous friends, indeed!—because they love to make themselves of consequence, by bawling and scampering about at an election!—And you would let such people draw you on, to ruin yourself."

"I will show you that they shall not," cried Vivian, seizing a sheet of paper, and sitting down immediately to write the copy of a circular letter to his friends, informing them, with many thanks, that he declined to stand for the county. Russell eagerly wrote copies of this letter, which Vivian declared should be sent early the next morning. But no sooner was Russell out of sight than Lady Mary Vivian resumed her arguments in favour of commencing his canvass immediately, and before his friends should cool. When she saw the letters that he had been writing, she was excessively indignant; and, by a torrent of female and maternal eloquence, he was absolutely overwhelmed. Auxiliaries poured in to her ladyship on all sides; horsemen after horsemen, freeholders of all degrees, now flocked to the house, hearing that Mr. Vivian had thoughts of standing for the county. They were unanimously loud in their assurances of success. Old and new copies of poll books were produced, and the different interests of the county counted and recounted, balanced and counterbalanced, again and again, by each person, after his own fashion: and it was proved to Mr. Vivian, in black and white, and as plain as figures could make it, that he had the game in his own hands; and that, if he would but declare himself, the other candidate would, the very next day, they would be bound for it, decline the contest. Vivian had a clear head, and a competent knowledge of arithmetic; he saw the fallacies and inaccuracies in their modes of computation; he saw, upon examining the books, that the state of the county interests was very different from what they pretended or believed; and he was convinced that the opposite candidate would not decline: but after Vivian had stated these reasons ten times, and his mother and his electioneering partisans had reiterated their assertions twenty times, he yielded, merely because they had said twice as much as he had, and because, poor easy man! he had not power to resist continuity of solicitation.

He declared himself candidate for the county; and was soon immersed in all the toil, trouble, vexation, and expense, of a contested election. Of course, his marriage was now to be postponed till the election should be over. Love and county politics have little affinity. What the evils of a contested election are can be fully known only to those by whom they have been personally experienced. The contest was bitter. The Glistonbury interest was the strongest which supported Vivian: Lord Glistonbury and his lordship's friends were warm in his cause. Not that they had any particular regard for Vivian; but he was to be their member, opposed to the court candidate, whom his lordship was anxious to keep out of the county. Lord Glistonbury had once been a strong friend to government, and was thought a confirmed courtier, especially as he had been brought up in high aristocratic notions; but he had made it his great object to turn his earldom into a marquisate; and government having delayed or refused to gratify him in this point, he quitted them with disgust, and set up his standard amongst the opposition. He was now loud and zealous on every occasion that could, as he said, annoy government; and merely because he could not be a marquis, he became a patriot. Mistaken, abused name! how glorious in its original, how despicable in its debased signification!—Lord Glistonbury's exertions were indefatigable.

Vivian felt much gratitude for this apparently disinterested friendship; and, during a few weeks, whilst this canvass was going on, he formed a degree of intimacy with the Glistonbury family, which, in any other circumstances, could scarcely have been brought about during months or years. An election, in England, seems, for the time, to level all distinctions, not only of rank, but even of pride: Lady Glistonbury herself, at this season, found it necessary to relax from her usual rigidity.—There was an extraordinary freedom of egress and regress; and the haughty code of Glistonbury lay dormant. Vivian, of course, was the centre of all interest; and, whenever he appeared, every individual of the family was eager to inquire, "What news?—What news?—How do things go on to-day?—How will the election turn out?—Have you written to Mr. Such-a-one?—Have you been to Mr. Such-a-one's?—I'll write a note for you—I'll copy a letter."—There was one common cause—Miss Strictland even deigned to assist Mr. Vivian, and to try her awkward hand to forward his canvass, for it was to support the Glistonbury interest; and "there was no impropriety could attach to the thing." Russell's extreme anxiety made Vivian call more frequently even than it was necessary at the castle, to quiet his apprehensions, and to assure him that things were going on well. Young Lord Lidhurst, who was really good-natured, and over whose mind Russell began to gain some ascendancy, used to stand upon the watch for Vivian's appearance, and would run up the back stairs to Russell's apartment, to give him notice of it, and to be the first to tell the news. Lady Sarah—the icy lady Sarah herself—began to thaw; and every day, in the same phrase, she condescended to say to Mr. Vivian, that she "hoped the poll was going on as well as could be expected." It was, of course, reported, that Vivian was to succeed the late representative of the county in all its honours. In eight days he was confidently given to Lady Sarah by the generous public; and the day of their nuptials was positively fixed. As the lady was, even by the account of her friends, two or three years older than Mr. Vivian, and four or five years older by her looks, and as she was peculiarly unsuited to his taste, he heard the report without the slightest apprehension for his own constancy to Selina. He laughed at the idea, as an excellent joke, when it was first mentioned to him by Russell. Lord Glistonbury's manners, however, and the cordial familiarity with which he treated Vivian, gave every day increasing credit to the report. "If he were his son, my lord could not be more anxious about Mr. Vivian," said one of the plain-spoken freeholders, in the presence of the Lady Lidhursts.—Lady Sarah pursed up her mouth, and threw back her head; but Lady Julia, archly looking at her sister, smiled. The vivacity of Lady Julia's manner did not appear excessive during this election time, when all the world seemed mad; on the contrary, there was, in her utmost freedom and raillery, that air of good-breeding and politeness, in which vulgar mirth and liberty are always deficient. Vivian began to think that she was become less childish, and that there was something of a mixture of womanish timidity in her appearance, which rendered her infinitely more attractive. One evening, in particular, when her father having sent her for her morning's work, she returned with a basket full of the Vivian cockade, which she had made with her own delicate hands, Vivian thought she looked "very pretty:" her father desired her to give them to the person for whom they were intended, and she presented them to Mr. Russell, saying, "They are for your friend, sir."—Vivian thought she looked "very graceful."—Lady Mary Vivian suppressed half a sigh, and thought she kept the whole of her mind to herself. These happy days of canvassing, and this freedom of election, could not last for ever. After polling the county to the last freeholder, the contest was at length decided, and Vivian was declared duly elected. He was chaired, and he scattered money with a lavish hand, as he passed over the heads of the huzzaing populace; and he had all the honours of an election: the horses were taken from his carriage, and he was drawn by men, who were soon afterwards so much intoxicated, that they retained no vestige of rationality. Not only the inferior, but the superior rank of electors, as usual upon such occasions, thought proper to do honour to their choice, and to their powers of judgment, by drinking their member's health at the expense of their own, till they could neither see, hear, nor understand. Our hero was not by any means fond of drinking, but he could not refuse to do as others did; and Lord Glistonbury swore, that now he had found out that Vivian could be such a pleasant companion over a bottle, he should never listen to his excuses in future.

A few days after this election, parliament met for the dispatch of business; and as some important question was to come on, all the members were summoned, by a peremptory call of the house. Vivian was obliged to go to town immediately, and compelled to defer his marriage. He regretted being thus hurried away from Selina; and with a thousand tender and passionate expressions, assured her, that the moment his attendance on public business could be spared, he should hasten to the country to claim his promised happiness. The castle would be finished by the time the session was over; the lawyers would also have completed their settlements; and Vivian said he should make every other necessary preparation whilst he was in town: therefore he urged Selina now to fix the time for their marriage, and to let it be the first week of the recess of parliament. But Miss Sidney, who had great delicacy of feeling and dignity of character, thought that Vivian had of late shown some symptoms of decreased affection, and that he had betrayed signs of unsteadiness of character. In the whole affair of the castle-building and of the election, he had evidently been led by others instead of following his own conviction:—she wisely dreaded that he might, in more important actions, yield his judgment to others; and then what security could she have for his principles? He might, perhaps, be led into all sorts of fashionable dissipation and vice. Besides these fears, she considered that Vivian was the possessor of a large fortune; that his mother had with difficulty consented to this match; that he was very young, had seen but little of the world, and might, perhaps, in future, repent of having made, thus early in life, a love match. She therefore absolutely refused to let him now bind himself to her by any fresh promises. She desired that he should consider himself as perfectly at liberty, and released from all engagement to her. It was evident, however, from the manner in which she spoke that she wished to restore her lover's liberty for his sake only; and that her own feelings, however they might be suppressed, were unchanged. Vivian was touched and charmed by her delicacy and generosity: in the fervour of his feelings he swore that his affections could never change; and he believed what he swore. Lady Mary Vivian was struck, also, with Miss Sidney's conduct at parting; and she acknowledged that it was impossible to show at once more tenderness and dignity. No one, however, not even Vivian, knew how much pain this separation gave Selina. Her good sense and prudence told her indeed, that it was best, both for her happiness and Vivian's, that he should see something more of the world, and that she should have some farther proof of the steadiness of his attachment, before she should unite herself with him irrevocably: but whilst she endeavoured to fortify her mind with these reflections, love inspired many painful fears; and, though she never repented having set him free from his promises and engagements, she trembled for the consequences of his being thus at liberty, in such scenes of temptation as a London life would present.

CHAPTER III

When our hero arrived in London, and when he was first introduced into fashionable society, his thoughts were so intent upon Selina Sidney, that he was in no danger of plunging into dissipation. He was surprised at the eagerness with which some young men pursued frivolous pleasures: he was still more astonished at seeing the apathy in which others of his own age were sunk, and the listless insignificance in which they lounged away their lives.

The call of the house, which brought Vivian to town, brought Lord Glistonbury also to attend his duty in the house of peers: with his lordship's family came Mr. Russell, whom Vivian went to see, as soon and as often as he could. Russell heard, with satisfaction, the indignant eloquence with which his friend spoke; and only wished that these sentiments might last, and that fashion might never lead him to imitate or to tolerate fools, whom he now despised.

"In the mean time, tell me how you go on yourself," said Vivian; "how do you like your situation here, and your pupil, and all the Glistonbury family? Let me behind the scenes at once; for, you know, I see them only on the stage."

Russell replied, in general terms, that he had hopes Lord Lidhurst would turn out well, and that therefore he was satisfied with his situation; but avoided entering into particulars, because he was a confidential person in the family. He thought that a preceptor and a physician were, in some respects, bound, by a similar species of honour, to speak cautiously of the maladies of their patients, or the faults of their pupils. Admitted into the secrets of families, they should never make use of the confidence reposed in them, to the disadvantage of any by whom they are trusted. Russell's strictly honourable reserve upon this occasion was rather provoking to Vivian, who, to all his questions, could obtain only the dry answer of—"Judge for yourself."—The nature of a town life, and the sort of intercourse which capital cities afford, put this very little in Vivian's power. The obligations he was under to Lord Glistonbury for assistance at the election made him anxious to show his lordship respect and attention; and the sort of intimacy which that election had brought on was, to a certain degree, kept up in town. Lady Mary Vivian was constantly one at Lady Glistonbury's card parties; and Vivian was frequently at his lordship's dinners. Considering the coldness and formality of Lady Glistonbury's manners, she was particularly attentive to Lady Mary Vivian; and our hero was continually an attendant upon the ladies of the Glistonbury family to all public places. This was by no means disagreeable to him, as they were persons of high consideration; and they were sure of drawing into their circle the very best company. Lady Mary Vivian observed that it was a great advantage to her son to have such a house as Lord Glistonbury's open to him, to go to whenever he pleased. Besides the advantage to his morals, her ladyship was by no means insensible to the gratification her pride received from her son's living in such high company. The report which had been raised in the country during the election, that Mr. Vivian was going to be married to Lady Sarah Lidhurst, now began to circulate in town. This was not surprising, since a young man in London, of any fortune or notoriety, can hardly dance three or four times successively with the same young lady, cannot even sit beside her, and converse with her in public half a dozen times, without its being reported that he is going to be married to her. Of this, Vivian, during his noviciate in town, was not perhaps sufficiently aware: he was soon surprised at being asked, by almost every one he met, when his marriage with Lady Sarah Lidhurst was to take place. At first he contented himself with laughing at these questions, and declaring that there was no truth in the report: but his asseverations were not to be believed; they were attributed to motives of discretion: he was told by his companions, that he kept his own counsel very well; but they all knew the thing was to be: he was congratulated upon his good fortune in making such an excellent match; for though, as they said, he would have but little money with Lady Sarah, yet the connexion was so great, that he was the luckiest fellow upon earth. The degree of importance which the report gave him among the young men of his acquaintance, and the envy he excited, amused and gratified his vanity. The sort of conversation he was now in the constant habit of hearing, both from young and old, in all companies, about the marriages of people in the fashionable world, where fortune, and rank, and connexion, were always the first things spoken of or considered, began insensibly to influence Vivian's mode of speaking, if not of judging. Before he mixed in this society, he knew perfectly well that these were the principles by which people of the world are guided; but whilst he had believed this only on hearsay, it had not appeared to him so entirely true and so important as when he saw and heard it himself. The effect of the opinions of a set of fine people, now he was actually in their society, and whilst all other society was excluded from his perception, was very different from what he had imagined it might be, when he was in the country or at college. To do our hero justice, however, he was sensible of this aberration in his own mind, he had sense enough to perceive from what causes it arose, and steadiness sufficient to adhere to the judgements he had previously and deliberately formed. He did not in material points change his opinion of his mistress; he thought her far, far superior to all he saw and heard amongst the belles who were most admired in the fashionable world; but, at the same time, he began to agree with his mother's former wish, that Selina, added to all other merits, had the advantage of high birth and connexions, or at least, of belonging to a certain class of high company. He determined that, as soon as she should be his wife, he would have her introduced to the very first society in town: he pleased his imagination with anticipating the change that would be made in her appearance, by the addition of certain elegancies of the mode: he delighted in thinking of the sensation she would produce, and the respect that would be paid to her as Mrs. Vivian, surrounded as he would take care that she should be, with all those external signs of wealth and fashion, which command immediate and universal homage from the great and little world.

One day, when Vivian was absorbed in these pleasing reveries, Russell startled him with this question: "When are you to be married to Lady Sarah Lidhurst?"

"From you such a question!" said Vivian.

"Why not from me? It is a question that every body asks of me, because I am your intimate friend; and I should really be obliged to you, if you would furnish me with an answer, that may give me an air of a little more consequence than that which I have at present, being forced to answer, 'I don't know.'"

"You don't know! but why do not you answer, 'Never!' as I do," said Vivian, "to all the fools who ask me the same question?"

"Because they say that is your answer, and only a come off."

"I can't help it—Is it my fault if they won't believe the truth?"

"Why, people are apt to trust to appearances in these cases; and if appearances are contrary to your assertions, you should not wonder that you are not believed."

"Well, time will show them their mistake!" said Vivian.—"But I don't know what appearances you mean.—What appearances are against me?—I never in my life saw a woman I was less disposed to like—whom it would be more impossible for me to love—than Lady Sarah Lidhurst; and I am sure I never gave her, or any of her family, the least reason to imagine I had a thought of her."

"Very likely; yet you are at Lord Glistonbury's continually, and you attend her ladyship to all public places. Is this the way, do you think, to put a stop to the report that has been raised?"

"I care not whether it stops or goes on," said Vivian.—"How!—Don't I know it is false?—That's enough for me."

"It may embarrass you yet," said Russell.

"Good Heavens!—Can you, who know me so well, Russell, fancy me so weak as to be embarrassed by such a report? Look—I would rather put this hand into that fire and let it be burned off, than offer it to Lady Sarah Lidhurst."

"Very likely.—I don't doubt you think so," said Russell.

"And I would do so," said Vivian.

"Possibly.—Yet you might be embarrassed nevertheless, if you found that you had raised expectations which you could not fulfil; and if you found yourself accused of having jilted this lady, if all her friends were to say you had used her very ill.—I know your nature, Vivian; these things would disquiet you very much: and is it not better to prevent them?"

"But neither Lady Sarah nor her friends blame me: I see no signs in the family of any of the thoughts or feelings you suppose."

"Ladies—especially young and fashionable ladies—do not always show their thoughts or feelings," said Russell.

"Lady Sarah Lidhurst has no thoughts or feelings," said Vivian, "any more than an automaton. I'll answer for her—I am sure I can do her the justice to proclaim, that she has always, from the first moment I saw her till this instant, conducted herself towards me with the same petrified and petrifying propriety."

"I do not know what petrified propriety exactly means," said Russell: "but let it mean what it may, it is nothing to the present purpose; for the question is not about the propriety of Lady Sarah Lidhurst's conduct, but of yours. Now, allowing you to call her ladyship a petrifaction, or an automaton, or by whatever other name you please, still, I apprehend, that she is in reality a human creature, and a woman; and I conceive it is the duty of a man of honour or honesty not to deceive her."

"I would not deceive her, or any woman living, upon any account," said Vivian. "But how is it possible I can deceive her, when I tell you I never said a word about love or gallantry, or any thing like it, to her in my life?"

"But you know language is conventional, especially in gallantry," said Russell.

"True; but I'll swear the language of my looks has been unequivocal, if that is what you mean."

"Not exactly: there are certain signs by which the world JUDGES in these cases—if a gentleman is seen often with the same lady in public."

"Absurd, troublesome, ridiculous signs, which would put a stop to all society; which would prevent a man from conversing with a woman, either in public or private; and must absolutely preclude one sex from obtaining any real knowledge of the characters and dispositions of the other."

"I admit all you say—I feel the truth of it—I wish this were changed in society; it is a great inconvenience, a real evil," said Russell: "but an individual cannot alter a custom; and, as you have not, by your own account, any particular interest in becoming more intimately acquainted with the character and disposition of Lady Sarah Lidhurst, you will do well not to expose yourself to any inconvenience on her account, by neglecting common received forms and opinions."

"Well! well!—say no more about it," said Vivian, impatiently; "spare me all farther logic and morality upon this subject, and I'll do what you please—only tell me what you would have me do."

"Gradually withdraw yourself for some time from this house, and the report will die away of itself."

"Withdraw myself!—that would be very hard upon me!" cried Vivian; "for this house is the most agreeable house in town to me;—because you live in it, in the first place; and then, though the women are as stiff as pokers, one is always sure of meeting all the pleasant and clever men at Glistonbury's good dinner. Let me tell you, good dinners, and good company, and good conversation, and good music, make altogether a very pleasant house, which I should be confoundedly sorry to be forced to give up."

"I don't doubt it," said Russell; "but we must often give up more even than this for the sake of acting with consistency and honour; we must sacrifice the less to the greater good; and it is on these occasions that people show strength or weakness of mind."

Vivian felt the justice of his friend's observations—resolved to follow his advice—and to withdraw himself gradually from the Glistonbury circle. He had not, however, steadiness enough to persist in this resolution; one engagement linked on another; and he would soon, probably, have relapsed into his habit of being continually of their parties, if accident had not for a time suspended this intimacy, by leading him into another, which seemed to him still more attractive.

Among the men of talents and political consequence whom he met at Lord Glistonbury's was Mr. Wharton, whose conversation particularly pleased Vivian, and who now courted his acquaintance with an eagerness which was peculiarly flattering. Vivian knew him only as a man of great abilities; with his real character he was not acquainted. Wharton had prepossessing manners, and wit sufficient whenever he pleased to make the worse appear the better reason. In private or in public debate he had at his command, and could condescend to employ, all sorts of arms, and every possible mode of annoyance, from the most powerful artillery of logic to the lowest squib of humour. He was as little nice in the company he kept as in the style of his conversation. Frequently associating with fools, and willing even to be thought one, he made alternately his sport and advantage of the weakness and follies of mankind. Wharton was philosophically, politically, and fashionably profligate. After having ruined his private fortune by unbounded extravagance, he lived on—nobody knew how—in careless profusion. In public life he made a distinguished figure; and seemed, therefore, to think himself raised above the necessity of practising any of the minor virtues of economy, prudence, or justice, which common people find essential to their well-being in society. Far from attempting to conceal, he gloried in his faults; for he knew full well, that as long as he had the voice of numbers with him, he could bully, or laugh, or shame plain reason and rigid principle out of countenance. It was his grand art to represent good sense as stupidity, and virtue as hypocrisy. Hypocrisy was, in his opinion, the only vice which merited the brand of infamy; and from this he took sufficient care to prove, or at least to proclaim, himself free. Even whilst he offended against the decencies of life, there seemed to be something frank and graceful in his manner of throwing aside all disguise. There appeared an air of superior liberality in his avowing himself to be governed by that absolute selfishness, which other men strive to conceal even from their own hearts. He dexterously led his acquaintance to infer that he would prove as much better than his professions, as other people are often found to be worse than theirs. Where he wished to please, it was scarcely possible to escape the fascination of his manner; nor did he neglect any mode of courting popularity. He knew that a good table is necessary to attract even men of wit; and he made it a point to have the very best cook, and the very best wines. He paid his cook, and his cook was the only person he did pay, in ready money. His wine-merchant he paid in words—an art in which he was a professed and yet a successful adept, as hundreds of living witnesses were ready to attest. But though Wharton could cajole, he could not attach his fellow-creatures—he had a party, but no friend. With this distribution of things he was perfectly satisfied; for he considered men only as beings who were to be worked to his purposes; and he declared that, provided he had power over their interests and their humours, he cared not what became of their hearts. It was his policy to enlist young men of talents or fortune under his banners; and consequently Vivian was an object worthy of his attention. Such was the disorder of Wharton's affairs, that either ready money or political power was necessary to his existence. Our hero could, at the same time, supply his extravagance and increase his consequence. Wharton thought that he could borrow money from Vivian, and that he might command his vote in parliament; but, to the accomplishment of these schemes, there were two obstacles—Vivian was attached to an amiable woman, and was possessed of an estimable friend. Wharton had become acquainted with Russell at Lord Glistonbury's; and, in many arguments which they had held on public affairs, had discovered that Russell was not a man who ever preferred the expedient to the right, nor one who could be bullied or laughed out of his principles. He saw also that Russell's influence over Vivian was so great, that it supplied him with that strength of mind in which Vivian was naturally deficient; and, if our hero should marry such a woman as Miss Sidney, Wharton foresaw that he should have no chance of succeeding in his designs; therefore his first objects were, to detach Vivian from his friend Russell and from Selina. One morning he called upon Vivian with a party of his friends, and found him writing.

"Poetry!" cried Wharton, carelessly looking at what he had, been writing, "poetry, I protest!—Ay, I know this poor fellow's in love; and every man who is in love is a poet, 'with a woeful ditty to his mistress's eyebrow.' Pray what colour may Miss Sidney's eyebrows be?—she is really a pretty girl—I think I remember seeing her at some races.—Why does she never come to town?—But of course she is not to blame for that, but her fortune I suppose.—Marrying a girl without a fortune is a serious thing in these expensive days; but you have fortune enough for both yourself and your wife, so you may do as you please. Well, I thank God, I have no fortune! If I had been a young man of fortune I should have been the most unhappy rascal upon earth, for I should have always suspected that every woman liked me for my wealth—I should have had no pleasure in the smiles of an angel—angels, or their mothers, are so venal now-a-days, and so fond of the pomps and vanities of this wicked world!"

"I hope," said Vivian, laughing, "you don't include the whole sex in your satire."

"No—there are exceptions—and every man has his angel of an exception, as every woman has her star:—it is well for weak women when these stars of theirs don't lead them astray; and well for weak men when these angel exceptions before marriage don't turn out very women or devils afterwards. But why do I say all this? because I am a suspicious scoundrel—I know and can't help it. If other fellows of my standing in this wicked world would but speak the truth, however, they would show as much suspicion and more than I do. Bad as I am, and such as I am, you see, and have the whole of me—

nobody can say Wharton's a hypocrite; that's some comfort. But, seriously, Vivian, I don't mean to laugh at love and angels—I can just remember the time when I felt all your sort of romance—but that is in the preterpluperfect tense with me—completely past—ambition is no bad cure for love. My head is, at this present moment, so full of this new bill that we are bringing into parliament, that Cupid might empty his quiver upon me in vain.—Look! here is an impenetrable shield!" added he, wrapping round him a thick printed copy of an act of parliament. "Come, Vivian, you must come along with us to the house,

'And, mix'd with men, a man you must appear.'"

Vivian felt much ashamed of having been detected in writing a sonnet, especially as it afforded Wharton such a fine subject for raillery. He accompanied the party to the House of Commons, where Wharton made a brilliant speech. It gained universal applause. Vivian sympathized in the general enthusiasm of admiration for Wharton's talents, accepted an invitation to sup with him, and was charmed by his convivial powers. From this day, he grew every hour more intimate with Wharton.

"I can enjoy," thought Vivian, "the pleasure of his society without being influenced by his libertine example."

Lady Mary Vivian saw the rise and progress of this intimacy, and was not insensible to its danger; yet she was gratified by seeing her son distinguished by a man of Wharton's political consequence; and she satisfied her conscience by saying, "He will bring my son forward in public life; and, as to the rest, Charles has too good principles ever to follow his example in private life."

Wharton had too much address to alarm Vivian's moral prejudices on a first acquaintance. He contented himself with ridiculing only the exaggeration of any of the virtues, still affecting to believe in virtue, and to love it, wherever it could be found genuine. By the success of his first petty attacks, he learned the power that ridicule had over our hero's mind; and he did not fail to make use of it continually. After having, as he perceived, succeeded in making Vivian ashamed of his sonnet to Selina, and of appearing as a romantic lover, he doubted not but in time he should make true love itself ridiculous; and Wharton thought it was now the moment to hazard another stroke, and to commence his attack against friendship.

"Vivian, my good fellow! why do you let yourself be ruled by that modern stoic in the form of Lord Lidhurst's tutor? I never saw any of these cold moralists who were real, warm-hearted, good friends. I have a notion I see more of Russell's play in the house where he has got than he thinks I do; and I can form a shrewd guess why he was so zealous in warning you of the report about Lady Sarah Lidhurst—he had his own snug reasons for wanting you away—Oh, trust me for scenting out self-interest, through all the doublings and windings of your cunning moralist!"

Reddening with indignation at this attack upon his friend, Vivian warmly replied, that Mr. Wharton ought to restrain his wit where the feelings of friendship and the character of a man of honour were concerned; that he did not, in the least, comprehend his insinuations with regard to Russell; but that, for his own part, he had such firm reliance upon his friend's attachment and integrity, that he was at any time ready to pledge his own honour for Russell's, and to answer for it with his life.

"Spare your heroics, my dear Vivian!" cried Wharton, laughing; "for we are not in the days of Pylades and Orestes;—yet, upon my soul, instead of being as angry with you as you are with me, at this instant I like you a thousand times the better for your enthusiastic credulity. For my part, I have, ever since I lived in the world and put away childish things, regretted that charming instinct of credulity, which experience so fatally counteracts. I envy you, my dear boy!—as to the rest, you know Russell's merits better than I do: I'll take him henceforward upon trust from you."

"Thus Wharton, finding that he was upon dangerous ground, made a timely retreat: the playful manner and open countenance with which he now spoke, and the quick transition that he made to other subjects of conversation, prevented Vivian from suspecting that any settled design had been formed to detach him from Russell. From this time forward, Wharton forbore raillery on love and friendship; and, far from seeming desirous of interfering in Vivian's private concerns, appeared quite absorbed in politics. Avowing, as he did, that he was guided solely by his interest in public life, he laughed at Vivian for professing more generous principles.

"I know," cried Wharton, "how to make use of a fine word, and to round a fine sentence, as well as the best of you; but what a simpleton he must be who is cheated by his own sophistry!—An artist, an enthusiastic artist, who is generally half a madman, might fall in love with a statue of his own making; but you never heard of a coiner, did you, who was cheated by his own bad shilling? Patriotism and loyalty are counterfeit coin; I can't be taken in by them at my time of day."

Vivian could not forbear to smile at the drollery and wit with which this profligate defended his want of integrity; yet he sometimes seriously and warmly asserted his own principles. Upon these occasions, Wharton either overpowered him by a fine flow of words, or else listened with the most flattering air of admiration, and silenced him by compliments to his eloquence. Vivian thought that he was quite secure of his own firmness; but the contagion of bad example sometimes affects the mind imperceptibly; as certain noxious atmospheres steal upon the senses, and excite the most agreeable sensations, while they secretly destroy the principles of health and life. A day was fixed when a question of importance was to come on in the House of Commons. Wharton was extremely anxious to have Vivian's vote. Vivian, according to the parliamentary phrase, had not made up his mind on the subject. A heap of pamphlets on the question lay uncut upon his table. Every morning he resolved to read them, that he might form his judgment, and vote according to his unbiassed opinion; but every morning he was interrupted by some of the fashionable idlers whom his facility of temper had indulged in the habit of haunting him daily. "Oh, Vivian! we are going to such and such a place, and you must come with us!" was a mode of persuasion which he could not resist.

"If I don't do as they do," thought he, "I shall be quite unfashionable. Russell may say what he pleases, but it is necessary to yield to one's companions in trifles.

'Whoever would be pleased and please,
Must do what others do with ease.'"

This couplet, which had been repeated to him by Wharton, recurred to him continually; and thus Wharton, by slight means, in which he seemed to have no interest or design, prepared Vivian for his purposes, by working gradually on the easiness of his disposition. He always argued, that it could not possibly signify what he did with an hour or two of his day, till at last Vivian found that he had no hours of his own, that his whole time was at the disposal of others; and now that he really wanted leisure to consider an important question,—when his credit, as a member of the senate, and as a man just entering political life, depended on this decision,—he literally could not command time to read over the necessary documents. So the appointed day arrived before Vivian's opinion was formed; and, from mere want of time to decide for himself, he voted as Wharton desired. Another and another political question came on; the same causes operated, and the same consequences ensued. Wharton managed with great address, so as to prevent him from feeling that he gave up his freewill. Before Vivian was aware of it, whilst he thought that he was perfectly independent of all parties, public opinion had enrolled him amongst Wharton's partisans. Of this Russell was the first to give him warning. Russell heard of it amongst the political leaders who met at Lord Glistonbury's dinners; and, knowing the danger there is of a young man's committing himself on certain points, he, with the eagerness of a true friend, wrote immediately to put Vivian upon his guard:—

"My Dear Vivian,

"I am just going into the country with Lord Lidhurst, and perhaps may not return for some time. I cannot leave you without putting you on your guard, once more, against Mr. Wharton. I understand that you are thought to be one of his party, and that he countenances the report. Take care that you are not bound hand and foot, before you know where you are.

"Your sincere friend,

"H. Russell."

With the natural frankness of his disposition, Vivian immediately spoke to Wharton upon the subject.

"What! people say that you are one of my party, do they?" said Wharton: "I never heard this before, but I am heartily glad to hear it. You are in for it now, Vivian: you are one of us; and with us you must stand or fall."

"Excuse me there!" cried Vivian; "I am not of any party; and am determined to keep myself independent."

"Do you remember the honest Quaker's answer to the man of no party?" said Wharton.

"No."

"I think it was about the year '40, when party disputes about Whig and Tory ran high—but no matter what year, it will do for any time. A gentleman of undeviating integrity, an independent man, just such a man as Mr. Vivian, offered himself candidate for a town in the east, west, north, or south of England— no matter where, it will do for any place; and the first person whose vote he solicited was a Quaker, who asked him whether he was a Whig or Tory?—'Neither. I am an independent, moderate man; and when the members of administration are right, I will vote with them—when wrong, against them.' 'And be these really thy principles?' quoth the Quaker; 'then a vote of mine thou shalt never have. Thou seest my door, it leadeth into the street; the right hand side of which is for the Tory, the left for the Whigs; and for a cold-blooded moderate man, like thee, there is the kennel, and into it thou wilt be jostled, for thou beest not decided enough for any other situation.'"

"But why should the moderate man be condemned to the kennel?" said Vivian. "Was there no middle to your Quaker's road? A stout man cannot be EASILY jostled into the kennel."

"Pshaw! pshaw!" said Wharton: "jesting out of the question, a man is nothing in public life, or worse than nothing, a trimmer, unless HE JOINS a party, and unless he abides by it, too."

"As long as the party is in the right, I presume, you mean," said Vivian.

"Right or wrong'" cried Wharton, "a man must abide by his party. No power, and no popularity, trust me, without it!—Better stride on the greasy heads of the mob than be trampled under their dirtier feet. An armed neutrality may be a good thing, but an unarmed neutrality is fit only for fools. Besides, in Russell's grand style, I can bring down the ancients upon you, and tell you that when the commonwealth is in danger he cannot be a good man who sides with neither party."

"If it be so necessary to join a party, and if, after once joining it, I must abide by it, right or wrong, for life," said Vivian, "it behoves me to consider well, before I commit myself; and, before I go into the ranks, I must see good reason to confide, not only in the abilities, but in the integrity and public virtue of my leader."

"Public virtue! sounds fresh from college," said Wharton; "I would as soon, and sooner, hear a schoolboy read his theme as hear a man begin to prose about public virtue—especially a member of parliament. Keep that phrase, my dear Vivian, till some of the treasury bench come to court you; then look superb, like a French tragic actor, swelling out your chest, and throwing the head over the left shoulder—thus—exclaim, 'Public virtue forbid!'—practise! practise!—for if you do it well, it may be worth a loud huzza to you yet; or better still, a snug place or pension. But stay till you're asked—stay till you're asked—that's the etiquette; never till then let me hear public virtue come out of your lips, else you'll raise suspicion of your virtue, and lower your price. What would you think of a pretty actress who began to talk to you of her reputation before you put it in any danger? Oh, Vivian! my honest fellow! unless you would make me think you no better than thousands that have gone before you, never let me hear from your lips again, till the proper time, the hypocritical state phrase—public virtue."

"I had always, till now, understood that it was possible to be a patriot without being a hypocrite," replied Vivian; "I always understood that Mr. Wharton was a patriot."

"A very fair sarcasm on me," said Wharton, laughing. "But you know, I'm a sad dog; never set myself up for a pattern man.—Come! let's home to dinner, and a truce with politics and morality. I find, Vivian, you're a sturdy fellow, and must have your own way; no bending, no leading you, I see. Well! it is a good thing to have so much strength of mind: I envy you."

It must be recorded to the credit of our hero, that in defiance of Wharton's raillery, he talked, and—oh! still more wonderful!—thought of public virtue, during nearly half of his first session in parliament. But, alas! whilst his political principles thus withstood the force of ridicule, temptation soon presented itself to Vivian in a new shape, and in a form so seducing, as to draw his attention totally away from politics, and to put his private, if not his public, honour, in the most imminent peril.

CHAPTER IV

One morning, as Vivian was walking with Mr. Wharton up Bond-street, they were met by a party of fashionable loungers, one of whom asked whether Mrs. Wharton was not come to town yet.

"Mrs. Wharton!" said Vivian, with an air of surprise.

"Yes, she came to town this morning," said Wharton, carelessly; then laughing, as he turned to look at Vivian, "Vivian, my good fellow! what smites you with such surprise? Did not you know I was married?"

"I suppose I must have heard it; but I really forgot it," said Vivian.

"There you had the advantage of me," said Wharton, still laughing. "But if you never heard of Mrs. Wharton before, keep your own secret; for I can tell you she would never forgive you, though I might. Put a good face on the matter, at any rate; and swear you've heard so much of her, that you were dying to see her. Some of these gentlemen, who have nothing else to do, will introduce you whenever you please."

"And cannot I," said Vivian, "have the honour of your introduction?"

"Mine! the worst you could possibly have. The honour, as you are pleased to call it, would be no favour, I assure you. The honour!—honour of a husband's introduction! What a novice you are, or would make me believe you to be! But, seriously, I am engaged to-day at Glistonbury's: so, good morning to you."

Accustomed to hear Wharton talk in the freest manner of women and marriage in general, and scarcely having heard him mention his own wife, Vivian had, as he said, absolutely forgotten that Wharton was a married man. When he was introduced to Mrs. Wharton, he was still more surprised at her husband's indifference; for he beheld a lady in all the radiance of beauty, and all the elegance of fashion: he was so much dazzled by her charms, that he had not immediately power or inclination to examine what her understanding or disposition might be; and he could only repeat to himself, "How is it possible that Wharton can be indifferent to such a beautiful creature!"

Incapable of feeling any of what he, called the romance of love, the passion, of course, had always been with Mr. Wharton of a very transient nature. Tired of his wife's person, he showed his indifference without scruple or ceremony. Notorious and glorying in his gallantries, he was often heard to declare, that no price was too high to be paid for beauty, except a man's liberty; but that was a sacrifice which he would never make to any woman, especially to a wife. Marriage vows and custom-house oaths he classed in the same order of technical forms,—nowise binding on the conscience of any but fools and dupes. Whilst the husband went on in this manner, the wife satisfied herself by indulgence in her strongest passions—the passion for dress and public admiration. Childishly eager to set the fashion in trifles, she spent unconscionable sums on her pretty person; and devoted all her days, or rather all her nights, to public amusements. So insatiable and restless is the passion for admiration, that she was never happy for half an hour together, at any place of public amusement, unless she fixed the gaze of numbers. The first winter after her marriage she enjoyed the prerogatives of a fashionable beauty; but the reign of fashion is more transient even than the bloom of beauty. Mrs. Wharton's beauty soon grew familiar, and faded in the public eye; some newer face was this season the mode. Mrs. Wharton appeared twice at the opera in the most elegant and becoming dresses; but no one followed her lead. Mortified and utterly dejected, she felt, with the keenest anguish, the first symptoms of the decline of public admiration. It was just at this period, when she was miserably in want of the consolations of flattery, that Vivian's acquaintance with her commenced. Gratified by the sort of delighted surprise which she saw in his countenance the first moment he beheld her, seeing that he was an agreeable man, and knowing that he was a man of fortune and family, she took pains to please him by all the common arts of coquetry. But his vanity was proof against these: the weakness of the lady's understanding and the frivolity of her character were, for some weeks, sufficient antidotes against all the power of her personal charms; so much so, that at this period he often compared, or rather contrasted, Mrs. Wharton and Selina, and blessed his happy fate. He wrote to his friend Russell soon after he was introduced to this celebrated beauty, and drew a strong and just parallel between the characters of these two ladies: he concluded with saying, "Notwithstanding your well-founded dread of the volatility of my character, you will not, I hope, my dear Russell, do me the injustice to apprehend that I am in any danger from the charms of Mrs. Wharton."

Vivian wrote with perfect sincerity; he believed it to be impossible that he could ever become attached to such a woman as Mrs. Wharton, even if she had not been married, and the wife of his friend. So, in all the security of conscious contempt, he went every day to wait upon her, or rather to meet agreeable company at her house,—a house in which all that was fashionable and dissipated assembled; where beauty, and talents, and rank, met and mingled; and where political or other arrangements prevented the host and hostess from scrupulously excluding some whose characters were not free from suspicion. Lady Mary Vivian never went to Mrs. Wharton's; but she acknowledged that she knew many ladies of unblemished reputation who thought it no impropriety to visit there; and Mrs. Wharton's own character she knew was hitherto unimpeached. "She is, indeed, a woman of a cold, selfish temper," said Lady Mary; "not likely to be led into danger by the tender passion, or by any of the delusions of the imagination."

Vivian agreed with his mother in this opinion, and went on paying his devoirs to her every day. It was the fashion of the times, and peculiarly the mode of this house, for the gentlemen to pay exclusive attention to matrons. Few of the young men seemed to think it worth while to speak to an unmarried woman in any company; and the few who might be inclined to it were, as they declared, deterred by the danger: for either the young ladies themselves, or their mothers, immediately formed expectations and schemes of drawing them into matrimony—the grand object of the ladies' wishes and of the gentlemen's fears. The men said they could not speak to an unmarried woman, or even dance with her more than twice, without its being reported that they were going to be married; and then the friends and relatives of the young ladies pretended to think them injured and ill-treated, if these reports were not realized. Our hero had some slight experience of the truth of these complaints in his own case with the Lady Sarah Lidhurst: he willingly took the rest upon trust—believed all the exaggerations of his companions—and began to think it prudent and necessary to follow their example, and to confine his attentions to married women. Many irresistible reasons concurred to make Mrs. Wharton the most convenient and proper person to whom he could pay this sort of homage: besides, she seemed to fall to his share by lot and necessity; for, at Wharton's house, every other lady and every other gentleman being engaged in gallantry, play, or politics, Mrs. Wharton must have been utterly neglected if Vivian had not paid her some attention. Common politeness absolutely required it; the attention became a matter of course, and was habitually expected. Still he had not the slightest design of going beyond the line of modern politeness; but, in certain circumstances, people go wrong a great way before they are aware that they have gone a single step. It was presently repeated to Mr. Vivian, by some of Mrs. Wharton's confidantes, in whispers, and under the solemn promise of secrecy, that he certainly was a prodigious favourite of hers. He laughed, and affected to disbelieve the insinuation: it made its impression, however; and he was secretly flattered by the idea of being a prodigious favourite with such a beautiful young creature. In some moments he saw her with eyes of compassion, pitying her for the neglect with which she was treated by her husband: he began to attribute much of her apparent frivolity, and many of her faults, more to the want of a guide and a friend than to a deficiency of understanding or to defects of character. Mrs. Wharton had just sufficient sense to be cunning—this implies but a very small portion: she perceived the advantage which she gained by thus working upon Vivian's vanity and upon his compassion. She continued her operations, without being violently interested in their success; for she had at first only a general wish to attract his attention, because he was a fashionable young man.

One morning when he called upon Wharton to accompany him to the House of Commons, he found Mrs. Wharton in tears, her husband walking up and down the room in evident ill-humour. He stopped speaking when Vivian entered; and Mrs. Wharton endeavoured, or seemed to endeavour, to conceal her emotion. She began to play on her harp; and Wharton, addressing himself to Vivian, talked of the politics of the day. There was some incoherence in the conversation; for Vivian's attention was distracted by the air that Mrs. Wharton was playing, of which he was passionately fond.

"There's no possibility of doing any thing while there is such a cursed noise in the room!" cried Wharton. "Here I have the heads of this bill to draw up—I cannot endure to have music wherever I go—"

He snatched up his papers and retired to an adjoining apartment, begging that Vivian would wait one quarter of an hour for him.—Mrs. Wharton's tears flowed afresh, and she looked beautiful in tears.

"You see—you see, Mr. Vivian—and I am ashamed you should see—how I am treated.—I am, indeed, the most unfortunate creature upon the face of the earth; and nobody in this world has the least compassion for me!"

Vivian's countenance contradicted this last assertion most positively.—Mrs. Wharton understood this; and her attitude of despondency was the most graceful imaginable.

"My dear Mrs. Wharton"—(it was the first time our hero had ever called her "his dear Mrs. Wharton;" but it was only a platonic dear)—"you take trifles much too seriously—Wharton was hurried by business—a moment's impatience must be forgiven."

"A moment!" replied Mrs. Wharton, casting up to heaven her beautiful eyes—"Oh! Mr. Vivian, how little do you know of him!—I am the most miserable creature that ever existed; but there is not a man upon earth to whom I would say so except yourself."

Vivian could not help feeling some gratitude for this distinction; and, as he leaned over her harp with an air of unusual interest, he said he hoped that he should ever prove himself worthy of her esteem and confidence.

At this instant Wharton interrupted the conversation, by passing hastily through the room.—"Come, Vivian," said he; "we shall be very late at the house."

"We shall see you again of course at dinner," said Mrs. Wharton to Vivian in a low voice. Our hero replied by an assenting bow.

Five minutes afterwards he repented that he had accepted the invitation, because he foresaw that he should resume a conversation which was at once interesting and embarrassing. He felt that it was not right to become the depository of this lady's complaints against her husband; yet he had been moved by her tears, and the idea that he was the only man in the world to whom she would open her heart upon such a delicate subject, interested him irresistibly in her favour. He returned in the evening, and was flattered by observing, that amongst the crowd of company by which she was surrounded he was instantly distinguished. He was perfectly persuaded of the innocence of her intentions; and, as he was attached to another woman, he fancied that he could become the friend of the beautiful Mrs. Wharton without danger. The first time he had an opportunity of speaking to her in private, he expressed this idea in the manner that he thought the most delicately flattering to her self-complacency. Mrs. Wharton seemed to be perfectly satisfied with this conduct; and declared, that unless she had been certain that he was not a man of gallantry, she should never have placed any confidence in his friendship.

"I consider you," said she, "quite as a married man:—by-the-bye, when are you to be married, and what sort of a person is Miss Sidney?—I am told she is excessively handsome, and amiable, and sensible.— What a happy creature she is!—just going to be united to the man she loves!" Here the lady gave a profound sigh; and Vivian had an opportunity of observing that she had the longest dark eyelashes that he had ever seen.

"I was married," continued she, "before I knew what I was about. You know Mr. Wharton can be so charming when he pleases—and then he was so much in love with me, and swore he would shoot himself if I would not have him—and all that sort of thing.—I protest I was terrified; and I was quite a child, you know. I had been out but six weeks, and I thought I was in love with him. That was because I did not know what love was—then;—besides, he hurried and teased me to such a degree!—After all, I'm convinced I married him more out of compassion than any thing else; and now you see how he treats me!—most barbarously and tyrannically!—But I would not give the least hint of this to any man living but yourself. I conjure you to keep my secret—and—pity me!—that is all I ask—pity me sometimes, when your thoughts are not absorbed in a happier manner."

Vivian's generosity was piqued: he could not be so selfish as to be engrossed exclusively by his own felicity. He thought that delicacy should induce him to forbear expatiating upon Selina's virtues and accomplishments, or upon his passion. He carried this delicacy so far, that sometimes for a fortnight or three weeks he never mentioned her name. He could not but observe that Mrs. Wharton did not like him the less for this species of sacrifice. It may be observed, that Mrs. Wharton managed her attack upon Vivian with more art than could be expected from so silly a woman; but we must consider that all her faculties were concentrated on one object; so that she seemed to have an instinct for coquetry. The most silly animals in the creation, from the insect tribe upwards, show, on some occasions, where their interests are immediately concerned, a degree of sagacity and ingenuity, which, compared with their usual imbecility, appears absolutely wonderful. The opinion which Vivian had early formed of the weakness of this lady's understanding prevented him from being on his guard against her artifices: he could not conceive it possible that he should be duped by a person so obviously his inferior. With a woman of talents and knowledge, he might have been suspicious; but there was nothing in Mrs. Wharton to alarm his pride or to awaken his fears: he fancied that he could extricate himself in a moment, and with the slightest effort, from any snares which she could contrive; and, under this persuasion, he neglected to make even that slight effort, and thus continued from hour to hour in voluntary captivity.

Insensibly Vivian became more interested for Mrs. Wharton; and, at the same time, submitted with increased facility to the influence of her husband. It was necessary that he should have some excuse to the world, and yet more to his own conscience, for being so constantly at Wharton's. The pleasure he took in Wharton's conversation was still a sort of involuntary excuse to himself for his intimacy with the lady. "Wharton's wit more than Mrs. Wharton's beauty," thought he, "is the attraction that draws me here—I am full as ready to be of his parties as of hers; and this is the best proof that all is as it should be."

Wharton's parties were not always such as Vivian would have chosen; but he was pressed on, without power of resistance. For instance, one night Wharton was going with Lord Pontipool and a set of dissipated young men, to the house of a lady who made herself fashionable by keeping a faro-bank.

"Vivian, you'll come along with us?" said Wharton. "Come, we must have you—unless you are more happily engaged."

His eye glanced with a mixture of contempt and jealousy upon his wife. Mrs. Wharton's alarmed and imploring countenance at the same moment seemed to say, "For Heaven's sake, go with him, or I am undone." In such circumstances it was impossible for Vivian to say no: he followed immediately; acting, as he thought, from a principle of honour and generosity. Wharton was not a man to give up the advantage which he had gained. Every day he showed more capricious jealousy of his wife, though he, at the same time, expressed the most entire confidence in the honour of his friend. Vivian still thought he could not do too much to convince him that his confidence was not misplaced; and thus, to protect Mrs. Wharton from suspicion, he yielded to all her husband's wishes. Vivian now felt frequently ashamed of his conduct, but always proud of his motives; and, with ingenious sophistry, he justified to himself the worst actions, by pleading that he did them with the best intentions.

CHAPTER V

By this time Lady Mary Vivian began to hear hints of her son's attachment to Mrs. Wharton; and, much alarmed, she repented having encouraged him to form a political or fashionable intimacy with the Whartons. Suddenly awakened to the perception of the danger, Lady Mary was too vehement in her terror. She spoke with so much warmth and indignation, that there was little chance of her counsels being of use.

"But, my dear madam, it is only a platonic attachment," argued Vivian, when his mother represented to him that the world talked loudly of his intimacy with Mrs. Wharton.

"A platonic attachment!—Fashionable, dangerous sophistry!" said Lady Mary.

"Why so, ma'am?" said her son, warmly; "and why should we mind what the world says? The world is so fond of scandal, that a man and woman cannot have any degree of friendship for one another without a hue and cry being immediately raised—and all the prudes and coquettes join at once in believing, or pretending to believe, that there must be something wrong. No wonder such a pretty woman as Mrs. Wharton cannot escape envy, and, of course, censure; but her conduct can defy the utmost malice of her enemies."

"I hope so," said Lady Mary; "and, at all events, I am not one of them. I know and care very little about Mrs. Wharton, whom I have always been accustomed to consider as a frivolous, silly woman; but what I wish to say, though I fear I have lost your confidence, and that my advice will not—"

"Frivolous! silly!" interrupted Vivian; "believe me, my dear mother, you and half the world are, and have been, under a great mistake about her understanding and character."

"Her forming a platonic friendship with a young man is no great proof of her sense or of her virtue," said Lady Mary. "The danger of platonic attachments, I thought, had been sufficiently understood. Pray, my dear Charles, never let me hear more from you of platonics with married women."

"I won't use the expression, ma'am, if you have any objection to it," said Vivian; "but, mother, you wish me to live in the most fashionable company, and yet you desire me not to live as they live, and talk as they talk: now, that is next to impossible. Pardon me, but I should not have thought," added he, laughing, "that you, who like most things that are fashionable, would object to platonics."

"Object to them!—I despise, detest, abhor them! Platonics have been the ruin of more women, the destruction of the peace of more families, than open profligacy ever could have accomplished. Many a married woman, who would have started with horror at the idea of beginning an intrigue, has been drawn in to admit of a platonic attachment. And many a man, who would as soon have thought of committing murder as of seducing his friend's wife, has allowed himself to commence a platonic attachment; and how these end, all the world knows."

Struck by these words, Vivian suddenly quitted his air of raillery, and became serious. Had his mother stopped there, and left the rest to his good sense and awakened perception of danger, all would have been well; but she was ever prone to say too much; and, in her ardour to prove herself to be in the right, forgot that people are apt to be shocked, by having it pointed out that they are utterly in the wrong.

"Indeed, the very word platonics," pursued she, "is considered, by those who have seen any thing of life, as the mere watchword of knaves or dupes; of those who deceive, or of those who wish to be deceived."

"Be assured, ma'am," said Vivian, "that Mrs. Wharton is not one of those who wish either to deceive or to be deceived; and, as to myself, I hope I am as far from any danger of being a dupe as of being a knave. My connexion with Mrs. Wharton is perfectly innocent; it is justified by the example of hundreds and thousands every day in the fashionable world; and I should do her and myself great injustice, if I broke off our intimacy suddenly, as if I acknowledged that it was improper."

"And what can be more improper? since you force me to speak plainly," cried Lady Mary; "what can be more improper than such an intimacy, especially in your circumstances?"

"My circumstances! What circumstances, ma'am?"

"Have you forgotten Miss Sidney?"

"By no means, ma'am," said Vivian, colouring deeply; "Mrs. Wharton is well apprized, and was, from the first moment of our friendship, clearly informed of my—engagements with Miss Sidney."

"And how do they agree with your attachment to Mrs. Wharton?"

"Perfectly well, ma'am—Mrs. Wharton understands all that perfectly well, ma'am."

"And Miss Sidney! do you think she will understand it?—and is it not extraordinary that I should think more of her feelings than you do?"

At these questions Vivian became so angry, that he was incapable of listening farther to reason, or to the best advice, even from a mother, for whom he had the highest respect. The mother and son parted with feelings of mutual dissatisfaction.

Vivian, from that spirit of opposition so often seen in weak characters, went immediately from his mother's lecture to a party at Mrs. Wharton's. Lady Mary, in the mean time, sat down to write to Miss Sidney. Whatever reluctance she had originally felt to her son's marriage with this young lady, it must be repeated, to her ladyship's credit, that Selina's honourable and disinterested conduct had won her entire approbation. She wrote, therefore, in the strongest terms to press the immediate conclusion of that match, which she now considered as the only chance of securing her son's morals and happiness. Her letter concluded with these words:—"I shall expect you in town directly. Do not, my dear, let any idle scruples prevent you from coming to my house. Consider that my happiness, your own, and my son's, depend upon your compliance. I am persuaded, that the moment he sees you, the moment you exert your power over him, he will be himself again. But, believe me, I know the young men of the present day better than you do: their constancy is not proof against absence. If he lose the habit of seeing and conversing with you, I cannot answer for the rest.—Adieu! I am so much harassed by my own thoughts, and by the reports I hear, that I scarcely know what I write. Pray come immediately, my dear Selina, that I may talk to you of many subjects on which I don't like to trust myself to write. My feelings have been too long repressed.—I must unburden my heart to you. You only can console and assist me; and, independently of all other considerations, you owe to my friendship for you, Selina, not to refuse this first request I ever made you.—Farewell! I shall expect to see you as soon as possible.

"Yours, &c.

"MARY VIVIAN."

"St. James's-street."

In this letter, Lady Mary Vivian had not explained the nature of her son's danger, or of her fears for him. Motives of delicacy had prevented her from explicitly telling Miss Sidney her suspicions that Vivian was attached to a married woman. "Selina," said her ladyship to herself, "must, probably, have heard the report from Mr. G—, who is so often at her mother's; therefore, there can be no necessity for my saying any more than I have done. She will understand my hints."

Unfortunately, however, Miss Sidney did not comprehend, or in the least suspect, the most material part of the truth; she understood simply, from Lady Mary's letter, that Vivian's affections wavered, and she imagined that he was, perhaps, on the point of making matrimonial proposals for some fashionable belle, probably for one of the Lady Lidhursts; but the idea of his becoming attached to a married woman never entered her thoughts. Many motives conspired to incline Selina to accept of the invitation. The certainty that Lady Mary would be highly offended by a refusal; the hint, that her influence over Vivian would operate immediately, and in all its force, if he were to see and converse with her; and that, on the contrary, absence might extinguish his passion for ever; curiosity to learn precisely the nature of the reports, which his mother had heard to his disadvantage; but, above all, a fond wish to be nearer to the man she loved, and to have daily opportunities of seeing him, prompted Selina to comply with Lady Mary's request. On the contrary, good sense and delicacy represented, that she had released Vivian from all promises, all engagements; that, at parting, she had professed to leave him perfectly at liberty: that it would, therefore, be as indelicate as imprudent to make such an attempt to reclaim his inconstant heart. She had told him, that she desired to have proof of the steadiness, both of his character and of his attachment, before she could consent to marry him. From this decision she could not, she would not, recede. She had the fortitude to persist in this resolution. She wrote to Lady Mary Vivian in the kindest, but, at the same time, in the most decided terms, declining the tempting invitation.

It happened that Vivian was with his mother at the moment when Selina's answer arrived. In the firm belief that such a pressing invitation as she had sent, to a person in Selina's circumstances and of Selina's temper, could not be refused, her ladyship had made it a point with her son to dine tête-à-tête with her this day; and she had been talking to him, in the most eloquent but imprudent manner, of the contrast between the characters of Mrs. Wharton and Miss Sidney. He protested that his esteem and love for Miss Sidney were unabated; yet, when his mother told him that he would, perhaps, in a few minutes see his Selina, he changed colour, grew embarrassed and melancholy, and thus by his looks effectually contradicted his words. He was roused from his reverie by the arrival of Selina's letter. His mother's disappointment and anger were expressed in the strongest terms, when she found that Selina declined her invitation; but such are the quick and seemingly perverse turns of the human heart, Vivian grew warm in Selina's defence the moment that his mother became angry with her: he read her letter with tender emotion, for he saw through the whole of it, the strength, as well as the delicacy of her attachment. All that his mother's praises had failed to effect, was immediately accomplished by this letter; and he, who but an instant before dreaded to meet Selina, now that she refused to come, was seized with a strong desire to see her; his impatience was so great, that he would willingly have set out that instant for the country. Men of such characters as Vivian's are peculiarly jealous of their free will; and, precisely because they know that they are easily led, they resist, in affairs of the heart especially, the slightest appearance of control.

Lady Mary was delighted to hear her son declare his resolution to leave town the next morning, and to see Miss Sidney as soon as possible; but she could not forbear reproaching him for not doing what she wanted precisely in the manner in which she had planned that it should be done.

"I see, my dear Charles," cried she, "that even when you do right, I must not flatter myself that it is owing to any influence of mine. Give my compliments to Miss Sidney, and assure her that I shall in future forbear to injure her in your opinion by my interference, or even by expressing my approbation of her character. My anger, it is obvious, has served her better than my kindness; and therefore she has no reason to regret that my affection has been lessened, as I confess it has been, by her late conduct."

The next morning, when Vivian was prepared to leave town, he called upon Wharton, to settle with him about some political, business which was to be transacted in his absence. Wharton was not at home—Vivian knew that it would be best to avoid seeing Mrs. Wharton; but he was afraid that she would be offended, and he could not help sacrificing a few minutes to politeness. The lady was alone; apparently very languid, and charmingly melancholy. Before Vivian could explain himself, she poured forth, in silly phrases, but in a voice that made even nonsense please, a rariety of reproaches for his having absented himself for such a length of time.—"Positively, she would keep him prisoner, now that she had him safe once more." To be kept prisoner by a fair lady was so flattering, that it was full an hour before he could prevail upon himself to assert his liberty—the fear of giving pain, indeed, influenced him still more than vanity. At last, when Mrs. Wharton spoke of her engagements for the evening, and seemed to take it for granted that he would be of her party, he summoned resolution sufficient—Oh! wonderful effort of courage!—to tell her, that he was under a necessity of leaving town immediately.

"Going, I presume, to—"

"To the country," said Vivian, firmly.

"To the country!—No, no, no; say at once, to Selina!—Tell me the worst in one word!"

Astonished beyond measure, Vivian had not power to move. The lady fell back on the sofa in violent hysterics. Our hero trembled lest any of her servants should come in, or lest her husband should at his return find her in this condition, and discover the cause. He endeavoured in vain to soothe and compose the weeping fair one; he could not have the barbarity to leave her in this state. By sweet degrees she recovered her recollection—was in the most lovely confusion—asked where she was, and what was going to happen. Vivian had not the rashness to run the risk of a second fit of hysterics; he gave up all thoughts of his journey for this day, and the lady recovered her spirits in the most flattering manner. Vivian intended to postpone his journey only for a single day; but, after he had yielded one point, he found that there was no receding. He was now persuaded that Mrs. Wharton was miserable; that she would never forgive herself for having betrayed the state of her heart. His self-love pleaded powerfully in her favour: he considered that her husband treated her with mortifying neglect, and provoked the spirit of retaliation by his gallantries. Vivian fancied that Mrs. Wharton's attachment to him might render her wretched, but would never make her criminal. With sophistical delicacy he veiled his own motives; and, instead of following the plain dictates of reason, he involved his understanding in that species of sentimental casuistry which confounds all principles of right and wrong. But the dread that he felt lest Wharton should discover what was going on might have sufficiently convinced him that he was not acting honourably. The suspicions which Mr. Wharton formerly showed of his wife seemed now to be completely lulled asleep; and he gave Vivian continually such proofs of confidence as stung him to the soul. By an absurd, but not an uncommon error of self-love, Vivian was induced to believe, that a man who professed to cheat mankind in general behaved towards him in particular with strict honour, and even with unparalleled generosity. Honesty was too vulgar a virtue for Wharton; but honour, the aristocratic, exclusive virtue of a gentleman, he laid claim to in the highest tone. The very frankness with which Wharton avowed his libertine principles with respect to women, convinced Vivian that he had not the slightest suspicion that these could be immediately applied to the ruin of his own wife.

"How can you, my dear Wharton, talk in this manner?" said Vivian once, when he had been speaking with great freedom.

"But it is better," added he, with a sigh, "to speak than to act like a villain."

"Villain!" repeated Wharton, with a sarcastic laugh; "you are grown quite ridiculous, Vivian: I protest, I don't understand you. Women now-a-days are surely able, if not willing enough, to take care of themselves; and villains, though they were very common in the time of Miss Clarissa Harlowe, and of all the tragedy queens of the last century, are not to be heard of in these days. Any strange tales of those male monsters called seducers could gain credit during the ages of ignorance and credulity; but now, the enlightened world cannot be imposed upon by such miracles; and a gentleman may be a man of gallantry—nay, even a lady may be a woman of gallantry—without being hooted out of society as a monster; at all events, the blame is, as it should be, equally divided between the parties concerned; and if modern lovers quarrel, they do not die of grief, but settle their differences in a court of law, where a spinster may have her compensation for a breach of contract of marriage; a father or a husband their damages for the loss of the company, affection, solace, services, &c., as the case may be, of his wife or daughter. All this is perfectly well understood; and the terrors of law are quite sufficient, without the terrors of sentiment. If a man punish himself, or let himself be punished, twice for the same offence, once by his conscience, and once by his king and his country, he is a fool; and, moreover, acts contrary to the spirit of the British law, which sayeth—see Blackstone and others—that no man shall be punished twice for the same offence.—Suffer your risible muscles to relax, I beseech you, Vivian; and do not affect a presbyterian rigidity, which becomes your face as ill as your age."

"I affect nothing—certainly I do not affect presbyterian rigidity," cried Vivian, laughing. "But, after all, Wharton, if you had a daughter or a sister, what would you think of any man, your friend for instance, who should attempt—"

"To cut your speech short at once," interrupted Wharton, "I should not think at all about the matter; I should blow his brains out, of course; and afterwards, probably, blow out my own. But treachery from a friend—from a man of honour—is a thing of which I can hardly form an idea. Where I give my confidence, I give it without any paltry mental reservation—I could not suspect a friend."

Vivian suffered, at this instant, all the agony which a generous mind, conscious of guilt, could endure. He thought that the confusion of his mind must be visible in his countenance—his embarrassment was so great that he could not utter a word. Wharton did not seem to perceive his companion's agitation, but passed on carelessly to other subjects of conversation; and at length completely relieved Vivian from fear of immediate detection, by asking a favour from him—a pecuniary favour.

"All is safe—Mrs. Wharton, at least, is safe, thank Heaven!" thought Vivian. "Had her husband the slightest suspicion, he never would condescend to accept of any favour from me."

With eagerness, and almost with tears of gratitude, Vivian pressed upon Wharton the money which he condescended to borrow—it was no inconsiderable sum.

"Wharton!" cried he, "you sometimes talk freely—too freely; but you are, I am convinced, the most open-hearted, unsuspicious, generous fellow upon earth—you deserve a better friend than I am."

Unable any longer to suppress or conceal the emotions which struggled in his heart, he broke away abruptly, hurried home, shut himself up in his own apartment, and sat down immediately to write to Mrs. Wharton. The idea that Mrs. Wharton loved him in preference to all the fashionable coxcombs and wits by whom she was surrounded had insensibly raised our hero's opinion of her understanding so much, that he now imagined that the world laboured under a prejudice against her abilities. He gave himself credit for having discovered that this beauty was not a fool; and he now spoke and wrote to her as if she had been a woman of sense. With eloquence which might have moved a woman of genius, with delicacy that might have touched a woman of feeling, he conjured her to fortify his honourable resolutions; and thus, whilst it was yet time, to secure her happiness and his own. "Instead of writing this letter," added he in a postscript, "I ought, perhaps, to fly from you for ever; but that would show a want of confidence in you and in myself; and, besides, upon the most mature reflection, I think it best to stay, and wait upon you to-morrow as usual, lest, by my precipitation, I should excite suspicion in Wharton's mind."

The weak apprehension that Mrs. Wharton should betray herself by another fit of hysterics, if he should leave town, and if his departure should be suddenly announced to her by her husband, or by some common acquaintance, induced him to delay a few days longer, that he might prepare her mind by degrees, and convince her of the necessity for their absolute separation. When he had finished his letter to Mrs. Wharton, he was sufficiently well pleased with himself to venture to write to Miss Sidney. His letters to her had of late been short and constrained; but this was written with the full flow of affection. He was now in hopes that he should extricate himself honourably from his difficulties, and that he might at last claim his reward from Selina.

CHAPTER VI

After he had despatched his two letters, he became excessively anxious to receive Mrs. Wharton's answer. By trifling but unavoidable accidents, it was delayed a few hours. At last it arrived; Vivian tore it open, and read with surprise these words:

"Your letter is just what I wished, and makes me the happiest of women—that is, if you are sincere—which, after all you've said, I can't doubt. I am so hurried by visitors, and annoyed, that I cannot write more; but shall have time to talk to-night at the opera."

At the opera Mrs. Wharton appeared in high spirits, and was dressed with more than usual elegance. It was observed that she had never been seen to look so beautiful. There was something in her manner that puzzled Vivian extremely; this extraordinary gaiety was not what he had reason to expect. "Is it possible," thought he, "that this woman is a mere coquette, who has been amusing herself at my expense all this time, and can now break off all connexion with me without a moment's regret?" Vivian's pride was piqued: though he wished to part from the lady, he could not bear that this parting should evidently cost her nothing. He was mortified beyond expression by the idea that he had been duped. After the opera was over, whilst Mrs. Wharton was waiting for her carriage, he had an opportunity of speaking to her without being overheard.

"I am happy," said he, with a constrained voice, "I am extremely happy to see you, madam, in such charming spirits to-night."

"But are not you a strange man to look so grave?" cried Mrs. Wharton. "I vow, I don't know what to make of you! But I believe you want to quarrel for the pleasure of making it up again. Now that won't do. By-the-bye, I have a quarrel with you, sir.—How came you to sign your name to that foolish stuff you wrote me yesterday? Never do so any more, I charge you, for fear of accidents. But what's the matter now?—You are a strange mortal!—Are you going to die upon the spot?—What is the matter?"

"My letter to you was not signed, I believe," said Vivian, in an altered voice.

"Indeed it was," said Mrs. Wharton. "It was signed Charles Vivian at full length. But why are you in such tremors about it? I only mentioned it to put you on your guard in future.—I've burnt the letter—people always get themselves into scrapes if they don't burn love-letters—as I've often heard Mr. Wharton say," added she, laughing.

To his unspeakable consternation, Vivian now discovered that he had sent the letter intended for Selina to Mrs. Wharton; and that which was designed for Mrs. Wharton he had directed to Miss Sidney. Vivian was so lost in thought, that the cry of "Mrs. Wharton's carriage stops the way!" was vociferated many times before he recovered sufficient presence of mind to hand the lady out of the house. He went home immediately, that he might reflect upon what was best to be done. His servant presently gave him a letter which a messenger had just brought from the country. The packet was from Selina.

"Enclosed, I return the letter which I received from you this morning. I read the first three lines of it before I perceived that it could not be intended for me—I went no farther.—I cannot help knowing for whom it was designed; but you may be assured that your secret shall be kept inviolably.—You have no reproaches to fear from me.—This is the last letter I shall ever write to you.—Leave it to me to explain my own conduct to my mother and to yours; if they think me capricious, I can bear it. I shall tell them that my sentiments are totally changed: I am sure I can say so with perfect truth.—Oh, Vivian, it is you who are to be pitied; every thing may be endured except remorse. Would to Heaven, I could save you from the reproaches of your own heart!—Adieu!

"SELINA SIDNEY."

The feelings of Vivian's mind, on reading this letter, cannot be described. Admiration, love, tenderness, remorse, successively seized upon his heart. Incapable of any distinct reflection, he threw himself upon his bed, and closed his eyes, endeavouring to compose himself to sleep, that he might forget his existence. But, motionless as he lay, the tumult of his mind continued unabated. His pulse beat high; and before morning he was in a fever. The dread that his mother should come to attend him, and to inquire into the cause of his illness, increased his agitation:—she came. Her kindness and anxiety were fresh torments to her unhappy son. Bitterly did he reproach himself as the cause of misery to those he loved and esteemed most in the world. He became delirious; and, whilst he was in this state, he repeated Mrs. Wharton's name sometimes in terms of endearment, sometimes in accents of execration. His mother's suspicions of his intrigue were confirmed by many expressions which burst from him, and which were thought by his attendants to be merely the ravings of fever. Lady Mary had, at this crisis, the prudence to conceal her doubts, and to keep every body, as much as possible, out of her son's apartment. In a few days his fever subsided, and he recovered to the clear recollection of all that had passed previously to his illness. He almost wished to be again delirious. The first time he was left alone, he rose from his bed, unlocked his bureau, and seized Selina's letter, which he read again and again, studying each line and word, as if he could draw from them every time a new meaning.

"She read but three lines of my letter," said he to himself; "then she only guesses that I have an intrigue with Mrs. Wharton, without knowing that in this very letter I used my utmost influence to recall Mrs. Wharton to—herself."

The belief that Selina thought worse of him than he deserved was some consolation to Vivian. He was resolved to recover her esteem: he determined to break off all connexion with Mrs. Wharton; and, full of this intention, he was impatient till the physicians permitted him to go abroad. When he was at last free from their dominion, had escaped from his chamber, and had just gained the staircase, he was stopped by his mother.

"Charles," said she, "before you quit me again, it is my duty to say a few words to you upon a subject of some importance."

Lady Mary led the way to her dressing-room with a dignified air; Vivian followed with a mixture of pride and alarm in his manner. From the bare idea of a maternal lecture his mind revolted: he imagined that she was going to repeat the remonstrance which she had formerly made against his intimacy with Mrs. Wharton, and against platonics in general; but he had not the least apprehension that she had discovered the whole truth: he was, therefore, both surprised and shocked, when she spoke to him in the following manner:

"The libertinism of the age in which we live has so far loosened all the bonds of society, and all the ties of nature, that I doubt not but a mother's anxiety for the morals of her son—her only son—the son over whose education she has watched from his infancy, may appear, even in his eyes, a fit subject for ridicule. I am well aware that my solicitude and my counsels have long been irksome to him, I have lost his affections by a steady adherence to my duty; but I shall persevere with the less reluctance, since the dread of my displeasure, or the hope of my approbation, cannot now touch his sensibility. During your illness, you have betrayed a secret—you have reason to start with horror. Is it possible that a son of mine, with the principles which I have endeavoured to instil into his mind, should become so far depraved? Do I live to hear, from his own lips, that he is the seducer of a married woman—and that woman the wife of his friend?"

Vivian walked up and down the room in great agony: his mother continued, with increased severity of manner, "I say nothing of your dissimulation with me, nor of all your platonic subterfuges—I know that, with a man of intrigue, falsehood is deemed a virtue. I shall not condescend to inquire farther into your guilty secrets—I now think myself fortunate in having no place in your confidence. But I here declare to you, in the most solemn manner, that I never will see you again until all connexion between you and Mrs. Wharton is utterly dissolved. I do not advise—I COMMAND, and must be obeyed—or I cast you off for ever."

Lady Mary left the room as she uttered these words. Her son was deeply struck with his mother's eloquence: he knew she was right, yet his pride was wounded by the peremptory severity of her manner:—his remorse and his good resolutions gave place to anger. The more he felt himself in the wrong, the less he could bear to be reproached by the voice of authority. Even because his mother commanded him to give up all connexion with Mrs. Wharton, he was inclined to disobey—he could not bear to seem to do right merely in compliance to her will. He went to visit Mrs. Wharton in a very different temper from that in which, half an hour before this conference with his mother, he had resolved to see the lady. Mrs. Wharton knew how to take advantage both of the weakness of his character and of the generosity of his temper. She fell into transports of grief when she found that Lady Mary Vivian and Miss Sidney were in possession of her secret. It was in vain that Vivian assured her that it would be kept inviolably; she persisted in repeating, "that her reputation was lost; that she had sacrificed every thing for a man who would, at last, desert her in the most treacherous and barbarous manner, leaving her at the mercy of her husband, the most profligate, hard-hearted tyrant upon earth. As to her being reconciled to him," she declared, "that was totally out of the question; his behaviour to her was such, that she could not live with him, even if her heart were not fatally prepossessed in favour of another." Her passions seemed wrought to the highest pitch. With all the eloquence of beauty in distress, she appealed to Vivian as her only friend; she threw herself entirely upon his protection; she vowed that she could not, would not, remain another day in the same house with Mr. Wharton; that her destiny, her existence, were at Vivian's mercy. Vivian had not sufficient fortitude to support this scene. He stood irresolute. The present temptation prevailed over his better resolutions. He was actually persuaded by this woman, whom he did not love, whom he could not esteem, to carry her off to the continent—whilst, at the very time, he admired, esteemed, and loved another. The plan of the elopement was formed and settled in a few minutes;—on Mrs. Wharton's part, apparently with all the hurry of passion; on Vivian's with all the confusion of despair. The same carriage, the very same horses, that had been ordered to carry our hero to his beloved Selina, conveyed him and Mrs. Wharton the first stage of their flight towards the continent. The next morning the following paragraph appeared in the newspapers:—

"Yesterday, the beautiful and fashionable Mrs. W—, whose marriage we announced last year to the celebrated Mr. W—, eloped from his house in St. James's-street, in company with C— V—, member for —shire. This catastrophe has caused the greatest sensation and astonishment in the circles of fashion; for the lady in question had always, till this fatal step, preserved the most unblemished reputation; and Mr. and Mrs. W— were considered as models of conjugal felicity. The injured husband was attending his public duty in the House of Commons; and, as we are credibly informed, was, with patriotic ardour, speaking in his country's cause, when this unfortunate event, which for ever bereaves him of domestic happiness, took place. What must increase the poignancy of his feelings upon the occasion remains to be stated—that the seducer was his intimate friend, a young man, whom he had raised into notice in public life, and whom he had, with all that warmth and confidence of heart for which he is remarkable, introduced into his house, and trusted with his beloved wife. Mr. W— is, we hear, in pursuit of the fugitives."

CHAPTER VII

In the modern fashionable code of honour, when a man has seduced or carried off his friend's wife, the next thing he has to do is to fight the man whom he has injured and betrayed. By thus appealing to the ordeal of the duel, he may not only clear himself from guilt; but, if it be done with proper spirit, he may acquire celebrity and glory in the annals of gallantry, and in the eyes of the fair and innocent. In our hero's place, most men of fashion would have triumphed in the notoriety of his offence, and would have rejoiced in an opportunity of offering the husband the satisfaction of a gentleman. But, unfortunately for Vivian, he had not yet suited his principles to his practice: he had acted like a man of fashion; but, alas! he still thought and felt like a man of virtue—as the following letter will show.

"TO THE REV. HENRY RUSSELL.

"Indignant as you will be, Russell, at all you hear of me, you cannot be more shocked than I am myself. I do not write to palliate or apologize—my conduct admits of no defence—I shall attempt none, private or public—I have written to my lawyer to give directions that no sort of defence shall be set up on my part, when the affair comes into Doctors' Commons—as it shortly will; for I understand that poor Wharton has commenced a prosecution. As to damages he has only to name them—any thing within the compass of my fortune he may command. Would to God that money could make him amends! But he is too generous, too noble a fellow—profligate as he is in some things, how incapable would he be of acting as basely as I have done! There is not, perhaps, at this moment, a human being who has so high an opinion of the man I have injured as I have myself:—he did not love his wife—but that is no excuse for me—his honour is as much wounded as if I had robbed him of her during the time he loved her most fondly:—he once doted upon her, and would have loved her again, when he was tired of his gallantries; and they might then have lived together as happily as ever, if I had not been—. What was I?—What am I?—Not a villain—or I should glory in what I have done—but the weakest of human beings—and how true it is, Russell, that 'all wickedness is weakness!'

"I understand that W—, wherever he goes, calls me a coward, as well as a scoundrel; and says that I have kept out of the way to avoid fighting him. He is mistaken. It is true, I had the utmost dread of having his life to answer for—and nothing should have provoked me to fire upon him;—but I had determined how to act—I would have met him, and have stood his fire. I should not be sorry, at present, to be put out of the world; and would rather fall by his hand than by any other. But since this is out of the question, and that things have taken another turn, I have only to live, as long as it shall please God, a life of remorse—and, at least, to try to make the unfortunate woman who has thrown herself upon my protection as happy as I can.

"If you have any remaining regard for a pupil who has so disgraced you, do me one favour—Go to Miss Sidney, and give her what comfort you can. Say nothing for me, or of me, but that I wish her to forget me as soon as possible. She discarded me from her heart when she first discovered this intrigue—before this last fatal step. Still I had hopes of recovering her esteem and affection; for I had resolved—But no matter what I resolved—all my resolutions failed; and now I am utterly unworthy of her love. This, and all that is good and happy in life, all the fair hopes and virtuous promises of my youth, I must give up. Early as it is in my day, my sun has set. I truly desire that she should forget me; for you know I am bound in honour—Honour! How dare I use the word? I am bound, after the divorce, to marry the woman I have seduced. Oh, Russell! what a wife for your friend!—What a daughter-in-law for my poor mother, after all her care of my education—all her affection—all her pride in me!—It will break her heart! Mine will not break. I shall drag on, perhaps, to a miserable old age. I am of too feeble a nature to feel these things as strong minds would—as you will for me; but do not blame yourself for my faults. All that man could do for me, you did. This must be some consolation to you, my dear and excellent friend! May I still call you friend?—or have I no friend left upon earth?

"C. VIVIAN."

From this letter some idea may be formed of what this unhappy man suffered at this period of his life, from "the reflections of a mind not used to its own reproaches." The view of the future was as dreadful as the retrospect of the past. His thoughts continually dwelt upon the public trial which was preparing— before him he saw all its disgraceful circumstances. Then the horror of marrying, of passing his whole future existence with a woman whom he could not esteem or trust! These last were secret subjects of anxiety and anguish, the more intensely felt, because he could not speak of them to any human being. Such as Mrs. Wharton was, she was to be his wife; and he was called upon to defend her against reproach and insult,—if possible, from contempt. During the course of six weeks, which they spent together in exile at Brussels, Vivian became so altered in his appearance, that his most intimate friends could scarcely have known him; his worst enemies, if he had had any, could not have desired the prolongation of his sufferings.

One evening, as he was sitting alone in his hotel, ruminating bitter thoughts, a letter was brought to him from Mr. Russell; the first he had received since he left England. Every one, who has been absent from his friends in a foreign country, must know the sort of emotion which the bare sight of a letter from home excites; but, in Vivian's circumstances, abandoned as he felt himself, and deserving to be abandoned by his best friends, the sight of a letter from Russell so struck him, that he gazed upon the direction for some minutes, almost without power or wish to open it. At last he opened, and read, "Return to your country, your friends, and yourself, Vivian! Your day is not yet over! Your sun is not yet set!—Resume your energy—recover your self-confidence—carry your good resolutions into effect—and you may yet be an honour to your family, a delight to your fond mother, and the pride of your friend Russell. Your remorse has been poignant and sincere; let it be salutary and permanent in its consequences: this is the repentance which religion requires. The part of a man of sense and virtue is to make his past errors of use to his future conduct. Whilst I had nothing to say that could give you pleasure, I forbore to answer your letter; I forbore to overwhelm a mind sinking under remorse. My sacred duty is to waken the sinner to repentance, not to shut the gates of mercy on the penitent. Now, I can relieve your mind from part of the load by which it has been justly oppressed. You know that nothing can palliate your conduct in an intrigue with a married woman—from this I had hoped your moral and religious education would have preserved you. But of the premeditated guilt of deceiving the husband, and laying a plan to seduce the wife, I never suspected you; and I may now tell you, that you have not betrayed Mr. Wharton; he has betrayed you. You have not seduced Mrs. Wharton; you have been seduced by her. You are not bound to marry her—Wharton cannot obtain a divorce—he dare not bring the affair to trial; if he does, he is undone. There has been collusion between the parties. The proof of this you will find in the enclosed paper, which will be sworn to, in due legal form, whenever it is necessary. Even when you see them, you will scarcely believe these 'damning proofs' of Wharton's baseness. But I always knew, I always told you, that this pretence to honour and candour, frankness and friendship, with this avowed contempt of all principle and all virtue, could not be safe, could not be sincere, would not stand the test.—No—nothing should make me trust to the private honour of a man so corrupt in public life as Mr. Wharton. A man who sells his conscience for his interest will sell it for his pleasure. A man who will betray his country will betray his friend. It is in vain to palter with our conscience: there are not two honours—two honesties. How I rejoice at this moment, in the reflection that your character, as a public man, is yet untarnished You have still this great advantage:—feel its value. Return, and distinguish yourself among your countrymen: distinguish yourself by integrity still more than by talents. A certain degree of talents is now cheap in England: integrity is what we want— true patriotism, true public spirit, noble ambition not that vile scramble for places and pensions, which some men call ambition; not that bawling, brawling, Thersites character, which other men call public spirit; not that marketable commodity with which Wharton, and such as he, cheat popular opinion for a season;—but that fair virtue which will endure, and abide by its cause to the last; which, in place or out, shall be the same; which, successful or unsuccessful, shall sustain the possessor's character through all changes of party; which, whilst he lives, shall command respect from even the most profligate of his contemporaries; upon which, when he is dying, he may reflect with satisfaction; which, after his death, shall be the consolation of his friends, and the glory of his country. All this is yet in your power, Vivian.— Come, then, and fulfil the promise of your early years! Come, and restore to your mother a son worthy of her!—Come, and surpass the hopes of your true friend,

"H. RUSSELL."

The rapid succession of feelings with which Vivian read this letter can scarcely be imagined. The paper it enclosed was from a former waiting-maid of Mrs. Wharton's; a woman who was expected to be the principal evidence on Mr. Wharton's side. She had been his mistress; one of those innumerable mistresses, to whom he had, of course, addressed his transferable promises of eternal constancy. She too, of course, had believed the vow, in spite of all experience and probability; and while she pardoned his infidelities to her mistress, &c. all which she deemed very natural for a gentleman like him, yet she was astonished and outrageous when she found him faithless to her own charms. In a fit of jealousy she flew to Mr. Russell, whom she knew to be Vivian's friend; and, to revenge herself on Wharton, revealed the secrets which she had in her power; put into Russell's hands the proofs of collusion between Mr. Wharton and his wife; and took malicious pains to substantiate her evidence, to a lawyer's full satisfaction; knowing that she might prevent the possibility of a divorce, and that she should thus punish her perjured inconstant in the most sensible manner, by at once depriving him of twenty thousand pounds damages, and by chaining him again to a wife whom he abhorred.

The same post which brought Vivian this woman's deposition and Russell's letter brought Mrs. Wharton notice that the whole plan of collusion was discovered: she was therefore prepared for Vivian's reproaches, and received the first burst of his astonishment and indignation with a studied Magdalen expression of countenance: then she attempted a silly apology, laying all the blame on her husband, and vowing that she had acted under terror, and that her life would not have been safe in his hands if she had not implicitly obeyed and executed his horrid plans. She wept and kneeled in vain. Finding Vivian immoveable in his purpose to return immediately to England, she suddenly rose from her knees, and, all beautiful as she was, looked in Vivian's eyes like a fiend, whilst, with an unnatural smile, she said to him, "You see, fool as I am thought to be, I have been too clever for some people; and I can tell Mr. Wharton that I have been too clever for him too. His heart is set upon a divorce; but he can't have it. He can't marry Miss P—, nor yet her fortune, nor ever shall! I shall remain at Brussels—I have friends here—and friends who were my friends before I was forced to give my hand to Mr. Wharton, or my smiles to you, sir!—people who will not tease me with talking of remorse and repentance, and such ungallant, ungentlemanlike stuff; nor sit bewailing themselves, like a country parson, instead of dashing out with me here in a fashionable style, as a man of any spirit would have done. But you!—you're neither good nor bad; and no woman will ever love you, nor ever did. Now you know my whole mind."

"Would to Heaven I had known it sooner!" said Vivian. "No—I rejoice that I did not sooner know, and that I never could have suspected, such depravity!—under such a form, too."

Mrs. Wharton's eye glanced with satisfaction upon the large mirror opposite to her. Vivian left her in utter disgust and horror. "Drive on!" cried he, as he threw himself into the chaise that was to carry him away; "Faster! faster!"

The words, "and no woman will ever love you, nor ever, did," rung upon Vivian's ear. "There she is mistaken, thank Heaven!" said he to himself: yet the words still dwelt upon his mind, and gave him exquisite pain. Upon looking again at Russell's letter, he observed that Selina Sidney's name was never mentioned; that she was neither directly nor indirectly alluded to in the whole letter. What omen to draw from this he could not divine. Again he read it; and all that Russell said of public life, and his exhortations to him to come and distinguish himself in public and in the political world, struck him in a new light. It seemed as if Russell was sensible that, there were no farther hopes of Selina, and that therefore he tried to turn Vivian's mind from love to ambition. Fourteen times he read over this letter before he reached England; but he could not discover from it any thing as to the point on which his heart was most interested. He reached London in this, uncertainty.

"Put me out of suspense, my best friend," cried he, the moment he saw Russell: "tell me, is Selina living?"

"Yes—she has been very ill, but is now recovered—quite recovered, and with your mother, who is grown fonder of her than ever she was."

"Selina alive! well! and with my mother!—and may I—I don't mean may I now,—but may I ever hope?—Believe me, I feel myself capable of any exertions, any forbearance, to obtain her forgiveness—to merit—May I ever hope for it?—Speak!"

Russell assured him that he need not dread Miss Sidney's resentment, for that she felt none; she had expressed pity more than anger—that she had taken pains to sooth his mother; and had expressed sincere satisfaction on hearing of his release from his unworthy bondage, and at his return home to his friends.

The tone in which Russell spoke, and the seriousness and embarrassment of his manner, alarmed Vivian inexpressibly. He stood silent, and dared not ask farther explanation for some minutes.—At length he broke silence, and conjured his friend to go immediately to Miss Sidney and his mother, and to request permission for him to see them both in each other's presence. Russell said, that if Vivian insisted, he would comply with his request; but that he advised him not to attempt to see Miss Sidney at present; not till he had been some time in London—till he had given some earnest of the steadiness of his conduct—till he had appeared again, and distinguished himself in public life. "This might raise you again in her esteem; and," continued Russell, "you must be aware that her love depends on her esteem—at least, that the one cannot exist without the other."

"Will you deliver a letter to her from me?" said Vivian. "If you think I had better not attempt to see her yet, you will deliver a letter for me?"

After some hesitation, or rather some deliberation, Russell answered, in a constrained voice, "I will deliver your letter, if you insist upon it."

Vivian wrote:—Russell undertook to deliver the letter, though with evident reluctance. In the mean time Vivian went to see his mother, whom he longed, yet dreaded to meet. Her manner was not now severe and haughty, as when she last addressed him; but mild and benign: she held out her hand to him, and said, "Thank God! my son is restored to me, and to himself!"

She could say no more; but embraced him tenderly. Russell had shown Lady Mary that her son had been the dupe of a preconcerted scheme to work upon his passions. She deplored his weakness, but she had been touched by his sufferings; and was persuaded that his remorse would guard him against future errors. Therefore not a word or look of reproach escaped from her. When he spoke of Selina, Lady Mary, with great animation of countenance and warmth of eulogium, declared, that it was the first wish of her heart to see her son married to a woman of such a noble character and angelic temper; "but," added her ladyship, her manner changing suddenly, as she pronounced the word but—before she could explain the but, Russell came into the room, and told Vivian that Miss Sidney desired to see him. Vivian heard the words with joy; but his joy was checked by the great gravity and embarrassment of his friend's countenance, and by a sigh of ill omen from his mother. Eager to relieve his suspense, he hastened to Selina, who, as Russell told him, was in Lady Mary's dressing-room—the room in which he had first declared his passion for her. Hope and fear alternately seized him—fear prevailed the moment that he beheld Selina. Not that any strong displeasure appeared in her countenance—no, it was mild and placid; but it was changed towards him, and its very serenity was alarming. Whilst she welcomed him to his native country and to his friends, and while she expressed hopes for his future happiness, all hope forsook him, and, in broken sentences, he attempted to stammer out some answer; then, throwing himself into a chair, he exclaimed, "I see all future happiness is lost for me—and I deserve it!"

"Do not reproach yourself," said Selina in a sweet voice; but the voice, though sweet, was so altered to him, that it threw him into despair. "It is my wish, not to inflict, but to spare you pain. I have, therefore, desired to see you as soon as possible, that you might not form false expectations."

"Then you no longer love me, Selina? Now, after all I have suffered, you have the cruelty to tell me so? And you, who could form my character to every thing that is good and honourable; you, who alone could restore me to myself—you reject, you cast me from you for ever?"

"I have suffered much," said Selina, in a trembling voice, "since we parted."

Vivian's eye quickly ran over her face and whole form as she spoke these words; and he saw, indeed, traces of sickness and suffering: with the idea of his power over her affections, his hopes revived; he seized the feeble hand, which lay motionless; but she withdrew it decidedly, and his hopes again forsook him, when she gently raised her head, and continued to speak, "I have suffered much since we parted, Mr. Vivian; and I hope you will spare me unnecessary and useless pain in this interview: painful to a certain degree it must be to both of us; for I cannot, even now that all feelings of passion have subsided, and that the possibility of my being united to you is past, tell you so, with all the composure which I had expected to do; nor with all the firmness of voice and manner which is necessary, perhaps, to convince you of the truth, and to restore your mind to itself."

"The possibility of my being united to you is past!—Why?" interrupted Vivian, incapable of understanding or listening to any thing else, till this question was answered.

"Do not force me to what may seem like cruel reproach; but let it suffice for me to say, that my sentiments have been so much altered by a year's experience, that it is impossible for me ever to become your wife. My love was founded on esteem. I had, indeed, always fears of the instability of your character; therefore, I put your resolution to the proof: the event has proved to me that my fears were but too just. I speak with difficulty; for I cannot easily give you so much pain as I know that I am inflicting at this moment. But," resumed she, in a more resolute tone, "it is absolutely necessary for your future peace of mind, as well as for my own, that I should convince you I am sincere, perfectly sincere, at this moment; that I know my own heart; that my determination has not been hastily formed, and cannot be altered. The deliberate manner in which I now speak to you will, I hope, persuade you of this truth. And if I have hesitated, or showed any agitation in this interview, attribute it to its real cause—the weakness of my health; feebleness of body, not of mind."

She rose to leave the room; but Vivian detained her, beseeching her, with all the eloquence of passion in despair, to hear him but for one moment; whilst he urged that there was no probability of his ever relapsing into errors from which he had suffered so much; that now his character was formed by adversity; and that such was the power which Selina possessed over his heart, that a union with her would, at this crisis, decide his fate; that her steadiness would give stability to his resolutions; and that his gratitude would so increase his affection, that he should have the strongest possible motives to make her a good husband; that when he was happy in domestic life, he should feel every energy of his mind revive; that he should exert all his powers to distinguish himself, and to justify the choice of the woman he adored.

In spite of the word adored, which has usually such power to confound female judgment, Selina perceived that all he said was merely a repetition of his former arguments, of which experience had proved the insufficiency. She was aware that, if before marriage his resolution and constancy had not been able to support the trial, it would be folly or madness to marry him with the vague hope that she might reform his character. She therefore continued steady to her resolution; and as she found that Vivian's disappointment was greater than she had expected, she immediately withdrew from his mother's house. The next morning, when Vivian came to breakfast, after having spent a sleepless night, planning new arguments or new intreaties in favour of his love, he found that Miss Sidney was gone. His mother and his friend Russell joined in representing to him that it would be useless to follow her, that it would only give himself and Selina unavailing pain. Vivian felt this stroke severely. His mind was, as it were, adrift again. After the first violence of his feelings had spent itself, and when he sunk into that kind of apathy which is the consequence of exhausted passion, his friend Russell endeavoured to excite him to honourable ambition. Vivian caught the idea, that if he distinguished himself in public life, and if he there displayed any steadiness of character, he might win back Selina's esteem and affection. Fired with this hope, he immediately turned his whole mind to the object; applied with indefatigable ardour, day and night, to make himself master of the subjects likely to be discussed in the ensuing session of parliament. At length his application and his energy were crowned with success. On a question of considerable political importance, which he had carefully considered, he made an excellent speech; a speech which directly made him of consequence in the house; which, in the language of the newspapers, "was received with unbounded applause, was distinguished for strength of argument, lucid order, and a happy choice of expression." But what encouraged our hero more than newspaper puffs or party panegyrics was the approbation of his friend Russell. Russell never praised violently; but a few words, or even a look of satisfaction from him, went farther than the most exaggerated eulogiums from others. Vivian pursued his course for some time with honour and increasing reputation. There was one man who never joined in any of the compliments paid to the rising orator; there was one man who always spoke of him with contempt, who pronounced that "Vivian would never go far in politics—that it was not in him—that he was too soft—que c'étoit bâtir sur de la boue, que de compter sur lui." This depreciator and enemy of Vivian was the man who, but a few months before, had been his political proneur and unblushing flatterer, Mr. Wharton. Exasperated by the consciousness of his own detected baseness, and provoked still more by his being frustrated in all his schemes, Wharton now practised every art that a malicious and unprincipled wit could devise to lower the opinion of Vivian's talents, and to prevent his obtaining either power or celebrity. Our hero was stimulated by this conduct to fresh exertions. So far Wharton's enmity was of service to him; but it was of disservice, by changing, in some measure, the purity of the motives from which he acted. With love and honourable ambition now mixed hatred, thoughts of vengeance, views of vulgar vanity and interest: he thought more of contradicting Mr. Wharton's prophecies than of fulfilling his own ideas of what was fair and right. He was anxious to prove, that he could "go far in politics, that it was in him, that he was not too soft, and that it was not building on mud to depend on him." These indefinite expressions operated powerfully and perniciously on his imagination. To prove that Wharton was mistaken in his prognostics, it was necessary to our hero to obtain the price and stamp of talents—it was essential to gain political power; and this could not be attained without joining a party. Vivian joined the party then in opposition. Wharton and he, though both in opposition, of course, after what had passed, could never meet in any private company; nor had they any communication in public, though on the same side of the question: their enmity was so great, that not only the business of the nation, but even the interests of their party, were often impeded by their quarrels. In the midst of these disputes, Vivian insensibly adopted more and more of the language and principles of the public men with whom he daily associated. He began to hear and talk of compensations and jobs, as they did; and to consider all measures proved to be necessary for the support of his party as expedient, if not absolutely right. His country could not be saved, unless he and his friends could obtain the management of affairs; and no men, be found, could gain parliamentary influence, or raise themselves into political power, without acting as a body. Then, of course, all subordinate points of right were to be sacrificed to the great good of promoting the views of the party. Still, however, his patriotism was upon the whole pure; he had no personal views of interest, no desire even to be in place, independently of a wish to promote the good of his country. Secret overtures were, about this time, made to him by government; and inquiries were made if there was any thing which could gratify him, or by which he could be induced to lay aside his opposition, and to assist in supporting their measures. Many compliments to his talents and eloquence, and all the usual commonplaces, about the expediency and propriety of strengthening the hands of government, were, of course, added. Something specific was at length mentioned: it was intimated, that as he was of an ancient family, it might gratify him that his mother should be made a baroness in her own right. The offer was declined, and the temptation was firmly withstood by our hero; his credit was now at its acme with his own coadjutors. Lady Mary whispered the circumstance, as a state secret, to all her acquaintance; and Russell took care that Miss Sidney should hear of it.

Vivian was now cited as an incorruptible patriot. Wharton's malice, and even his wit, was almost silenced; yet he was heard to say, amidst the din of applause, "This is only the first offer; he is in the right to make a show of resistance: he will coquet for a time, and keep philandering on till he suits himself, and then he'll jilt us, you'll see."

Such speeches, though they reached Vivian's ear by the kind officiousness of friends, were never made by Mr. Wharton so directly that he could take hold of them; and Russell strenuously advised him not to seek occasion to quarrel with a man who evidently desired only to raise his own reputation by making Vivian angry, getting him in the wrong, and forcing him into an imprudent duel.

"Let your actions continue to contradict his words, and they can never injure you," said Russell.

For some time Vivian adhered to his friend's advice, and he proudly felt the superiority of principle and character. But, alas! there was one defence that his patriotism wanted—economy. Whilst he was thus active in the public cause, and exulting in his disinterestedness, his private affairs were getting into terrible disorder. The expense of building his castle had increased beyond all his calculations—the expense of his election—the money he had lost at play whilst he was in Wharton's society—the sums he had lent to Wharton—the money he had spent abroad,—all these accumulated brought him to great difficulties: for though his estate was considerable, yet it was so settled and tied up that he could neither sell nor mortgage. His creditors became clamorous—he had no means of satisfying or quieting them: an execution was actually sent down to his castle, just as it was finished. Lady Mary Vivian was in the greatest alarm and distress: she had no means of extricating her son. As to his fashionable friends— no hopes from such extravagant and selfish beings. What was to be done? At this critical moment, the offers from a certain quarter were renewed in another, and, as it seemed, a more acceptable form,—a pension was proffered instead of a title; and it was promised that the business should be so managed, and the pension so held in another name, that nothing of the transaction should transpire; and that his seceding from opposition should be made to appear a change of sentiments from conviction, not from interested motives. Vivian's honourable feelings revolted from these offers, and abhorred these subterfuges; but distress—pecuniary distress! he had never before felt its pressure; he had never till now felt how powerful, how compulsatory it is over even generous and high-spirited souls. Whilst Vivian was thus oppressed with difficulties, which his imprudence had brought upon him; whilst his mind was struggling with opposing motives, he was, most fortunately for his political integrity, relieved, partly by accident, and partly by friendship. It happened that the incumbent of the rich living, of which Vivian had the presentation, was dying just at this time; and Russell, instead of claiming the living which Vivian had promised to him, relinquished all pretensions to it, and insisted upon his friend's disposing of his right of presentation. The sum which this enabled Vivian to raise was fully sufficient to satisfy the execution which had been laid on his castle; and the less clamorous creditors were content to be paid by instalments, annually, from his income. Thus he was saved for the present; and he formed the most prudent resolves for the future. He was most sincerely grateful to his disinterested friend. The full extent of the sacrifice which Russell made him was not, however, known at this time, nor for some years afterwards.

But, without anticipation, let us proceed with our story. Amongst those fashionable and political friends with whom our hero had, since his return to England, renewed his connexion, was my Lord Glistonbury. His lordship, far from thinking the worse of him for his affair with Mrs. Wharton, spoke of it in modish slang, as "a new and fine feather in his cap;" and he congratulated Vivian upon his having "carried off the prize without paying the price." Vivian's success as a parliamentary orator had still further endeared him to his lordship, who failed not to repeat, that he had always prophesied Vivian would make a capital figure in public life; that Vivian was his member, &c. At the recess, Lord Glistonbury insisted upon carrying Vivian down to spend the holidays with him at Glistonbury Castle.

"You must come, Vivian: so make your fellow put your worldly goods into my barouche, which is at the door; and we are to have a great party at Glistonbury, and private theatricals, and the devil knows what; and you must see my little Julia act, and I must introduce you to the Rosamunda. Come, come! you can't refuse me!—Why, you have only a bachelor's castle of your own to go to; and that's a dismal sort of business, compared with what I have in petto for you—'the feast of reason, and the flow of soul,' in the first style, I assure you. You must know, I always—even in the midst of the wildest of my wild oats—had a taste for the belles-lettres, and philosophy, and the muses, and the literati, and so forth—always a touch of the Mecaenas about me.—And now my boy's growing up, it's more particularly proper to bring these sort of people about him; for, you know, clever men who have a reputation can sound a flourish of trumpets advantageously before 'a Grecian youth of talents rare' makes his appearance on the stage of the great world—Ha! hey!—Is not this what one may call prudence?—Ha!—Good to have a father who knows something of life, and of books too, hey? Then, for my daughters, too—daughter, I mean; for Lady Sarah's Lady Glistonbury's child: her ladyship and Miss Strictland have manufactured her after their own taste and fashion; and I've nothing to say to that—But my little Julia—Ah, I've got a different sort of governess about her these few months past—not without family battles, you may guess. But when Jupiter gives the nod, you know, even Juno, stately as she is, must bend. So I have my Rosamunda for my little Julia—who, by-the-bye, is no longer my little Julia, but a prodigious fine woman, as you shall see. But, all this time, is your fellow putting your things up? No!—Hey? how? Oh, I understand your long face of hesitation—you have not seen the ladies since the Wharton affair, and you don't know how they might look.—Never fear! Lady Glistonbury shall do as I please, and look as I please. Besides, entre nous, I know she hates the Whartons; so that her morality will have a loophole to creep out of; and you'll be safe and snug, whilst all the blame will be thrown on them—Hey!—Oh, I understand things—pique myself on investigating the human heart. Come, we have not a moment to lose; and you'll have your friend Russell, too—Come, come! to have and to hold, as the lawyers say—"

Seizing Vivian's arm, Lord Glistonbury carried him off before he had half understood all his lordship had poured forth so rapidly; and before he had decided whether he wished or not to accept of this invitation.

CHAPTER VIII

On his way to Glistonbury Castle, Vivian had full leisure to repent of having accepted of this invitation, recollecting, as he did, all the former reports about himself and Lady Sarah Lidhurst. He determined, therefore, that his visit should be as short as possible; and the chief pleasure he promised himself was the society of his friend Russell.

On his arrival at the castle, he was told that Mr. Russell was out riding; and that every body else was in the theatre at a rehearsal, except Lady Glistonbury, the Lady Sarah, and Miss Strictland. He found these three ladies sitting in form in the great deserted drawing-room, each looking like a copy of the other, and all as if they were deploring the degeneracy of the times. Vivian approached with due awe; but, to his great surprise and relief, at his approach their countenances exhibited some signs of life. Lord Glistonbury presented him on his return from abroad: Lady Glistonbury's features relaxed to a smile, though she seemed immediately to repent of it, and to feel it incumbent upon her to maintain her rigidity of mien. Whilst she, and of course Miss Strictland and the Lady Sarah, were thus embarrassed between the necessity of reprobating the sin, and the desire of pleasing the sinner, Lord Glistonbury ran on with one of his speeches, of borrowed sense and original nonsense, and then would have carried him off to the rehearsal, but Lady Glistonbury called Vivian back, begging, in her formal manner, "that her lord would do her the favour to leave Mr. Vivian with her for a few minutes, as it was so long since she had the pleasure of seeing him at Glistonbury." Vivian returned with as good a grace as he could; and, to find means of breaking the embarrassing silence that ensued, took up a book which lay upon the table, "Toplady's Sermons"—no hope of assistance from that: he had recourse to another—equally unlucky, "Wesley's Diary:" another—"The Pilgrim's Progress." He went no farther; but, looking up, he perceived that the Lady Sarah was motioned by her august mother to leave the room. Vivian had again recourse to "Toplady."

"Very unfashionable books, Mr. Vivian," said Miss Strictland, bridling and smiling as in scorn.

"Very unfashionable books!" repeated Lady Glistonbury, with the same inflection of voice, and the same bridling and smiling. "Very different," continued her ladyship, "very different from what you have been accustomed to see on some ladies' tables, no doubt, Mr. Vivian! Without mentioning names, or alluding to transactions that ought to be buried in eternal oblivion, and that are so very distressing to your friends here to think of, sir, give me leave to ask, Mr. Vivian, whether it be true what I have heard, that the prosecution, and every thing relative to it, is entirely given up?"

"Entirely, madam."

"Then," said Lady Glistonbury, glancing her eye at Miss Strictland, "we may welcome Mr. Vivian with safe consciences to Glistonbury; and since the affair will never become public, and since Lady Sarah knows none of the improper particulars; and since she may, and, from her education, naturally will, class all such things under the head of impossibilities and false reports, of which people, in our rank of life especially, are subject every hour to hear so many; there cannot, as I am persuaded you will agree with me in thinking, Miss Strictland, be any impropriety in our and Lady Sarah's receiving Mr. Vivian again on the same footing as formerly."

Miss Strictland bowed her formal assent: Vivian bowed, because he saw that a bow was expected from him; and then he pondered on what might be meant by the words, on the same footing as formerly; and he had just framed a clause explanatory and restrictive of the same, when he was interrupted by the sound of laughter, and of numerous, loud, and mingled voices, coming along the gallery that led to the drawing-room. As if these were signals for her departure, and as if she dreaded the intrusion and contamination of the revel rout, Lady Glistonbury arose, looked at her watch, pronounced her belief that it was full time for her to go to dress, and retired through a Venetian door, followed by Miss Strictland, repeating the same belief, and bearing her ladyship's tapestry work: her steps quickened as the door at the opposite end of the room opened; and, curtsying (an unnecessary apology to Mr. Vivian) as she passed, she left him to himself. And now,

"He sees a train profusely gay,
Come pranckling o'er the place."

Some were dressed for comic, some for tragic characters; but all seemed equally gay, and talked equally fast. There had been a dressed rehearsal of "The Fair Penitent," and of "The Romp;" and all the spectators and all the actors were giving and receiving exuberant compliments. Vivian knew many of the party,—some of them bel-esprits, some fashionable amateurs; all pretenders to notoriety, either as judges or performers. In the midst of this motley group, there was one figure who stood receiving and expecting universal homage: she was dressed as "The Fair Penitent;" but her affected vivacity of gesture and countenance was in striking contrast to her tragic attire; and Vivian could hardly forbear smiling at the minauderies with which she listened and talked to the gentlemen round her; now languishing, now coquetting; rolling her eyes, and throwing herself into a succession of studied attitudes, dealing repartees to this side and to that; and, in short, making the greatest possible exhibition both of her person and her mind.

"Don't you know her? Did you never see her before?—No! you've been out of England; but you've heard of her, certainly?—Rosamunda,"—whispered Lord Glistonbury to Vivian.

"And who is Rosamunda?" said Vivian; "an actress."

"Actress!—Hush!—Bless you! no—but the famous poetess. Is it possible that you hav'n't read the poems of Rosamunda?—They were in every body's hands a few months ago; but you were abroad—better engaged, or as well, hey? But, as I was going to tell you, that's the reason she's called The Rosamunda—I gave her the name, for I patronized her from the first. Her real name is Bateman; and Lady Glistonbury and her set call her Miss Bateman still, but nobody else. She's an amazing clever woman, I assure you—more genius than any of 'em since the time of Rousseau!—Devil of a salary!—and devil of a battle I had to fight with some of my friends before I could fix her here; but I was determined I would follow my own ideas in Julia's education. Lady Glistonbury had her way and her routine with Lady Sarah; and it's all very well, vastly well—

'Virtue for her too painful an endeavour,
Content to dwell in decencies for ever.'

You know the sort of thing! Yes, yes; but I was not content to have my Julia lost among the mediocres, as I call them: so I took her out of Miss Strictland's hands; and the Rosamunda's her governess."

"Her governess!" repeated Vivian, with uncontrollable astonishment; "Lady Julia Lidhurst's governess!"

"Yes, you may well be surprised," pursued Lord Glistonbury, mistaking the cause of the surprise: "no one in England could have done it but myself; she refused innumerable applications,—immense offers; and, after all, you know, she does not appear as governess titrée—only as a friend of the family, who directs Lady Julia Lidhurst's literary talents. Oh, you understand, a man of the world knows how to manage these things—sacrifices always to the vanity of the sex, or the pride, as the case may be, I never mind names, but things, as the metaphysicians say—distinguish betwixt essentials and accidents—sound philosophy that, hey? And, thank Heaven! a gentleman or a nobleman need not apologize in these days for talking of philosophy before ladies, even if any body overheard us, which, as it happens, I believe nobody does. So let me, now that you know your Paris, introduce you to 'The Rosamunda.'—Mr. Vivian—the Rosamunda. Rosamunda—Mr. Vivian."

After Vivian had for a few minutes acted audience, very little to his own satisfaction, he was relieved by Lord Glistonbury's exclaiming, "But Julia! where's Julia all this time?"

Rosamunda looked round, with the air of one interrupted by a frivolous question which requires no answer; but some one less exalted, and more attentive to the common forms of civility, told his lordship that Lady Julia was in the gallery with her brother. Lord Glistonbury hurried Vivian into the gallery. He was struck the moment he met Lady Julia with the great change and improvement in her appearance. Instead of the childish girl he had formerly seen flying about, full only of the frolic of the present moment, he now saw a fine graceful woman with a striking countenance that indicated both genius and sensibility. She was talking to her brother with so much eagerness, that she did not see Vivian come into the gallery; and, as he walked on towards the farther end, where she was standing, he had time to admire her.

"A fine girl, faith! though she is my daughter," whispered Lord Glistonbury; "and would you believe that she is only sixteen?"

"Only sixteen!"

"Ay: and stay till you talk to her—stay till you hear her—you will be more surprised. Such genius! such eloquence! She's my own girl. Well, Julia, my darling!" cried he, raising his voice, "in the clouds, as usual?"

Lady Julia started—but it was a natural, not a theatric start—colouring at the consciousness of her own absence of mind. She came forward with a manner that apologized better than words could do, and she received Mr. Vivian so courteously, and with such ingenuous pleasure in her countenance, that he began to rejoice in having accepted the invitation to Glistonbury; at the same instant, he recollected a look which his mother had given him when he first saw Lady Julia on the terrace of the castle.

"Well, what was she saying to you, Lidhurst? hey! my boy?"

"We were arguing, sir."

"Arguing! Ay, ay, she's the devil for that!—words at will!—'Persuasive words, and more persuasive sighs!' Ah, woman! woman for ever! always talking us out of our senses! and which of the best of us would not wish it to be so? 'Oh! let me, let me be deceived!' is the cream of philosophy, epicurean and stoic—at least, that's my creed. But to the point: what was it about that she was holding forth so charmingly—a book or a lover? A book, I'll wager: she's such a romantic little fool, and so unlike other women: leaves all her admirers there in the drawing-room, and stays out here, talking over musty books with her brother. But come, what was the point? I will have it argued again before me—Let's see the book."

Lord Lidhurst pointed out a speech in "The Fair Penitent," and said that they had been debating about the manner in which it should be recited. Lord Glistonbury called upon his daughter to repeat it: she showed a slight degree of unaffected timidity at first; but when her father stamped and bid her let him see no vulgar bashfulness, she obeyed—recited charmingly—and, when urged by a little opposition from her brother, grew warm in defence of her own opinion—displayed in its support such sensibility, with such a flow of eloquence, accompanied with such animated and graceful, yet natural gesture, that Vivian was transported with sudden admiration. He was astonished at this early development of feeling and intellect; and if, in the midst of his delight, he felt some latent disapprobation of this display of talent from so young a woman, yet he quickly justified her to himself, by saying that he was not a stranger; that he had formerly been received by her family on a footing of intimacy. Then he observed farther, in her vindication, that there was not the slightest affectation or coquetry in any of her words or motions; that she spoke with this eagerness not to gain admiration, but because she was carried away by her enthusiasm, and, thoughtless of herself, was eager only to persuade and to make her opinions prevail. Such was the enchantment of her eloquence and her beauty, that after a quarter of an hour spent in her company, our hero did not know whether to wish that she had more sedateness and reserve, or to rejoice that she was so animated and natural. Before he could decide this point, his friend Russell returned from riding. After the first greetings were over, Russell drew him aside, and asked, "Pray, my dear Vivian, what brings you here?"

"Lord Glistonbury—to whom I had not time to say no, he talked so fast. But, after all, why should I say no? I am a free man—a discarded lover. I am absolutely convinced that Selina Sidney's refusal will never be retracted; my mother, I know, is of that opinion. You suggested, that if I distinguished myself in public life, and showed steadiness, I might recover her esteem and affection; but I see no chance of it. My mother showed me her last letter—no hopes from that—so I think it would be madness, or folly, to waste my time, and wear out my feelings, in pursuit of a woman, who, however amiable, is lost to me."

"Of that you are the best judge," said Russell, gravely. "I am far from wishing—from urging you to waste your time. Lady Mary Vivian must know more of Miss Sidney, and be better able to judge of the state of her heart than I can be. It would not be the part of a friend to excite you to persevere in a pursuit that would end in disappointment; but this much, before we quit the subject for ever, I feel it my duty to say—that I think Miss Sidney the woman of all others the best suited to your character, the most deserving of your love, the most calculated to make you exquisitely and permanently happy."

"All that's very true," said Vivian, impatiently; "but, since I can't have her, why make me miserable about her?"

"Am I to understand," resumed Russell, after a long pause, "am I to understand that, now you have regained your freedom, you come here with the settled purpose of espousing the Lady Sarah Lidhurst?"

"Heaven forfend!" cried Vivian, starting back.

"Then I am to go over again, on this subject, with indefatigable patience and in due logical order, all the arguments, moral, prudential, and conventional, which I had the labour of laying before you about a twelvemonth ago."

"Save yourself the trouble, my dear friend!" said Vivian; "I shall set all that upon a right footing immediately, by speaking of the report at once to some of the family. I was going to rise to explain this morning, when I was with Lady Glastonbury; but I felt a sort of delicacy—it was an awkward time—and at that moment somebody came into the room."

"Ay," said Russell, "you are just like the hero of a novel, stopped from saying what he ought to say by somebody's coming into the room.—Awkward time! Take care you don't sacrifice yourself at last to these awkwardnesses and this sort of delicacies. I have still my fears that you will get into difficulties about Lady Sarah."

Vivian could not help laughing at what he called his friend's absurd fears.

"If you are determined, my dear Russell, at all events to fear for me, I'll suggest to you a more reasonable cause of dread. Suppose I should fall desperately in love with Lady Julia!—I assure you there's some danger of that. She is really very handsome and very graceful; uncommonly clever and eloquent—as to the rest, you know her—what is she?"

"All that you have said, and more. She might be made any thing—every thing; an ornament to her sex— an honour to her country—were she under the guidance of persons fit to direct great powers and a noble character; but yet I cannot, Vivian, as your friend, recommend her to you as a wife."

"I am not thinking of her as a wife," said Vivian: "I have not had time to think of her at all yet. But you said, just now, that in good hands she might be made every thing that is good and great. Why not by a husband, instead of a governess? and would not you call mine good hands?"

"Good, but not steady—not at all the husband fit to guide such a woman. He must be a man not only of superior sense, but of superior strength of mind."

Vivian was piqued by this remark, and proceeded to compare the fitness of his character to such a character as Lady Julia's. Every moment he showed more curiosity to hear further particulars of her disposition; of the different characters of her governesses, and of all her relations; but Russell refused to say more. He had told him what he was called upon, as his friend, to reveal; he left the rest to Vivian's own observation and judgment. Vivian set himself to work to observe and judge with all his might.

He soon perceived that all Russell had told him of the mismanagement of Lady Julia's education was true. In this house there were two parties, each in extremes, and each with their systems and practice carried to the utmost excess. The partisans of the old and the new school were here to be seen at daggers-drawing. Lady Glastonbury, abhorrent of what she termed modern philosophy, and classing under that name almost all science and literature, especially all attempts to cultivate the understanding of women, had, with the assistance of her double, Miss Strictland, brought up Lady Sarah in all the ignorance and all the rigidity of the most obsolete of the old school; she had made Lady Sarah precisely like herself; with virtue, stiff, dogmatical, and repulsive; with religion, gloomy and puritanical; with manners, cold and automatic. In the course of eighteen years, whilst Lady Glistonbury went on, like clock-work, the same round, punctual to the letter but unfeeling of the spirit of her duties, she contrived, even by the wearisome method of her minuted diary of education, to make her house odious to her husband. Some task, or master, or hour of lesson, continually, and immitigably plagued him: he went abroad for amusement, and found dissipation. Thus, by her unaccommodating temper, and the obstinacy of her manifold virtues, she succeeded in alienating the affections of her husband. In despair he one day exclaimed,

"Ah que de vertus vous me faites haïr;"

and, repelled by virtue in this ungracious form, he flew to more attractive vice. Finding that he could not have any comfort or solace in the society of his wife, he sought consolation in the company of a mistress. Lady Glistonbury had, in the mean time, her consolation in being a pattern-wife; and in hearing that at card-tables it was universally said, that Lord Glistonbury was the worst of husbands, and that her ladyship was extremely to be pitied. In process of time, Lord Glistonbury was driven to his home again by the united torments of a virago mistress and the gout. It was at this period that he formed the notion of being at once a political leader and a Mecaenas; and it was at this period that he became acquainted with both his daughters, and determined that his Julia should never resemble the Lady Sarah. He saw his own genius in Julia; and he resolved, as he said, to give her fair play, and to make her one of the wonders of the age. After some months' counteraction and altercation, Lord Glistonbury, with a high hand, took his daughter from under the control of Miss Strictland; and, in spite of all the representations, prophecies, and denunciations of her mother, consigned Julia to the care of a governess after his own heart—a Miss Bateman; or, as he called her, The Rosamunda. From the moment this lady was introduced into the family there was an irreconcileable breach between the husband and wife. Lady Glistonbury was perfectly in the right in her dread of such a governess as Miss Bateman for her daughter. Her ladyship was only partially and accidentally right: right in point of fact, but wrong in the general principle; for she objected to Miss Bateman, as being of the class of literary women; to her real faults, her inordinate love of admiration, and romantic imprudence, Lady Glistonbury did not object, because she did not at first know them; and when she did, she considered them but as necessary consequences of the cultivation and enlargement of Miss Bateman's understanding. "No wonder!" her ladyship would say; "I knew it must be so; I knew it could not be otherwise. All those clever women, as they are called, are the same. This comes of literature and literary ladies."

Thus moralizing in private with Miss Strictland and her own small party, Lady Glistonbury appeared silent and passive before her husband and his adherents. After prophesying how it all must end in the ruin of her daughter Julia, she declared that she would never speak on this subject again: she showed herself ready, with maternal resignation, and in silent obduracy, to witness the completion of the sacrifice of her devoted child.

Lord Glistonbury was quite satisfied with having silenced opposition. His new governess, established in her office, and with full and unlimited powers, went on triumphant and careless of her charge; she thought of little but displaying her own talents in company. The castle was consequently filled with crowds of amateurs; novels and plays were the order of the day; and a theatre was fitted up, all in open defiance of poor Lady Glistonbury. The daughter commenced her new course of education by being taught to laugh at her mother's prejudices. Such was the state of affairs when Vivian commenced his observations; and all this secret history he learnt by scraps, and hints, and inuendoes, from very particular friends of both parties—friends who were not troubled with any of Mr. Russell's scruples or discretion.

Vivian's attention was now fixed upon Lady Julia; he observed with satisfaction, that, notwithstanding her governess's example and excitement, Lady Julia did not show any exorbitant desire for general admiration; and that her manners were free from coquetry and affectation: she seemed rather to disdain the flattery, and to avoid both the homage and the company of men who were her inferiors in mental qualifications; she addressed her conversation principally to Vivian and his friend Russell; with them, indeed, she conversed a great deal, with much eagerness and enthusiasm, expressing all her opinions without disguise, and showing on most occasions more imagination than reason, and more feeling than judgment. Vivian perceived that it was soon suspected by many of their observers, and especially by Lady Glistonbury and the Lady Sarah, that Julia had a design upon his heart; but he plainly discerned that she had no design whatever to captivate him; and that though she gave him so large a share of her company, it was without thinking of him as a lover: he saw that she conversed with him and Mr. Russell, preferably to others, because they spoke on subjects which interested her more; and because they drew out her brother, of whom she was very fond. Her being capable, at so early an age, to appreciate Russell's character and talents; her preferring his solid sense and his plain sincerity to the brilliancy, the fashion, and even the gallantry of all the men whom her father had now collected round her, appeared to Vivian the most unequivocal proof of the superiority of her understanding and of the goodness of her disposition. On various occasions, he marked with delight the deference she paid to his friend's opinion, and the readiness with which she listened to reason from him—albeit unused and averse from reason in general. Impatient as she was of control, and confident, both in her own powers and in her instinctive moral sense (about which, by-the-bye, she talked a great deal of eloquent nonsense), yet a word or a look from Mr. Russell would reclaim her in her highest flights. Soon after Vivian commenced his observations upon this interesting subject, he saw an instance of what Russell had told him of the ease with which Lady Julia might be guided by a man of sense and strength of mind.

The tragedy of "The Fair Penitent," Calista by Miss Bateman, was represented with vast applause to a brilliant audience at the Glistonbury theatre. The same play was to be reacted a week afterwards to a fresh audience—it was proposed that Vivian should play Lothario, and that Lady Julia should play Calista: Miss Bateman saw no objection to this proposal: Lord Glistonbury might, perhaps, have had the parental prudence to object to his daughter's appearing in public at her age, in such a character, before a mixed audience: but, unfortunately, Lady Glistonbury bursting from her silence at this critical moment, said so much, and in such a prosing and puritanical manner, not only against her daughter's acting in this play, and in these circumstances, but against all stage plays, playwrights, actors, and actresses whatsoever, denouncing and anathematizing them all indiscriminately; that immediately Lord Glistonbury laughed— Miss Bateman took fire—and it became a trial of power between the contending parties. Lady Julia, who had but lately escaped from the irksomeness of her mother's injudicious and minute control, dreaded, above all things, to be again subjected to her and Miss Strictland; therefore, without considering the real propriety or impropriety of the point in question, without examining whether Miss Bateman was right or wrong in the licence she had granted, Lady Julia supported her opinion warmly; and, with all her eloquence, at once asserted her own liberty, and defended the cause of the theatre in general. She had heard Mr. Russell once speak of the utility of a well-regulated public stage; of the influence of good theatric representations in forming the taste and rousing the soul to virtue: he had shown her Marmontel's celebrated letter to Rousseau on this subject; consequently, she thought she knew what his opinion must be on the present occasion: therefore she spoke with more than her usual confidence and enthusiasm. Her eloquence and her abilities transported her father and most of her auditors, Vivian among the rest, with astonishment and admiration: she enjoyed, at this moment, what the French call un grand succès; but, in the midst of the buzz of applause, Vivian observed that her eye turned anxiously upon Russell, who stood silent, and with a disapproving countenance.

"I am sure your friend, Mr. Russell, is displeased at this instant—and with me.—I must know why.—Let us ask him.—Do bring him here."

Immediately she disengaged herself from all her admirers, and, making room for Mr. Russell beside her, waited, as she said, to hear from him ses vérités. Russell would have declined speaking, but her ladyship appealed earnestly and urgently for his opinion, saying, "Who will speak the truth to me if you will not? On whose judgment can I rely if not on yours?—You direct my brother's mind to every thing that is wise and good; direct mine: I am as desirous to do right as he can be: and you will find me—self-willed and volatile, as I know you think me—you will find me a docile pupil. Then tell me frankly—did I, just now, speak too much or too warmly? I thought I was speaking your sentiments, and that I must be right. But perhaps it was not right for a woman, or so young a woman as I am, to support even just opinions so resolutely. And yet is it a crime to be young?—And is the honour of maintaining truth to be monopolized by age?—No, surely; for Mr. Russell himself has not that claim to stand forth, as he so often does, in its defence. If you think that I ought not to act Calista; if you think that I had better not appear on the stage at all, only say so!—All I ask is your opinion; the advantage of your judgment. And you see, Mr. Vivian, how difficult it is to obtain it!—But his friend, probably, never felt this difficulty!"

With a degree of sober composure, which almost provoked Vivian, Mr. Russell answered this animated lady. And with a sincerity which, though politely shown, Vivian thought severe and almost cruel, Russell acknowledged that her ladyship had anticipated some, but not all of his objections. He represented that she had failed in becoming respect to her mother, in thus publicly attacking and opposing her opinions, even supposing them to be ill-founded; and declared that, as to the case in discussion, he was entirely of Lady Glistonbury's opinion, that it would be unfit and injurious to a young lady to exhibit herself, even on a private stage, in the character in which it had been proposed that Lady Julia should appear.

Whilst Russell spoke, Vivian was charmed with the manner in which Lady Julia listened: he thought her countenance enchantingly beautiful, alternately softened as it was by the expression of genuine humility, and radiant with candour and gratitude. She made no reply, but immediately went to her mother; and, in the most engaging manner acknowledged that she had been wrong, and declared that she was convinced it would be improper for her to act the character she had proposed. With that cold haughtiness of mien, the most repulsive to a warm and generous mind, the mother turned to her daughter, and said that, for her part, she had no faith in sudden conversions, and starts of good conduct made little impression upon her; that, as far as she was herself concerned, she forgave, as in charity it became her, all the undutiful insolence with which she had been treated; that, as to the rest, she was glad to find, for Lady Julia's own sake, that she had given up her strange, and, as she must say, scandalous intentions. "However," added Lady Glistonbury, "I am not so sanguine as to consider this as any thing but a respite from ruin; I am not so credulous as to believe in sudden reformations; nor, despicable as you and my lord do me the honour to think my understanding—am I to be made the dupe of a little deceitful fondling!"

Julia withdrew her arms, which she had thrown round her mother; and Miss Strictland, after breaking her netting silk with a jerk of indignation, observed, that, for her part, she wondered young ladies should go to consult their brother's tutor, instead of more suitable, and, perhaps, as competent advisers. Lady Julia, now indignant, turned away, and was withdrawing from before the triumvirate, when Lady Sarah, who had sat looking, even more stiff and constrained than usual, suddenly broke from her stony state, and, springing forward, exclaimed, "Stay, Julia!—Stay, my dear sister!—Oh, Miss Strictland! do my sister justice!—When Julia is so candid, so eager to do right, intercede for her with my mother!"

"First, may I presume to ask," said Miss Strictland, drawing herself up with starch malice; "first, may I presume to ask, whether Mr. Vivian, upon this occasion, declined to act Lothario?"

"Miss Strictland, you do not do my sister justice!" cried Lady Sarah: "Miss Strictland, you are wrong—very wrong!"

Miss Strictland, for a moment struck dumb with astonishment, opening her eyes as far as they could open, stared at Lady Sarah, and, after a pause, exclaimed, "Lady Sarah! I protest I never saw any thing that surprised me so much in my whole life!—Wrong!—very wrong!—I?—My Lady Glistonbury, I trust your ladyship—"

Lady Glistonbury, at this instant, showed, by a little involuntary shake of her head, that she was inwardly perturbed: Lady Sarah, throwing herself upon her knees before her mother, exclaimed, "Oh, madam!—mother! forgive me if I failed in respect to Miss Strictland!—But, my sister! my sister—!"

"Rise, Sarah, rise!" said Lady Glistonbury; "that is not a fit attitude!—And you are wrong, very wrong, to fail in respect to Miss Strictland, my second self, Sarah. Lady Julia Lidhurst, it is you who are the cause of this—the only failure of duty your sister ever was guilty of towards me in the whole course of her life—I beg of you to withdraw, and leave me my daughter Sarah."

"At least, I have found a sister, and when I most wanted it," said Lady Julia. "I always suspected you loved me, but I never knew how much till this moment," added she, turning to embrace her sister; but Lady Sarah had now resumed her stony appearance, and, standing motionless, received her sister's embrace without sign of life or feeling.

"Lady Julia Lidhurst," said Miss Strictland, "you humble yourself in vain: I think your mother, my Lady Glistonbury, requested of you to leave your sister, Lady Sarah, to us, and to her duty."

"Duty!" repeated Lady Julia, her eyes flashing indignation: "Is this what you call duty?—Never will I humble myself before you again—I will leave you—I do leave you—now and for ever—DUTY!"

She withdrew:—and thus was lost one of the fairest occasions of confirming a young and candid mind in prudent and excellent dispositions. After humbling herself in vain before a mother, this poor young lady was now to withstand a father's reproaches; and, after the inexorable Miss Strictland, she was to encounter the exasperated Miss Bateman. Whether the Gorgon terrors of one governess, or the fury passions of the other, were most formidable, it was difficult to decide. Miss Bateman had written an epilogue for Lady Julia to recite in the character of Calista; and, with the combined irritability of authoress and governess, she was enraged at the idea of her pupil's declining to repeat these favourite lines. Lord Glistonbury cared not for the lines; but, considering his own authority to be impeached by his daughter's resistance, he treated his Julia as a traitor to his cause, and a rebel to his party.

But Lady Julia was resolute in declining to play Calista; and Vivian admired the spirit and steadiness of her resistance to the solicitations and the flattery with which she was assailed by the numerous hangers-on of the family, and by the amateurs assembled at Glistonbury. Russell, who knew the warmth of her temper, however, dreaded that she should pass the bounds of propriety in the contest with her father and her governess; and he almost repented having given any advice upon the subject. The contest happily terminated in Lord Glistonbury's having a violent fit of the gout, which, as the newspapers informed the public, "ended for the season the Christmas hospitalities and theatrical festivities at Glistonbury Castle!"

Whilst his lordship suffered this fit of torture, his daughter Julia attended him with so much patience and affection, that he forgave her for not being willing to be Calista; and, upon his recovery, he announced to Miss Bateman that it was his will and pleasure that his daughter Julia should do as she liked on this point, but that he desired it to be understood that this was no concession to Lady Glistonbury's prejudices, but an act of his own pure grace.

To celebrate his recovery, his lordship determined to give a ball; and Miss Bateman persuaded him to make it a fancy ball. In this family, unfortunately, every occurrence, even every proposal of amusement, became a subject of dispute and a source of misery. Lady Glistonbury, as soon as her lord announced his intention of giving this fancy ball, declined taking the direction of an entertainment which approached, she said, too near to the nature of a masquerade to meet her ideas of propriety. Lord Glistonbury laughed, and tried the powers of ridicule and wit:

"But on th'impassive ice the lightnings play'd."

The lady's cool obstinacy was fully a match for her lord's petulance: to all he could urge, she repeated, "that such entertainments did not meet her ideas of propriety." Her ladyship, Lady Sarah, and Miss Strictland, consequently declared it to be their resolution, "to appear in their own proper characters, and their own proper dresses, and no others."

These three rigid seceders excepted, all the world at Glistonbury Castle, and within its sphere of attraction, were occupied with preparations for this ball. Miss Bateman was quite in her element, flattered and flattering, consulting and consulted, in the midst of novels, plays, and poetry, prints, and pictures, searching for appropriate characters and dresses. This preceptress seemed to think and to expect that others should deem her office of governess merely a subordinate part of her business: she considered her having accepted of the superintendence of the education of Lady Julia Lidhurst as a prodigious condescension on her part, and a derogation from her rank and pretensions in the literary and fashionable world; a peculiar and sentimental favour to Lord Glistonbury, of which his lordship was bound in honour to show his sense, by treating her as a member of his family, not only with distinguished politeness, but by deferring to her opinion in all things, so as to prove to her satisfaction that she was considered only as a friend, and not at all as a governess. Thus she was raised as much above that station in the family in which she could be useful, as governesses in other houses have been sometimes depressed below their proper rank. Upon this, as upon all occasions, Miss Bateman was the first person to be thought of—her character and her dress were the primary points to be determined; and they were points of no easy decision, she having proposed for herself no less than five characters— the fair Rosamond, Joan of Arc, Cleopatra, Sigismunda, and Circe. After minute consideration of the dresses, which, at a fancy ball, were to constitute these characters, fair Rosamond was rejected, "because the old English dress muffled up the person too much; Joan of Arc would find her armour inconvenient for dancing; Cleopatra's diadem and royal purple would certainly be truly becoming, but then her regal length of train was as inadmissible in a dancing-dress as Joan of Arc's armour." Between Sigismunda and Circe, Miss Bateman's choice long vibrated. The Spanish and the Grecian costume had each its claims on her favour: for she was assured they both became her remarkably. Vivian was admitted to the consultation: he was informed that there must be both a Circe and a Sigismunda; and that Lady Julia was to take whichever of the two characters Miss Bateman declined. Pending the deliberation, Lady Julia whispered to Vivian, "For mercy's sake! contrive that I may not be doomed to be Circe; for Circe is no better than Calista."

Vivian was charmed with her ladyship's delicacy and discretion; he immediately decided her governess, by pointing out the beautiful head-dress of Flaxman's Circe, and observing that Miss Bateman's hair (which was a wig) might easily be arranged, so as to produce the same effect. Lady Julia rewarded Vivian for this able and successful manoeuvre by one of her sweetest smiles. Her smiles had now powerful influence over his heart. He rebelled against Russell's advice, to take more time to consider how far his character was suited to hers: he was conscious, indeed, that it would be more prudent to wait a little longer before he should declare his passion, as Lady Julia was so very young and enthusiastic, and as her education had been so ill managed; but he argued that the worse her education, and the more imprudent the people about her, the greater was her merit in conducting herself with discretion, and in trying to restrain her natural enthusiasm. Russell acknowledged this, and gave all due praise to Lady Julia; yet still he represented that Vivian had been acquainted with her so short time that he could not be a competent judge of her temper and disposition, even if his judgment were cool; but it was evident that his passions were now engaged warmly in her favour. All that Russell urged for delay so far operated, however, upon Vivian, that he adopted a half measure, and determined to try what chance he might have of pleasing her before he should either declare his love to her ladyship, or make his proposal to her father. A favourable opportunity soon occurred. On the day appointed for the fancy ball, the young Lord Lidhurst, who was to be Tancred, was taken ill of a feverish complaint: he was of a very weakly constitution, and his friends were much alarmed by his frequent indispositions. His physicians ordered quiet; he was confined to his own apartment; and another Tancred was of course to be sought for: Vivian ventured to offer to assume the character; and his manner, when he made this proposal to his fair Sigismunda, though it was intended to be merely polite and gallant, was so much agitated, that she now, for the first time, seemed to perceive the state of his heart. Colouring high, her ladyship answered, with hesitation unusual to her, "that she believed—she fancied—that is, she understood from her brother—that he had deputed Mr. Russell to represent Tancred in his place."

Vivian was not displeased by this answer: the change of colour and evident embarrassment appeared to him favourable omens; and he thought that whether the embarrassment arose from unwillingness to let any man but her brother's tutor, a man domesticated in the family, appear as her Tancred, or whether she was afraid of offending Mr. Russell, by changing the arrangement her brother had made; in either case Vivian felt ready, though a man in love, to approve of her motives. As to the rest, he was certain that Russell would decline the part assigned him; and, as Vivian expected, Russell came in a few minutes to resign his pretensions, or rather to state that though Lord Lidhurst had proposed it, he had never thought of accepting the honour; and that he should, in all probability, not appear at the ball, because he was anxious to stay as much as possible with Lord Lidhurst, whose indisposition increased instead of abating. Lord Glistonbury, after this explanation, came in high spirits, and with much satisfaction in his countenance and manner, said he was happy to hear that his Sigismunda was to have Mr. Vivian for her Tancred. So far all was prosperous to our hero's hopes.

But when he saw Lady Julia again, which was not till dinner time, he perceived an unfavourable alteration in her manner; not the timidity or embarrassment of a girl who is uncertain whether she is or is not pleased, or whether she should or should not appear to be pleased by the first approaches of a new lover; but there was in her manner a decided haughtiness, and an unusual air of displeasure and reserve. Though he sat beside her, and though in general her delightful conversation had been addressed either to him or Mr. Russell, they were now both deprived of this honour; whatever she said, and all she said, was unlike herself, was directed to persons opposite to her, even to the captain, the lawyer, and the family parasites, whose existence she commonly seemed to forget. She ate as well as spoke in a hurried manner, and as if in defiance of her feelings. Whilst the courses were changing, she turned towards Mr. Vivian, and after a rapid examining glance at his countenance, she said, in a low voice—"You must think me, Mr. Vivian, very unreasonable and whimsical, but I have given up all thoughts of being Sigismunda. Will you oblige me so far as not to appear in the dress of Tancred to-night? You will thus spare me all farther difficulty. You know my mother and sister have declared their determination not to wear any fancy dress; and though my father is anxious that I should, I believe it may be best that, in this instance, I follow my own judgment.—May I expect that you will oblige me?"

Vivian declared his entire submission to her ladyship's judgment: and he now was delighted to be able to forgive her for all seeming caprice; because he thought he saw an amiable motive for her conduct— the wish not to displease her mother, and not to excite the jealousy of her sister.

The hour when the ball was to commence arrived; the room filled with company; and Vivian, who flattered himself with the pleasure of dancing all night with Lady Julia, as the price of his prompt obedience, looked round the room in search of his expected partner, but he searched in vain. He looked to the door at every new entrance—no Lady Julia appeared. Circe, indeed, was every where to be seen and heard, and an uglier Circe never touched this earth; but she looked happily confident in the power of her charms. Whilst she was intent upon fascinating Vivian, he was impatiently waiting for a moment's intermission of her volubility, that he might ask what had become of Lady Julia.

"Lady Julia?—She's somewhere in the room, I suppose.—Oh! no: I remember, she told me she would go and sit a quarter of an hour with her brother. She will soon make her appearance, I suppose; but I am so angry with her for disappointing us all, and you in particular, by changing her mind about Sigismunda!—Such a capital Tancred as you would have made! and now you are no character at all! But then, you are only on a par with certain ladies. Comfort yourself with the great Pope's (I fear too true) reflection, that

'Most women have no characters at all.'"

Miss Bateman's eye glanced insolently, as she spoke, upon Lady Glistonbury's trio, who passed by at this instant, all without fancy dresses. Vivian shocked by this ill-breeding towards the mistress of the house, offered his arm immediately to Lady Glistonbury, and conducted her with Lady Sarah and Miss Strictland to their proper places, where, having seated themselves, each in the same attitude precisely, they looked more like martyrs prepared for endurance, than like persons in a ball-room. Vivian stayed to speak a few words to Lady Glistonbury, and was just going away, when her ladyship, addressing him with more than her usual formality, said, "Mr. Vivian, I see, has not adopted the fashion of the day; and as he is the only gentleman present, whose fancy dress does not proclaim him engaged to some partner equally fanciful, I cannot but wish that my daughter, Lady Sarah, should, if she dance at all to-night, dance with a gentleman in his own proper character."

Vivian, thus called upon, felt compelled to ask the honour of Lady Sarah's hand; but he flattered himself, that after the first dance he should have done his duty, and that he should be at liberty by the time Julia should make her appearance. But, to his great disappointment, Mr. Russell, who came in just as he had finished the first two dances, informed him that Lady Julia was determined not to appear at the ball, but to stay with her brother, who wished for her company. So poor Vivian found himself doomed to be Lady Sarah's partner for the remainder of the night. It happened that, as he was handing her ladyship to supper, in passing through an antechamber where some of the neighbours of inferior rank had been permitted to assemble to see the show, he heard one farmer's wife say to another, "Who beas that there, that's handing of Lady Sarah?"—They were detained a little by the crowd, so that he had time to hear the whole answer.—"Don't you know?" was the answer. "That there gentleman is Mr. Vivian of the new castle, that is to be married to her directly, and that's what he's come here for; for they've been engaged to one another ever since the time o' the election."

This speech disturbed our hero's mind considerably; for it awakened a train of reflections which he had wilfully left dormant. Will it, can it be believed, that after all his friend Russell's exhortations, after his own wise resolutions, he had never yet made any of those explanatory speeches he had intended?

"Positively," said he to himself, "this report shall not prevail four-and-twenty hours longer. I will propose for Lady Julia Lidhurst before I sleep. Russell, to be sure, advises me not to be precipitate—to take more time to study her disposition; but I am acquainted with her sufficiently;" (he should have said, I am in love with her sufficiently;) "and really now, I am bound in honour immediately to declare myself—it is the best possible way of putting a stop to a report which will be ultimately injurious to Lady Sarah."

Thus Vivian made his past irresolution an excuse for his present precipitation, flattering himself, as men often do when they are yielding to the impulse of their passions, that they are submitting to the dictates of reason. At six o'clock in the morning the company dispersed. Lord Glistonbury and Vivian were the last in the ball-room. His lordship began some raillery upon our hero's having declined appearing as Tancred, and upon his having devoted himself all night to Lady Sarah. Vivian seized the moment to explain his real feelings, and he made his proposal for Lady Julia. It was received with warm approbation by the father, who seemed to rejoice the more in this proposal, because he knew that it would disappoint and mortify Lady Glistonbury. The interests of his hatred seemed, indeed, to occupy his lordship more than the interests of Vivian's love; but politeness threw a decent veil over these feelings; and, after saying all that could be expected of the satisfaction it must be to a father to see his daughter united to a man of Mr. Vivian's family, fortune, talents, and great respectability; and after having given, incidentally and parenthetically, his opinions, not only concerning matrimony, but concerning all other affairs of human life, he wished his future son-in-law a very good night, and left him to repose. But no rest could Vivian take—he waited with impatience, that made every hour appear at least two, for the time when he was again to meet Lady Julia. He saw her at breakfast; but he perceived by her countenance that she as yet knew nothing of his proposal. After breakfast Lord Glistonbury said, "Come with me, my little Julia! it is a long time since I've had a walk and a talk with you." His lordship paced up and down the terrace, conversing earnestly with her for some time: he then went on to some labourers, who were cutting down a tree at the farther end of the avenue. Vivian hastened out to meet Lady Julia, who, after standing deep in thought for some moments, seemed returning towards the castle.

CHAPTER IX

"Mr. Vivian, I trust that I am not deficient in maidenly modesty," said Lady Julia, "when it is not incompatible with what I deem a higher virtue—sincerity. Now and ever, frankness is, and shall be, my only policy. The confidence I am about to repose in you, sir, is the strongest proof of my esteem, and of the gratitude I feel for your attachment.—My heart is no longer in my power to bestow. It is—young as I am, I dare to pronounce the words—irrevocably fixed upon one who will do honour to my choice. Your proposal was made to my father—Why was it not made to me?—Men—all men but one—treat women as puppets, and then wonder that they are not rational creatures!—Forgive me this too just reproach. But, as I was going to say, your proposal has thrown me into great difficulties—the greater because my father warmly approves of it. I have a strong affection for him; and, perhaps, a year or two ago, I should, in the ignorance in which I was dogmatically brought up, have thought it my duty to submit implicitly to parental authority, and to receive a husband from the hands of a father, without consulting either my own heart or my own judgment. But, since my mind has been more enlightened, and has opened to higher views of the dignity of my sex, and higher hopes of happiness, my ideas of duty have altered; and, I trust, I have sufficient courage to support my own idea of the rights of my sex, and my firm conviction of what is just and becoming."

Vivian was again going to say something; but, whether against or in favour of the rights of the sex, he had not clearly decided; when her ladyship saved him the trouble, by proceeding with the train of her ideas.

"My sincerity towards my father will, perhaps, cost me dear; but I cannot repent of it. As soon as I knew the state of my own heart—which was not till very lately—which was not, indeed, till you gave me reason to think you seriously liked me—I openly told my father all I knew of my own heart. Would you believe it?—I am sure I should not, unless I had seen and felt it—my father, who, you know, professes the most liberal opinions possible; my father, who, in conversation is 'All for love, and the world well lost;' my father, who let Miss Bateman put the Heloise into my hands, was astonished, shocked, indignant, at his own daughter's confession, I should say, assertion of her preference of a man of high merit, who wants only the advantages, if they be advantages, of rank and fortune.

"Mr. Vivian," continued she, "may I hope that now, when you must be convinced of the inefficacy of any attempt either to win or to control my affections, you will have the generosity to spare me all unnecessary contest with my father? It must render him more averse from the only union that can make his daughter happy; and it may ruin the fortunes of—the first, in my opinion, of human beings. I will request another favour from you—and let my willingness to be obliged by you convince you that I appreciate your character—I request that you will not only keep secret all that I have said to you; but that, if accident, or your own penetration, should hereafter discover to you the object of my affection, you will refrain from making any use of that discovery to my disadvantage. You see how entirely I have thrown myself on your honour and generosity."

Vivian assured her that the appeal was powerful with him; and that, by mastering his own passions, and sacrificing his feelings to hers, he would endeavour to show his strong desire to secure, at all events, her happiness.

"You are truly generous, Mr. Vivian, to listen to me with indulgence, to wish for my happiness, whilst I have been wounding your feelings. But, without any impeachment of your sincerity, or yet of your sensibility, let me say, that yours will be only a transient disappointment. Your acquaintance with me is but of yesterday, and the slight impression made on your mind will soon be effaced; but upon my mind there has been time to grave a deep, a first charactery of love, that never, whilst memory holds her seat, can be erased.—I believe," said Julia, checking herself, whilst a sudden blush overspread her countenance—"I am afraid that I have said too much, too much for a woman. The fault of my character, I know, I have been told, is the want of what is called RESERVE."

Blushing still more deeply as she pronounced these last words, the colour darting up to her temples, spreading over her neck, and making its way to the very tips of her fingers, "Now I have done worse," cried she, covering her face with her hands. But the next moment, resuming, or trying to resume her self-possession, she said, "It is time that I should retire, now that I have revealed my whole heart to you. It has, perhaps, been imprudently opened; but for that, your generosity, sir, is to blame. Had you shown more selfishness, I should assuredly have exerted more prudence, and have treated you with less confidence."

Lady Julia quitted him, and Vivian remained in a species of amaze, from which he could not immediately recover. Her frankness, her magnanimity, her enthusiastic sensibility, her eloquent beauty, had altogether exalted, to the highest ecstasy, his love and admiration. Then he walked about, beating his breast in despair at the thought of her affections being irrecoverably engaged,—next quarrelled with the boldness of the confession, the assertion of her love—then decided, that, with all her shining qualities and noble dispositions, she was not exactly the woman a man should desire for a wife: there was something too rash, too romantic about her; there was in her character, as she herself had said, and as Russell had remarked, too little reserve. Something like jealousy and distrust of his friend arose in Vivian's mind: "What!" said he to himself, "and is Russell my rival? and has he been all this time in secret my rival? Is it possible that Russell has been practising upon the affections of this innocent young creature—confided to him too? All this time, whilst he has been cautioning me against her charms, beseeching me not to propose for her precipitately, is it possible that he wanted only to get, to keep the start of me?—No—impossible! utterly impossible! If all the circumstances, all the evidence upon earth conspired, I would not believe it."

Resolved not to do injustice, even in his inmost soul, to his friend, our hero repelled all suspicion of Russell, by reflecting on his long and tried integrity, and on the warmth and fidelity of his friendship. In this temper he was crossing the castle-yard to go to Russell's apartment, when he was met and stopped by one of the domesticated friends of the family, Mr. Mainwaring, the young lawyer: he was in the confidence of Lord Glistonbury, and, proud to show it, he let Mr. Vivian know that he was apprised of the proposal that had been made, and congratulated him, and all the parties concerned, on the prospect of such an agreeable connexion. Vivian was quite unprepared to speak to any one, much less to a lawyer, upon this subject; he had not even thought of the means of obeying Lady Julia, by withdrawing his suit; therefore, with a mixture of vexation and embarrassment in his manner, he answered in commonplace phrases, meant to convey no precise meaning, and endeavoured to disengage himself from his companion; but the lawyer, who had fastened upon him, linking his arm in Vivian's, continued to walk him up and down under the great gateway, saying that he had a word or two of importance for his private ear. This man had taken much pains to insinuate himself into Vivian's favour, by the most obsequious and officious attentions: though his flattery had at first been disgusting, yet, by persevering in his show of civility, he had at length inclined Vivian to think that he was too harsh in his first judgment, and to believe that, "after all, Mainwaring was a good friendly fellow, though his manner was against him."

Mr. Mainwaring, with many professions of regard for Vivian, and with sundry premisings that he hazarded himself by the communication, took the liberty of hinting, that he guessed, from Mr. Vivian's manner this morning, that obstacles had arisen on the part of a young lady who should be nameless; and he should make bold to add that, in his private opinion, the said obstacles would never be removed whilst a certain person remained in the castle, and whilst the young lady alluded to was allowed to spend so much of her time studying with her brother when well, or nursing him when sick. Mr. Mainwaring declared that he was perfectly astonished at Lord Glistonbury's blindness or imprudence in keeping this person in the house, after the hints his lordship had received, and after all the proofs that must or may have fallen within his cognizance, of the arts of seduction that had been employed. Here Vivian interrupted Mr. Mainwaring, to beg that he would not keep him longer in suspense by inuendoes, but that he would name distinctly the object of his suspicions. This, however, Mr. Mainwaring begged to be excused from doing: he would only shake his head and smile, and leave people to their own sagacity and penetration. Vivian warmly answered, that, if Mr. Mainwaring meant Mr. Russell, he was well assured that Mr. Mainwaring was utterly mistaken in attributing to him any but the most honourable conduct.

Mr. Mainwaring smiled, and shook his head—smiled again, and sighed, and hoped Mr. Vivian was right, and observed that time would show; and that, at all events, he trusted Mr. Vivian would keep profoundly secret the hint which his friendship had, indiscreetly perhaps, hazarded.

Scarcely had Mr. Mainwaring retired, when Captain Pickering met and seized upon Vivian, led to the same subject, and gave similar hints, that Russell was the happy rival who had secretly made himself master of Lady Julia's heart. Vivian, though much astonished, finding that these gentlemen agreed in their discoveries or their suspicions, still defended his friend Russell, and strongly protested that he would be responsible for his honour with his life, if it were necessary. The captain shrugged his shoulders, said it was none of his business, that, as Mr. Vivian took it up so warmly, he should let it drop; for it was by no means his intention to get into a quarrel with Mr. Vivian, for whom he had a particular regard. This said, with all the frankness of a soldier, Captain Pickering withdrew, adding, as the clergyman passed at this instant, "There's a man who could tell you more than any of us, if he would, but snug's the word with Wicksted."

Vivian, in great anxiety and much curiosity, appealed to Mr. Wicksted: he protested that he knew nothing, suspected nothing, at least could venture to say nothing; for these were very delicate family matters, and every gentleman should, on these occasions, make it a principle to see with his own eyes. Gradually, however, Mr. Wicksted let out his opinion, and implied infinitely more than Captain Pickering or Mr. Mainwaring had asserted. Vivian still maintained, in the warmest terms, that it was impossible his friend Russell should be to blame. Mr. Wicksted simply pronounced the word friend with a peculiar emphasis, and, with an incredulous smile, left him to his reflections. Those reflections were painful; for, though he defended Russell from the attacks of others, yet he had not sufficient firmness of mind completely to resist the suggestions of suspicion and jealousy, particularly when they had been corroborated by so many concurring testimonies. He had no longer the courage to go immediately to Russell, to tell him of his proposal for Lady Julia, or to speak to him of any of his secret feelings; but, turning away from the staircase that led to his friend's apartment, he determined to observe Russell with his own eyes, before he should decide upon the truth or falsehood of the accusations which had been brought against him. Alas! Vivian was no longer in a condition to observe with his own eyes; his imagination was so perturbed, that he could neither see nor hear any thing as it really was. When he next saw Russell and Lady Julia together, he wondered at his blindness in not having sooner perceived their mutual attachment: notwithstanding that Lady Julia had now the strongest motives to suppress every indication of her passion, symptoms of it broke out continually, the more violent, perhaps, from her endeavours to conceal them. He knew that she was passionately in love with Russell; and that Russell should not have perceived what every other man, even every indifferent spectator, had discovered, appeared incredible. Russell's calm manner and entire self-possession sometimes provoked Vivian, and sometimes quelled his suspicions; sometimes he looked upon this calmness as the extreme of art, sometimes as a proof of innocence, which could not be counterfeit. At one moment he was so much struck with Russell's friendly countenance, that, quite ashamed of his suspicions, he was upon the point of speaking openly to him; but, unfortunately, these intentions were frustrated by some slight obstacle. At length Miss Strictland, who had lately been very courteous to Mr. Vivian, took an opportunity of drawing him into one of the recessed windows; where, with infinite difficulty in bringing herself to speak on such a subject, after inconceivable bridlings of the head, and contortions of every muscle of her neck, she insinuated to him her fears, that my Lord Glistonbury's confidence had been very ill placed in Lord Lidhurst's tutor: she was aware that Mr. Russell had the honour of Mr. Vivian's friendship, but nothing could prevent her from speaking, where she felt it to be so much her duty; and that, as from the unfortunate circumstances in the family she had no longer any influence over Lady Julia Lidhurst, nor any chance of being listened to on such a subject with patience by Lord Glistonbury, she thought the best course she could take was to apply to Mr. Russell's friend, who might possibly, by his interference, prevent the utter disgrace and ruin of one branch of a noble family.

Miss Strictland, in all she said, hinted not at Vivian's attachment to Lady Julia, and gave him no reason to believe that she was apprised of his having proposed for her ladyship: she spoke with much moderation and candour; attributed all Lady Julia's errors to the imprudence of her new governess, Miss Bateman. Miss Strictland now showed a desire not to make, but to prevent mischief; even the circumlocutions and stiffness of her habitual prudery did not, on this occasion, seem unseasonable; therefore what she suggested made a great impression on Vivian. He still, however, defended Russell, and assured Miss Strictland that, from the long experience he had himself had of his friend's honour, he was convinced that no temptation could shake his integrity. Miss Strictland had formed her opinion on this point, she said, and it would be in vain to argue against it. Every new assertion; the belief of each new person who spoke to him on the subject; the combination, the coincidence of all their opinions, wrought his mind to such a height of jealousy, that he was now absolutely incapable of using his reason. He went in search of Russell, but in no fit mood to speak to him as he ought. He looked for him in his own, in Lord Lidhurst's apartment, in every sitting-room in the castle; but Mr. Russell was not to be found: at last Lady Sarah's maid, who heard him inquiring for Mr. Russell from the servants, told him, "she fancied that if he took the trouble to go to the west walk, he might find Mr. Russell, as that was a favourite walk of his." Vivian hurried thither, with a secret expectation of finding Lady Julia with him—there they both were in earnest conversation: as he approached, the trees concealed him from view; and Vivian heard his own name repeated. "Stop!" cried he, advancing: "let me not overhear your secrets—I am not a traitor to my friends!"

As he spoke, his eyes fixed with an expression of concentrated rage upon Russell. Terrified by Vivian's sudden appearance and strange address, and still more by the fierce look he cast on Russell, Lady Julia started and uttered a faint scream. With astonishment, but without losing his self-command, Russell advanced towards Vivian, saying, "You are out of your senses, my dear friend!—I will not listen to you in your present humour. Take a turn or two with me to cool yourself. The anger of a friend should always be allowed three minutes' grace, at least," added Russell, smiling, and endeavouring to draw Vivian away: but Vivian stood immoveable; Russell's calmness, instead of bringing him to his senses, only increased his anger; to his distempered imagination this coolness seemed perfidious dissimulation.

"You cannot deceive me longer, Mr. Russell, by all your art!" cried he. "Though I am the last to open my eyes, I have opened them. Why did you pretend to be my counsellor and friend, when you were my rival?—when you knew that you were my successful rival?—Yes, start and affect astonishment! Yes—look, if you can, with innocent surprise upon that lady!—Say that you have not betrayed her father's confidence!—say, that you have not practised upon her unguarded heart!—say, that you do not know that she loves you to distraction!"

"Oh! Mr. Vivian, what have you done?" cried Lady Julia: she could say no more, but fell senseless on the ground. Vivian's anger was at once sobered by this sight.

"What have I done!" repeated he, as they raised her from the ground. "Wretch! dishonourable villain that I am! I have betrayed her secret—But I thought every body knew it!—Is it possible that you did not know it, Russell?"

Russell made no reply, but ran to the river which was near them for some water—Vivian was incapable of affording any assistance, or even of forming a distinct idea. As soon as Lady Julia returned to her senses, Russell withdrew; Vivian threw himself on his knees before her, and said something about the violence of his passion—his sorrow—and her forgiveness. "Mr. Vivian," said Lady Julia, turning to him with a mixture of despair and dignity in her manner, "do not kneel to me; do not make use of any commonplace phrases—I cannot, at this moment, forgive you—you have done me an irreparable injury. I confided a secret to you—a secret known to no human being but my father and yourself—you have revealed it, and to whom?—Sooner would I have had it proclaimed to the whole world than to —; for what is the opinion of the whole world to me, compared to his?—Sir, you have done me, indeed, an irremediable injury!—I trusted to your honour—your discretion—and you have betrayed, sacrificed me."

"Vile suspicions!" cried Vivian, striking his forehead: "how could I listen to them for a moment!"

"Suspicions of Mr. Russell!" cried Julia, with a look of high indignation—"Suspicions of your noble-minded friend!—What wickedness, or what weakness!"

"Weakness!—miserable weakness!—the sudden effect of jealousy; and could you know, Lady Julia, by what means, by what arts, my mind was worked up to this insanity!"

"I cannot listen to this now, Mr. Vivian," interrupted Lady Julia: "my thoughts cannot fix upon such things—I cannot go back to the past—what is done cannot be undone—what has been said cannot be unsaid.—You cannot recall your words—they were heard—they were understood. I beg you to leave me, sir, that I may have leisure to think—if possible, to consider what yet remains for me to do. I have no friend—none, none willing or capable of advising me! I begged of you to leave me, sir."

Vivian could not, at this moment, decide whether he ought or ought not to tell Lady Julia that her secret was known, or at least suspected, by many individuals of the family.

"There's a servant on the terrace who seems to be looking for us," said Vivian; "I had something of consequence to say—but this man—"

"My lady, Miss Bateman desired me to let you know, my lady, that there is the Lady Playdels, and the colonel, and Sir James, in the drawing-room, just come;—and she begs, my lady, you will be pleased to come to them; for Miss Bateman's waiting for you, my lady, to repeat the verses, she bid me say, my lady."

"Go to them, Mr. Vivian; I cannot go."

"My lady," persisted the footman, "my lord himself begged you to come; and he and all the gentlemen have been looking for you every where."

"Return to my father, then, and say that I am coming immediately."

"Forced into company!" thought Lady Julia, as she walked slowly towards the house; "compelled to appear calm and gay, when my heart is—what a life of dissimulation! How unworthy of me, formed, as I was once pronounced to be, for every thing that is good and great!—But I am no longer mistress of myself—no soul left but for one object. Why did I not better guard my heart?—No!—rather, why can I not follow its dictates, and at once avow and justify its choice?"

Vivian interrupted Lady Julia's reverie by pointing out to her, as they passed along the terrace, a group of heads, in one of the back windows of the castle, that seemed to be watching them very earnestly. Miss Strictland's face was foremost; half her body was out of the window; and as she drew back, they heard her say—"It is not he!—It is not he!"—As they passed another front of the castle, another party seemed to be upon the watch at a staircase window;—the lawyer, the captain, the clergyman's heads appeared for a moment, and vanished.

"They seem all to be upon the watch for us," said Vivian.

"Meanness!" cried Lady Julia. "To watch or to be watched, I know not which is most degrading; but I cannot think they are watching us."

"My dear Lady Julia!—yet let me call you dear this once—my hopes are gone!—even for your forgiveness I have no right to hope—but let me do you one piece of service—let me put your open temper on its guard. You flatter yourself that the secret you confided to me is not known to any body living but to your father—I have reason to believe that it is suspected, if not positively known, by several other persons in this castle."

"Impossible!"

"I am certain, too certain, of what I say."

Lady Julia made a sudden stop; and, after a pause, exclaimed—

"Then farewell hope! and, with hope, farewell fear!"

"My lady, my lord sent me again, for my lord's very impatient for you, my lady," said the same footman, returning. Lord Glistonbury met them in the hall.—"Why, Julia! where have you been all this time?" he began, in an imperious tone; but seeing Mr. Vivian, his brow grew smooth and his voice good-humoured instantly.—"Ha!—So! so!—Hey! well!—All right! all right!—Good girl! good girl!—Time for every thing— Hey! Mr. Vivian?—'Que la solitude est charmante!' as Voltaire says—Beg pardon for sending for you; but interruption, you know, prevents têtes-à-têtes on the stage from growing tiresome; and the stage, they say, holds the mirror up to nature. But there's no nature now left to hold the mirror up to, except in a few odd instances, as in my Julia here!—Where so fast, my blushing darling?"

"I thought you wished, sir, that I should go to Lady Playdel and Sir James."

"Ay, ay, I sent for you to repeat those charming verses for them that I could not clearly remember.—Go up! go up!—We'll follow you!—We have a word or two to say about something—that's nothing to you."

Lord Glistonbury kept Vivian for a full hour in a state of considerable embarrassment, talking to him of Lady Julia, implying that she was favourably disposed towards him, but that she had a little pride, that might make her affect the contrary at first. Then came a disquisition on pride, with quotations and commonplaces;—then an eulogium, by his lordship, on his lordship's own knowledge of the human heart, and more especially of that "moving toyshop," the female heart; then anecdotes illustrative, comprising the gallantries of thirty years in various ranks of life, with suitable bon-mots and embellishments;—then a little French sentiment, by way of moral, with some philosophical axioms, to show that, though he had led such a gay life, he had been a deep thinker, and that, though nobody could have thought that he had had time for reading, his genius had supplied him, he could not himself really tell how, with what other people with the study of years could not master:—all which Vivian was compelled to hear, whilst he was the whole time impatient to get away, that he might search for Mr. Russell, with whom he was anxious to have an explanation. But, at last, when Lord Glistonbury set him free, he was not nearer to his object. Mr. Russell, he found upon inquiry, had not returned to the castle, nor did he return to dinner; he sent word that he was engaged to dine with a party of gentlemen at a literary club, in a country town nine miles distant. Vivian spent the greatest part of the evening in Lord Lidhurst's apartment, expecting Russell's return; but it grew so late, that Lord Lidhurst, who was still indisposed, went to bed; and when Vivian quitted his lordship, he met Russell's servant in the gallery, who said his master had been come in an hour ago: "but, sir," added the man, "my master won't let you see him, I am sure; for he would not let me in, and he said, that, if you asked for him, I was to answer, that he could not see you to-night."—Vivian knocked in vain at Russell's door; he could not gain admission; so he went reluctantly to bed, determined to rise very early, that he might see his friend as soon as possible, obtain his forgiveness for the past, and ask his advice for the future.

CHAPTER X

Suspense, curiosity, love, jealousy, remorse, any one of which is enough to keep a person awake all night, by turns agitated poor Vivian so violently, that for several hours he could not close his eyes; but at last, when quite exhausted, he fell into a profound sleep. The first image that came before his mind, when he awoke in the morning, was that of Lady Julia; his next recollection was of Russell.

"Is Mr. Russell up yet?" said Vivian to his servant, who was bringing in his boots.

"Up, sir! Oh, yes, hours ago!—He was off at daybreak!"

"Off!" cried Vivian, starting up in his bed; "off!—Where is he gone?"

"I can't say, sir. Yes, indeed, sir, I heard Mr. Russell's man say, that his master was going post to the north, to some old uncle that was taken ill, which he heard about at dinner from some of those gentlemen where he dined yesterday; but I can't say positively. But here's a letter he left for you with me."

"A letter!—Give it me!—Why didn't you give it me sooner?"

"Why really, sir, you lay so sound, I didn't care to waken you; and I was up so late myself, too, last night."

"Leave me now; I'll ring when I want you."

"TO C. VIVIAN, ESQ.

"I would not see you, after what passed yesterday, because I feared that I should not speak to you with temper. Lest you should misinterpret any thing I have formerly said, I must now solemnly assure you, that I never had the slightest suspicion of the secret you revealed to me till the moment when it was betrayed by your indiscretion. Still I can scarcely credit what appears to me so improbable; but, even under this uncertainty, I think it my duty to leave this family. Had the slightest idea of what you suggested ever crossed my imagination, I should then have acted as I do now. I say this, not to justify myself, but to convince you, that what I formerly hinted about reserve of manners and prudence was merely a general reflection.

"For my own part, I seem to act HEROICALLY; but I must disclaim that applause to which I am not entitled. All powerful as the temptation must appear to you, dangerous as it must have been, in other circumstances, to me, I cannot claim any merit for resisting its influence. My safety I owe neither to my own prudence or fortitude. I must now, Vivian, impart to you a secret which you are at liberty to confide where and when you think necessary—my heart is, and has long been, engaged. Whilst you were attached to Miss Sidney, I endeavoured to subdue my love for her; and every symptom of it was, I hope and believe, suppressed. This declaration cannot now give you any pain; except so far as it may, perhaps, excite in your mind some remorse for having unwarrantably, unworthily, and weakly, suffered yourself to feel suspicions of a true friend. Well as I know the infirmity of your character, and willing as I have always been to make allowance for a fault which I thought time and experience would correct, I was not prepared for this last stroke; I never thought your weakness of mind would have shown itself in suspicion of your best, your long-tried friend.—But I am at last convinced that your mind is not strong enough for confidence and friendship. I pity, but I see that I can no longer serve; and I feel that I can no longer esteem you. Farewell! Vivian. May you find a friend, who will supply to you the place of H. RUSSELL."

Vivian knew Russell's character too well to flatter himself that the latter part of this letter was written in anger that would quickly subside; from the tone of the letter he felt that Russell was deeply offended. In the whole course of his life he had depended on Russell's friendship as a solid blessing, of which he could never be deprived by any change of circumstances—by any possible chance in human affairs; and now to have lost such a friend by his own folly, by his own weakness, was a misfortune of which he could hardly believe the reality. At the same moment, too, he learned how nobly Russell had behaved towards him, in the most trying situation in which the human heart can be placed. Russell's love for Selina Sidney, Vivian had never till this instant suspected. "What force, what command of mind!—What magnanimity!—What a generous friend he has ever been to me!—and I—"

Poor Vivian, always sinning and always penitent, was so much absorbed by sorrow for the loss of Russell's friendship, that he could not for some time think even of the interests of his love, or consider the advantage which he might derive from the absence of his rival, and from that rival's explicit declaration, that his affections were irrevocably engaged. By degrees these ideas rose clearly to Vivian's view; his hopes revived. Lady Julia would see the absolute impossibility of Russell's returning, or of his accepting her affection; her good sense, her pride, would in time subdue this hopeless passion; and Vivian was generous enough, or sufficiently in love, to feel that the value of her heart would not be diminished, but rather increased in his opinion, by the sensibility she had shown to the talents and virtues of his friend. His friend, Vivian ventured now to call him; for with the hopes of love, the hopes of friendship rose.

"All may yet be well!" said he to himself. "Russell will forgive me when he hears how I was worked upon by those parasites and prudish busybodies, who infused their vile suspicions into my mind. Weak as it is, I never will allow that it is incapable of confidence or of friendship!—No! Russell will retract that harsh sentence. When he is happy, as I am sure I ardently hope he will be, in Selina's love, he will restore me to his favour. Without his friendship, I could not be satisfied with myself, or happy in the full accomplishment of all my other fondest hopes."

By the time that hope had thus revived and renovated our hero's soul; by the time that his views of things had totally changed, and that the colour of his future destiny had turned from black to white—from all gloom to all sunshine; the minute-hand of the clock had moved with unfeeling regularity, or, in plain unmeasured prose, it was now eleven o'clock, and three times Vivian had been warned that breakfast was ready. When he entered the room, the first thing he heard, as usual, was Miss Bateman's voice, who was declaiming upon some sentimental point, in all "the high sublime of deep absurd." Vivian, little interested in this display, and joining neither in the open flattery nor in the secret ridicule with which the gentlemen wits and amateurs listened to the Rosamunda, looked round for Lady Julia. "She breakfasts in her own room this morning," whispered Lord Glistonbury, before Vivian had even pronounced her ladyship's name.

"So!" said Mr. Pickering, "we have lost Mr. Russell this morning!"

"Yes," said Lord Glistonbury, "he was forced to hurry away to the north, I find, to an old sick uncle."

"Lord Lidhurst, I'm afraid, will break his heart for want of him," cried the lawyer, in a tone that might either pass for earnest or irony, according to the fancy of the interpreter.

"Lord Lidhurst, did you say?"—cried the captain: "are you sure you meant Lord Lidhurst? I don't apprehend that a young nobleman ever broke his heart after his tutor. But I was going to remark—"

What farther the captain was going to remark can never be known to the world; for Lord Glistonbury so startled him by the loud and rather angry tone in which he called for the cream, which stood with the captain, that all his few ideas were put to flight. Mr. Pickering, who noticed Lord Glistonbury's displeasure, now resumed the conversation about Mr. Russell in a new tone; and the lawyer and he joined in a eulogy upon that gentleman. Lord Glistonbury said not a word, but looked embarrassed. Miss Strictland cleared her throat several times, and looked infinitely more rigid and mysterious than usual. Lady Glistonbury and Lady Sarah, ditto—ditto. Almost every body, except such visitors as were strangers at the castle, perceived that there was something extraordinary going on in the family; and the gloom and constraint spread so, that, towards the close of breakfast, nothing was uttered, by prudent people, but awkward sentences about the weather—the wind—and the likelihood of there being a mail from the continent. Still through all this, regardless and unknowing of it all, the Rosamunda talked on, happily abstracted, egotistically secured from the pains of sympathy or of curiosity by the all-sufficient power of vanity. Even her patron, Lord Glistonbury, was at last provoked and disgusted. He was heard, under his breath, to pronounce a contemptuous Pshaw! and, as he rose from the breakfast table he whispered to Vivian, "There's a woman, now, who thinks of nothing living but herself!—All talkèe talkèe!—I begin to be weary of her.—Gentlemen," continued his lordship, "I've letters to write this morning.—You'll ride— you'll walk—you're for the billiard-room, I suppose.—Mr. Vivian, I shall find you in my study, I hope, an hour hence; but first I have a little business to settle." With evident embarrassment Lord Glistonbury retired. Lady Glistonbury, Lady Sarah, and Miss Strictland, each sighed; then, with looks of intelligence, rose and retired. The company separated soon afterwards; and went to ride, to walk, or to the billiard-room, and Vivian to the study, to wait there for Lord Glistonbury, and to meditate upon what might be the nature of his lordship's business. As Vivian crossed the gallery, the door of Lady Glistonbury's dressing-room opened, and was shut again instantaneously by Miss Strictland; but not before he saw Lady Julia kneeling at her father's feet, whilst Lady Glistonbury and Lady Sarah were standing like statues, on each side of his lordship. Vivian waited a full hour afterwards in tedious suspense in the study. At last he heard doors open and footsteps, and he judged that the family council had broken up; he laid down a book, of which he had read the same page over six times, without any one of the words it contained having conveyed a single idea to his mind. Lord Glistonbury came in, with papers and parchments in his hands.

"Mr. Vivian, I am afraid you have been waiting for me—have a thousand pardons to ask—I really could not come any sooner—I wished to speak to you—Won't you sit down?—We had better sit down quietly—there's no sort of hurry."

His lordship, however, seemed to be in great agitation-of spirits; and Vivian was convinced that his mind must be interested in an extraordinary manner, because he did not, as was his usual practice, digress to fifty impertinent episodes before he came to the point. He only blew his nose sundry times; and then at once said, "I wish to speak to you, Mr. Vivian, about the proposal you did me the honour to make for my daughter Julia. Difficulties have occurred on our side—very extraordinary difficulties—Julia, I understand, has hinted to you, sir, the nature of those difficulties.—Oh, Mr. Vivian," said Lord Glistonbury, suddenly quitting the constrained voice in which he spoke, and giving way to his natural feelings, "you are a man of honour and feeling, and a father may trust you!—Here's my girl—a charming girl she is; but knowing nothing of the world—self-willed, romantic, open-hearted, imprudent beyond conception; do not listen to any of the foolish things she says to you. You are a man of sense, you love her, and you are every way suited to her; it is the first wish of my heart—I tell you frankly—to see her your wife: then do not let her childish folly persuade you that her affections are engaged—don't listen to any such stuff. We all know what the first loves of a girl of sixteen must be—But it's our fault—my fault, my fault, since they will have it so. I care not whose fault it is; but we have had very improper people about her—very!—very!—But all may be well yet, if you, sir, will be steady, and save her—save her from herself. I would farther suggest—"

Lord Glistonbury was going on, probably, to have weakened by amplification the effect of what he had said, when Lady Julia entered the room; and, advancing with dignified determination of manner, said, "I have your commands, father, that I should see Mr. Vivian again:—I obey."

"That is right—that is my darling Julia; I always knew she would justify my high opinion of her." Lord Glistonbury attempted to draw her towards him fondly; but, with an unaltered manner, that seemed as if she suppressed strong emotion, she answered, "I do not deserve your caresses, father; do not oppress me with praise that I cannot merit: I wish to speak to Mr. Vivian without control and without witness."

Lord Glistonbury rose; and growing red and almost inarticulate with anger, exclaimed, "Remember, Julia! remember, Lady Julia Lidhurst! that if you say what you said you would say, and what I said you should not say—I—Lord Glistonbury, your father—I, as well as all the rest of your family, utterly disclaim and cast you off for ever!—You'll be a thing without fortune—without friends—without a name—without a being in the world—Lady Julia Lidhurst!"

"I am well aware of that," replied Lady Julia, growing quite pale, yet without changing the determination of her countenance, or abating any thing from the dignity of her manner: "I am well aware, that on what I am about to do depends my having, or my ceasing from this moment to have, fortune, friends, and a father."

Lord Glistonbury stood still for a moment—fixed his eyes upon her as if he would have read her soul; but, without seeking to elude his inquiry, her countenance seemed to offer itself to his penetration.

"By Heaven, there is no understanding this girl!" cried his lordship. "Mr. Vivian, I trust her to your honour—to your knowledge of the world—to your good sense;—in short, sir, to your love and constancy."

"And I, sir," said Lady Julia, turning to Vivian, after her father had left the room, and looking at Vivian so as to stop him short as he approached, and to disconcert him in the commencement of a passionate speech; "and I, too, sir, trust to your honour, whilst I deprecate your love. Imprudent as I was in the first confidence I reposed in you, and much as I have suffered by your rashness, I now stand determined to reveal to you another yet more important, yet more humiliating secret—You owe me no gratitude, sir!—I am compelled, by the circumstances in which I am placed, either to deceive or to trust you. I must either become your wife, and deceive you most treacherously; or I must trust you entirely, and tell you why it would be shameful that I should become your wife—shameful to me and to you."

"To me!—Impossible!" cried Vivian, bursting into some passionate expressions of love and admiration.

"Listen to me, sir; and do not make any of those rash professions, of which you will soon repent. You think you are speaking to the same Lady Julia you saw yesterday—No!—you are speaking to a very different person—a few hours have made a terrible change. You see before you, sir, one who has been, till this day, the darling and pride of her father; who has lived in the lap of luxury; who has been flattered, admired, by almost all who approached her; who had fortune, and rank, and fair prospects in life, and youth, and spirits, and all the pride of prosperity; who had, I believe, good dispositions, perhaps some talents, and, I may say, a generous heart; who might have been,—but that is all over—no matter what she might have been—she is

'A tale for ev'ry prating she.'

Fallen!—fallen! fallen under the feet of those who worshipped her!—fallen below the contempt of the contemptible!—Worse! worse! fallen in her own opinion—never to rise again."

Lady Julia's voice failed, and she was forced to pause. She sunk upon a seat, and hid her face—for some moments she neither saw nor heard; but at last, raising her head, she perceived Vivian.

"You are in amazement, sir! and I see you pity me; but let me beg of you to restrain your feelings—my own are as much as I can bear. O that I could recall a few hours of my existence! But I have not yet been able to tell you what has passed. My father, my friends, wish to conceal it from you: but, whatever I have done, however low I have sunk, I will not deceive, nor be an accomplice in deceit. From my own lips you shall hear all. This morning at daybreak, not being able to sleep, and having some suspicion that Mr. Russell would leave the castle, I rose, and whilst I was dressing, I heard the trampling of horses in the court. I looked out of my window, and saw Mr. Russell's man saddling his master's horse. I heard Mr. Russell, a moment afterwards, order the servant to take the horses to the great gate on the north road, and wait for him there, as he intended to walk through the park. I thought these were the last words I should ever hear him speak.—Love took possession of me—I stole softly down the little staircase that leads from my turret to one of the back doors, and got out of the castle, as I thought, unobserved: I hurried on, and waited in the great oak wood, through which I knew Mr. Russell would pass. When I saw him coming nearer and nearer to me, I would have given the world to have been in my own room again—I hid myself among the trees—yet, when he walked on in reverie without noticing me, taking me probably for one of the servants, I could not bear to think that this was the last moment I should ever see him, and I exclaimed—I know not what; but I know that at the sound of my voice Mr. Russell started, and never can I forget the look—Spare me the rest!—No!—I will not spare myself—I offered my heart, my hand,—and they were rejected!—In my madness I told him I regarded neither wealth, nor rank, nor friends, nor—That I would rather live with him in obscurity than be the greatest princess upon earth—I said this and more—and I was rejected—And even at this moment, instead of the vindictive passions which are said to fill the soul of a woman scorned, I feel admiration for your noble friend: I have not done him justice; I cannot repeat his words, or describe his manner. He persuaded, by his eloquence compelled, me to return to this castle. He took from me all hope; he destroyed by one word all my illusions—he told me that he loves another. He has left me to despair, to disgrace; and yet I love, esteem, and admire him, above all human beings! Admire one who despises me!—Is it possible? I know not, but it is so—I have more to tell you, sir!—As I returned to the castle, I was watched by Miss Strictland. How she knew all that had passed, I cannot divine; perhaps it was by means of some spy who followed me, and whom I did not perceive: for I neither saw nor heard any thing but my passion. Miss

Strictland communicated her discovery immediately to my father. I have been these last two hours before a family tribunal. My mother, with a coldness a thousand times worse than my poor father's rage, says, that I have only accomplished her prophecies; that she always knew and told my father that I should be a disgrace to my family. But no reproaches are equal to my own; I stand self-condemned. I feel like one awakened from a dream. A few words!—a single look from Mr. Russell!—how they have altered all my views, all my thoughts! Two hours' reflection—Two hours, did I say?—whole years—a whole existence—have passed to me in the last two hours: I am a different creature. But it is too late— too late!—Self-esteem is gone!—happiness is over for me in this world."

"Happiness over for you!" exclaimed Vivian in a tone expressive of the deep interest he felt for her; "Self-esteem gone!—No! Lady Julia; do not blame yourself so severely for what has passed! Blame the circumstances in which you have been placed; above all, blame me—blame my folly—my madness; your secret never would have been known, if I had not—"

"I thank you," interrupted Lady Julia, rising from her seat; "but no consolation can be of any avail. It neither consoles nor justifies me that others have been to blame."

"Permit me, at least," pursued Vivian, "to speak of my own sentiments for one moment. Permit me to say, Lady Julia, that the confidence with which you have just honoured me, instead of diminishing my attachment, has so raised my admiration for your candour and magnanimity, that no obstacles shall vanquish my constancy. I will wait respectfully, and, if I can, patiently, till time shall have effaced from your mind these painful impressions; I shall neither ask nor accept of the interference or influence of your father, nor of any of your friends; I shall rely solely on the operation of your own excellent understanding, and shall hope for my reward from your noble heart."

"You do not think it possible," said Lady Julia, looking at Vivian with dignified determination, "you do not think it possible, after all that has passed, after all that I have told you, that I could so far degrade myself or you, as to entertain any thoughts of becoming your wife? Farewell! Mr. Vivian.—You will not see me again. I shall obtain permission to retire, and live with a relation in a distant part of the country; where I shall no more be seen or heard of. My fortune will, I hope, be of use to my sister.—My poor father!—I pity him; he loves me: he loses his daughter for ever; worse than loses her! My mother, too—I pity her! for, though she does not love me, she will suffer for me; she will suffer more than my father, by the disgrace that would be brought upon my family, if ever the secret should be publicly known. My brother!—Oh, my beloved brother! he knows nothing yet of all this!—But why do I grieve you with my agony of mind? Forget that Lady Julia Lidhurst ever existed!—I wish you that happiness which I can never enjoy—I wish you may deserve and win a heart capable of feeling real love!—Adieu!"

CHAPTER XI

Convinced that all farther pursuit of Lady Julia Lidhurst would be vain, that it could tend only to increase her difficulties and his mortification, Vivian saw that the best thing he could possibly do was to leave Glistonbury. Thus he should relieve the whole family from the embarrassment of his presence; and, by immediate change of scene and of occupation, he had the best chance of recovering from his own disappointment. If Lady Julia was to quit the castle, he could have no inducement to stay; if her ladyship remained, his continuing in her society would be still more dangerous to his happiness. Besides, he felt offended with Lord Glistonbury, who evidently had wished to conceal from him the truth; and, without considering what was just or honourable, had endeavoured to secure, at all events, an establishment for his daughter, and a connexion for his family. To the weight of these reasons must be added a desire to see Mr. Russell, and to effect a reconciliation with him. The accumulated force of all these motives had power to overcome Vivian's habitual indecision: his servant was surprised by an order to have every thing ready for his journey to town immediately. Whilst his man prepared to obey, or at least to meditate upon the cause of this unusually decided order, our hero went in quest of Lord Glistonbury, to pay his compliments to his lordship previous to his departure. His lordship was in his daughter Julia's dressing-room, and could not be seen; but presently he came to Vivian in great hurry and distress of mind.

"A sad stroke upon us, Mr. Vivian!—a sad stroke upon us all—but most upon me; for she was the child of my expectations—I hear she has told you every thing—you, also, have been very ill-used—Never was astonishment equal to mine when I heard Miss Strictland's story. I need not caution you, Mr. Vivian, as to secrecy; you are a man of honour, and you see the peace of our whole family is at stake. The girl is going to a relation of ours in Devonshire.—Sha'n't stay here—sha'n't stay here—Disgrace to my family— She who was my pride—and, after all, says she will never marry.—Very well!—very well!—I shall never see her again, that I am determined upon.—I told her, that if she did not behave with common sense and propriety, in her last interview with you, I would give her up—and so I will, and so I do.—The whole is Lady Glistonbury's fault—she never managed her rightly when she was a child. Oh! I should put you on your guard in one particular—Miss Bateman knows nothing of what has happened—I wish Miss Strictland knew as little—I hate her. What business had she to play the spy upon my daughter? She does well to be a prude, for she is as ugly as sin. But we are in her power. She is to go to-morrow with Julia to Devonshire. It will make a quarrel between me and Miss Bateman—no matter for that; for now, the sooner we get rid of that Rosamunda, too, the better—she talks me dead, and will let no one talk but herself. And, between you and me, all this could not have happened, if she had looked after her charge properly.—Not but what I think Miss Strictland was still less fit to guide a girl of Julia's genius and disposition. All was done wrong at first, and I always said so to Lady Glistonbury. But, if the secret can be kept—and that depends on you, my dear friend—after six months' or a twelve-month's rustication with our poor parson in the country, you will see how tamed and docile the girl will come back to us. This is my scheme; but nobody shall know my whole mind but you—I shall tell her I will never see her again; and that will pacify Lady Glistonbury, and frighten Julia into submission. She says she'll never marry.— Stuff! Stuff!—You don't believe her!—What man who has seen any thing of the world ever believes such stuff?"

Vivian's servant came into the room to ask his master some question about horses.

"Going!—where? Going!—when? Going!—how?" cried Lord Glistonbury, as soon as the servant withdrew. "Surely, you are not going to leave us, Mr. Vivian?"

Vivian explained his reasons—Lord Glistonbury would not allow them any weight, entreated and insisted that he should stay at least a few days longer; for his going "just at this moment would seem quite like a break up in the family, and would be the most unfriendly and cruel thing imaginable." Why Lord Glistonbury so earnestly pressed his stay, perhaps even his lordship himself did not exactly know; for, with all the air of being a person of infinite address and depth of design, his lordship was in reality childishly inconsistent; what the French call inconséquent. On any subject, great or small, where he once took it into his head, or, as he called it, made it a point, that a thing should be so or so, he was as peremptory, or, where he could not be peremptory, as anxious, as if it were a matter of life and death. In his views there was no perspective, no keeping—all objects appeared of equal magnitude; and even now, when it might be conceived that his whole mind was intent upon a great family misfortune, he, in the course of a few minutes, became as eager about a mere trifle as if he had nothing else in the world to think of. From the earnestness with which Lord Glistonbury urged him to stay a few days, at least one day longer, Vivian was induced to believe that it must be a matter of real consequence to his lordship—"And, in his present state of distress, I cannot refuse such a request," thought Vivian. He yielded, therefore, to these solicitations, and consented to stay a few days longer; though he knew the prolonging his visit would be, in every respect, disagreeable.

At dinner Lord Glistonbury announced to the company that the physician had advised change of air immediately for Lord Lidhurst; and that, in consequence, his son would set out early the next morning for Devonshire—that his daughter Julia wished to go with her brother, and that Miss Strictland would accompany them. Lord Glistonbury apologized for his daughter's absence, "preparations for her journey so suddenly decided upon," &c. Lady Glistonbury and Lady Sarah looked terribly grim whilst all this was saying; but the gravity and stiffness of their demeanour did not appear any thing extraordinary to the greater part of the company, who had no idea of what was going forward. The lawyer, the captain, and the chaplain, however, interchanged significant looks; and many times, during the course of the evening, they made attempts to draw out Vivian's thoughts, but they found him impenetrable. There was an underplot of a quarrel between Miss Strictland and Miss Bateman, to which Vivian paid little attention; nor was he affected, in the slightest degree, by the Rosamunda's declaration to Lord Glistonbury, that she must leave his family, since she found that Miss Strictland had a larger share than herself of his lordship's confidence, and was, for what reason she could not divine, to have the honour of accompanying Lady Julia into Devonshire. Vivian perceived these quarrels, and heard the frivolous conversation of the company at Glistonbury Castle without interest, and with a sort of astonishment at the small motives by which others were agitated, whilst his whole soul was engrossed by love and pity for Lady Julia. In vain he hoped for another opportunity of seeing and speaking to her. She never appeared. The next morning he rose at daybreak that he might have the chance of seeing her: he begged Miss Strictland to entreat her ladyship would allow him to say a few words before she set out; but Miss Strictland replied, that she was assured the request would be vain; and he thought he perceived that Miss Strictland, though she affected to lament Lady Julia's blindness to her own interests and contumacy, in opposing her father's wishes, was, in reality, glad that she persisted in her own determination. Lord Lidhurst, on account of the weak state of his health, was kept in ignorance of every thing that could agitate him; and, when Vivian took leave of him, the poor young man left many messages of kindness and gratitude for Mr. Russell.

"I am sorry that he was obliged to leave me; for, ill or well, there is no human being, I will not except any one but my sister Julia, whom I should so much wish to have with me. Tell him so; and tell him—be sure you remember my very words, for perhaps I shall never see him again—tell him, that, living or dying, I shall feel grateful to him. He has given me tastes and principles very different from those I had when he came into this house. Even in sickness, I feel almost every hour the advantage of my present love for literature. If I should live and recover, I hope I shall do him some credit; and I trust my family will join in my gratitude. Julia, my dear sister! why do you weep so bitterly?—If I had seen you come into the room, I would not have spoken of my health."

Lord Glistonbury came up to tell them that Miss Strictland was ready. "Mr. Vivian," cried his lordship, "will you hand Julia into the carriage?—Julia, Mr. Vivian is offering you his services."

Vivian, as he attended Lady Julia, had so much respect for her feelings, that, though he had been waiting with extreme impatience for an opportunity to say a few words, yet now he would not speak, but handed her along the gallery, down the staircase, and across the great hall, in profound silence. She seemed sensible of this forbearance; and, turning to him at a moment when they could not be overheard, said, "It was not from unkindness, Mr. Vivian, I refused to see you again, but to convince you that my mind is determined—if you have any thing to say, I am ready to hear it."

"Is there nothing to be hoped from time?" said Vivian. "Your father, I know, has hopes that—All I ask is, that you will not make any rash resolutions."

"I make none; but I tell you, for your own sake, not to cherish any vain hope. My father does not know my mind sufficiently, therefore he may deceive you; but I will not.—I thought, after the manner in which I spoke to you yesterday, you would have had too much strength of mind to have rendered this repetition of my sentiments necessary.—Attach yourself elsewhere as soon as you can.—I sincerely wish your happiness. Miss Strictland is waiting.—Farewell!"

She hurried forward to the carriage; and, when she was gone, Vivian repented that he had seen her again, as it had only given them both additional and fruitless pain.

What passed during some succeeding days at Glistonbury Castle he scarcely knew; no trace remained in his mind of anything but the confused noise of people, who had been talking, laughing, and diverting themselves in a manner that seemed to him incomprehensible. He exerted himself, however, so far as to write to Russell, to implore his forgiveness, and to solicit a return of his friendship, which, in his present state of unhappiness, was more necessary to him than ever. When he had finished and despatched this letter, he sunk again into a sort of reckless state, without hope or determination, as to his future life. He could not decide whether he should go to his mother immediately on leaving Glistonbury, or to Mr. Russell, or (which he knew was the best course he could pursue) attend his duty in parliament, and, by plunging at once into public business, change the course of his thoughts, and force his mind to resume its energy. After altering his determination twenty times, after giving at least a dozen contradictory orders about his journey, his servant at last had his ultimatum, for London—the carriage to be at the door at ten o'clock the next morning. Every thing was ready at the appointed hour. Breakfast over, Vivian waited only to pay his compliments to Lady Glistonbury, who had breakfasted in her own apartment. Lady Sarah, with a manner as formal as usual, rose from the breakfast-table, and said she would let her mother know that Mr. Vivian was going. Vivian waited half an hour—an hour—two hours. Lady Glistonbury did not appear, nor did Lady Sarah return. The company had dispersed after the first half-hour. Lord Glistonbury began to believe that the ladies did not mean to make their appearance. At length a message came from Lady Glistonbury.—"Lady Glistonbury's compliments to Mr. Vivian—her ladyship was concerned that it was out of her power to have the pleasure of seeing Mr. Vivian, as she was too much indisposed to leave her room.—She and Lady Sarah wished him a very good journey."

Vivian went up to his room for his gloves, which he missed at the moment when he was going. Whilst he was opening the empty drawers one after another, in search of his gloves, and, at the same time, calling his servant to find them, he heard a loud scream from an adjoining apartment. He listened again—all was silent; and he supposed that what he had heard was not a scream: but, at that moment, Lady Sarah's maid flung open his door, and, running in with out-stretched arms, threw herself at Vivian's feet. Her sobs and tears prevented his understanding one syllable she said. At last she articulated intelligibly, "Oh, sir!—don't be so cruel to go—my lady!—my poor lady! If you go, it will kill Lady Sarah!"

"Kill Lady Sarah?—Why I saw her in perfect health this morning at breakfast!"

"Dear, dear sir! you know nothing of the matter!" said the maid, rising, and shutting the door: "you don't know what a way she has been in ever since the talk of your going—fits upon fits every night, and my lady, her mother, and I up holding her—and none in the house knowing it but ourselves. Very well at breakfast! Lord help us! sir. How little you know of what she has suffered! Lord have mercy upon me! I would not be a lady to be so much in love, and left so, for any thing in the whole world. And my Lady Sarah keeps every thing so to herself;—if it was not for these fits they would never have knowed she cared no more for you than a stone."

"And, probably you are quite mistaken," said Vivian; "and that I have nothing to do with the young lady's illness. If she has fits, I am very sorry for it; but I can't possibly—Certainly, you are quite mistaken!"

"Lord, sir!—mistaken! As if I could be mistaken, when I know my lady as well as I know myself! Why, sir, I know from the time of the election, when you was given to her by all the country—and to be sure when we all thought it would be a match directly—and the Lord knows what put it off!—I say, from that time, her heart was set upon you. Though she never said a word to me, or any one, I knew how it was, through all her coldness—And to be sure, when you was in Lon'on so much with us, all the town said, as all the country did afore, that to be sure it was to be a match—But then that sad affair, with that artfullest of women, that took you off from all that was good, and away, the Lord knows where, to foreign parts!—Well! to be sure, I never shall forget the day you come back again to us!—and the night of the ball!—and you dancing with my lady, and all so happy; then, to be sure, all were sarten it was to be immediately—And now to go and break my poor lady's heart at the last—Oh, sir, sir! if you could but see her, it would touch a heart of marble!"

Vivian's astonishment and dismay were so great, that he suffered the girl, who was an unpractised creature, to go on speaking without interruption: the warmth of affection with which she spoke of her lady, also, surprised him: for, till this instant, he had no idea that any one could love Lady Sarah Lidhurst; and the accounts she gave of the lady's sufferings not only touched his compassion, but worked upon his vanity. "This cold, proud young lady that never loved none before, to think," as her maid said, "that she should come to such a pass, as to be in fits about him. And it was her belief that Lady Sarah never would recover it, if he went away out of the castle this day."

The ringing of a bell had repeatedly been heard, whilst Lady Sarah's maid was speaking; it now rang violently, and her name was called vehemently from the adjoining apartment. "I must go, I must go!—Oh, sir! one day, for mercy's sake! stay one day longer!"

Vivian, though he had been moved by this girl's representations, was determined to effect his retreat whilst it was yet in his power; therefore he ran down stairs, and had gained the hall, where he was shaking hands with Lord Glistonbury, when my Lady Glistonbury's own woman came in a great hurry to say, that her lady, finding herself a little better now, and able to see Mr. Vivian, begged he would be so good as to walk up to her dressing-room.

Vivian, with a heavy heart and slow steps, obeyed; there was no refusing, no evading such a request. He summoned all his resolution, at the same time saying to himself, as he followed his conductor along the gallery, "It is impossible that I can ever be drawn in to marry Lady Sarah.—This is a concerted plan, and I shall not be so weak as to be the dupe of so gross an artifice."

Lady Glistonbury's maid showed him into her lady's dressing-room and retired. Lady Glistonbury was seated, and, without speaking, pointed to a chair which was set opposite to her. "So! a preparation for a scene," thought Vivian. He bowed, but, still keeping his hat in his hand, did not sit down:—he was extremely happy to hear, that her ladyship found herself something better—much honoured by her permitting him to pay his respects, and to offer his grateful acknowledgments to her ladyship before his departure from Glistonbury.

Her ladyship, still without speaking, pointed to the chair. Vivian sat down, and looked as if he had "screwed his courage to the sticking place." Lady Glistonbury had sometimes a little nervous trembling of her head, which was the only symptom of internal agitation that was ever observable in her; it was now increased to a degree which Vivian had never before seen.

"Are you in haste, sir, to be gone?" said Lady Glistonbury.

"Not if her ladyship had any commands for him; but otherwise, he had intended, if possible, to reach town that night."

"I shall not delay you many minutes, Mr. Vivian," said her ladyship. "You need not be under apprehension that Lady Glistonbury should seek to detain you longer than your own inclinations induce you to stay; it is, therefore, unnecessary to insult her with any appearance of haste or impatience."

Vivian instantly laid down his hat, and protested that he was not in the slightest degree impatient: he should be very ungrateful, as well as very ill-bred, if, after the most hospitable manner in which he had been received and entertained at Glistonbury Castle, he could be in haste to quit it. He was entirely at her ladyship's orders.

Lady Glistonbury bowed formally—was again silent—the trembling of her head very great—the rest of her form motionless.

"I have sent for you, Mr. Vivian," said she, "that I might, before you leave this castle, set you right on a subject which much concerns me. From the representations of a foolish country girl, a maid-servant of my daughter, Lady Sarah Lidhurst, which I have just discovered she has made to you, I had reason to fear that you might leave Glistonbury with very false notions—"

A cry was heard at this moment from the inner apartment, which made Vivian start; but Lady Glistonbury, without noticing it, went on speaking.

"With notions very injurious to my daughter Sarah; who, if I know any thing of her, would rather, if it were so ordained, go out of this world, than condescend to any thing unbecoming her sex, her education, and her family."

Vivian, struck with respect and compassion for the mother, who spoke to him in this manner, was now convinced that there had been no concerted plan to work upon his mind, that the maid had spoken without the knowledge of her lady; and the more proudly solicitous Lady Glistonbury showed herself to remove what she called the false impression from his mind, the more he was persuaded that the girl had spoken the truth. He was much embarrassed between his good-nature and his dread of becoming a sacrifice to his humanity.

He replied in general terms to Lady Glistonbury, that he had the highest respect for Lady Sarah Lidhurst, and that no opinion injurious to her could be entertained by him.

"Respect she must command from all," said Lady Glistonbury; "that it is out of any man's power to refuse her: as to the rest, she leaves you, and I leave you, sir, to your own conscience."

Lady Glistonbury rose, and so did Vivian. He hoped that neither her ladyship nor Lady Sarah had any cause—He hesitated; the words, to reproach, to complain, to be displeased, all came to his lips; but each seemed improper; and, none other being at hand to convey his meaning, he could not finish his sentence: so he began another upon a new construction, with "I should be much concerned if, in addition to all my other causes of regret in leaving Glistonbury Castle, I felt that I had incurred Lady Glistonbury's or Lady Sarah's displea—disapprobation."

"As to that, sir," said Lady Glistonbury, "I cannot but have my own opinion of your conduct; and you can scarcely expect, I apprehend, that a mother, such as I am, should not feel some disapprobation of conduct, which has—Sir, I beg I may not detain you—I have the honour to wish you a good journey and much happiness."

An attendant came from an inner apartment with a message! from Lady Sarah, who was worse, and wished to see her mother—"Immediately!—tell her, immediately!"

The servant returned with the answer. Vivian was retiring, but he came back, for he saw at that moment a convulsive motion contract Lady Glistonbury's face: she made an effort to walk; but if Vivian had not supported her instantly, she must have fallen. She endeavoured to disengage herself from his assistance, and again attempted to walk.

"For God's sake, lean upon me, madam!" said Vivian, much alarmed. With his assistance, she reached the door of the inner room: summoning all the returning powers of life, she then withdrew her arm from his, and pointing back to the door at which Vivian entered, she said, "That is your way, sir."

"Pardon me—I cannot go—I cannot leave you at this moment," said Vivian.

"This is my daughter's apartment, sir," said Lady Glistonbury, stopping, and standing still and fixed. Some of the attendants within, hearing her ladyship's voice, opened the door; Lady Glistonbury made an effort to prevent it, but in vain: the chamber was darkened, but as the door opened, the wind from an open window blew back the curtain, and some light fell upon a canopy bed, where Lady Sarah lay motionless, her eyes closed, and pale as death; one attendant chafing her temples, another rubbing her feet: she looked up just after the door opened, and, raising her head, she saw Vivian—a gleam of joy illumined her countenance, and coloured her cheek.

"Sir," repeated Lady Glistonbury, "this is my daughter's—"

She could articulate no more. She fell across the threshold, struck with palsy. Her daughter sprang from the bed, and, with Vivian's assistance, raised and carried Lady Glistonbury to an arm-chair near the open window, drew back the curtain, begged Vivian to go to her father, and instantly to despatch a messenger for medical assistance. Vivian sent his own servant, who had his horse ready at the door, and he bid the man go as fast as he could.

"Then you don't leave Glistonbury to-day, sir?" said the servant.

"Do as I order you—Where's Lord Glistonbury?"

His lordship, with the newspapers and letters open in his hand, came up—but they dropped on hearing the intelligence that Vivian communicated. His lordship was naturally humane and good-natured; and the shock was greater, perhaps, to him, from the sort of enmity in which he lived with Lady Glistonbury.

"I dread to go up stairs," said he. "For God's sake, Vivian, don't leave me in this distress!—do order your carriage away!—Put up Mr. Vivian's carriage."

Lady Sarah's maid came to tell them that Lady Glistonbury had recovered her speech, and that she had asked, "if Mr. Vivian was gone?"

"Do come up with me," cried Lord Glistonbury, "and she will see you are not gone."

"Here's my lord and Mr. Vivian, my lady," said the girl.

Then, turning to Lady Glistonbury's woman, she added, in a loud whisper, "Mr. Vivian won't go to-day."

Lady Sarah gave her maid some commission, which took her out of the room. Lady Sarah, no longer the formal, cold, slow personage whom Vivian detested, now seemed to him, and not only seemed but was, quite a different being, inspired with energy, and quickness, and presence of mind: she forgot herself, and her illness, and her prudery, and her love, and every other consideration, in the sense of her mother's danger. Lady Glistonbury had but imperfectly recovered her recollection. At one moment she smiled on Vivian, and tried to stretch out her hand to him, as she saw him standing beside Lady Sarah. But when he approached Lady Glistonbury, and spoke to her, she seemed to have some painful recollection, and, looking round the room, expressed surprise and uneasiness at his being there. Vivian retired; and Lord Glistonbury, who was crying like a child, followed, saying, "Take me out with you—Dr. G— ought to be here before now—I'll send for another physician!—Very shocking—very shocking—at Lady Glistonbury's time of life, too—for she is not an old woman by any means. Lady Glistonbury is eighteen months younger than I am!—Nobody knows how soon it may be their turn!—It's very shocking!—If I had known she was ill, I would have had advice for her sooner. She is very patient—too patient—a great deal too patient. She never will complain—never tells what she feels, body or mind—at least never tells me; but that may be my fault in some measure. Should be very sorry Lady Glistonbury went out of the world with things as they are now between us. Hope to God she will get over this attack!—Hey! Mr. Vivian?"

Vivian said whatever he could to fortify this hope, and was glad to see Lord Glistonbury show feelings of this sort. The physician arrived, and confirmed these hopes by his favourable prognostics. In the course of the day and night her face, which had been contracted, resumed its natural appearance; she recovered the use of her arm: a certain difficulty of articulation, and thickness of speech, with what the physician called hallucination of mind, and a general feebleness of body, were all the apparent consequences of this stroke. She was not herself sensible of the nature of the attack, or clear in her ideas of any thing that had passed immediately previous to it. She had only an imperfect recollection of her daughter's illness, and of some hurry about Mr. Vivian's going away. She was, however, well enough to go into her dressing-room, where Vivian went to pay his respects to her, with Lord Glistonbury. By unremitting exertions, and unusual cheerfulness, Lady Sarah succeeded in quieting her mother's confused apprehensions on her account. When out of Lady Glistonbury's hearing, all the attendants and the physicians repeatedly expressed fear that Lady Sarah would over-fatigue and injure herself by this extraordinary energy; but her powers of body and mind seemed to rise with the necessity for exertion; and, on this great occasion, she suddenly discovered a warmth and strength of character, of which few had ever before discerned even the slightest symptoms.

"Who would have expected this from Sarah?" whispered Lord Glistonbury to Vivian. "Why, her sister did not do more for me when I was ill! I always knew she loved her mother, but I thought it was in a quiet, commonplace way—Who knows but she loves me too?—or might—" She came into the room at this moment—"Sarah, my dear," said his lordship, "where are my letters and yesterday's papers, which I never read?—I'll see if there be any thing in them that can interest your mother."

Lord Glistonbury opened the papers, and the first article of public news was, "a dissolution of parliament confidently expected to take place immediately." This must put an end to Vivian's scheme of going to town to attend his duty in parliament. "But, may be, it is only newspaper information." It was confirmed by all Lord Glistonbury and Vivian's private letters. A letter from his mother, which Vivian now for the first moment had time to peruse, mentioned the dissolution of parliament as certain; she named her authority, which could not be doubted; and, in consequence, she had sent down supplies of wine for an election; and she said that she would "be immediately at Castle Vivian, to keep open house and open heart for her son. Though not furnished," she observed, "the castle would suit the better all the purposes of an election; and she should not feel any inconvenience, for her own part, let the accommodations be what they might."

Lord Glistonbury directly proposed and insisted upon Lady Mary Vivian's making Glistonbury her head-quarters. Vivian objected: Lady Glistonbury's illness was an ostensible and, he hoped, would be a sufficient excuse for declining the invitation. But Lord Glistonbury persisted: "Lady Glistonbury, he was sure, would wish it—nothing would be more agreeable to her." His lordship's looks appealed to Lady Sarah, but Lady Sarah was silent; and, when her father positively required her opinion, by adding, "Hey! Sarah?" she rather discouraged than pressed the invitation. She said, that though she was persuaded her mother would, if she were well, be happy to have the pleasure of seeing Lady Mary Vivian; yet she could not, in her mother's present situation, venture to decide how far her health might be able to stand any election bustle.

Lady Sarah said this with a very calm voice, but blushed extremely as she spoke; and, for the first time, Vivian thought her not absolutely plain; and, for the first time, he thought even the formality and deliberate coolness of her manner were not disagreeable. He liked her more, at this moment, than he had ever imagined it possible he could like Lady Sarah Lidhurst; but he liked her chiefly because she did not press him into her service, but rather forwarded his earnest wish to get away from Glistonbury.

Lord Glistonbury appealed to the physician, and asked whether company and amusement were not "the best things possible for his patient? Lady Glistonbury should not be left alone, surely! Her mind should be interested and amused; and an election would be a fortunate circumstance just at present!"

The physician qualified the assent which his lordship's peremptory tone seemed to demand, by saying, "that certainly moderate amusement, and whatever interested without agitating her ladyship, would be salutary." His lordship then declared that he would leave it to Lady Glistonbury herself to decide: quitting the end of the room where they were holding their consultation, he approached her ladyship to explain the matter. But Lady Sarah stopped him, beseeching so earnestly that no appeal might be made to her mother, that Vivian was quite moved; and he settled the business at once to general satisfaction, by declaring that, though neither he nor Lady Mary Vivian could think of intruding as inmates at present, yet that they should, as soon as Lady Glistonbury's health would permit, be as much at Glistonbury Castle as possible; and that the short distance from his house would make it, he hoped, not inconvenient to his lordship for all election business. Lord Glistonbury acceded, and Lady Sarah appeared gratefully satisfied. His lordship, who always took the task of explanation upon himself, now read the paragraph about the dissolution aloud to Lady Glistonbury; informed her, that Lady Mary Vivian was coming immediately to the country; and that they should hope to see Lady Mary and Mr. Vivian almost every day, though he could not prevail upon them to take up their abode during the election at Glistonbury. Lady Glistonbury listened, and tried, and seemed to understand—bowed to Mr. Vivian and smiled, and said she remembered he was often at Glistonbury during the last election—that she was happy to hear she should have the pleasure to see Lady Mary Vivian—that some people disliked election times, but for her part she did not, when she was strong. Indeed, the last election she recollected with particular pleasure—she was happy that Lord Glistonbury's interest was of service to Mr. Vivian. Then "she hoped his canvass to-day had been successful?"—and asked some questions that showed her mind had become confused, and that she was confounding the past with the present. Lady Sarah and Mr. Vivian said a few words to set her right—she looked first at one, and then at the other, listening, and then said—"I understand—God bless you both." Vivian took up his hat, and looked out of the window, to see if his carriage was at the door.

"Mr. Vivian wishes you a good morning, madam," said Lady Sarah: "he is going to Castle Vivian, to get things ready for Lady Mary's arrival."

"I wish you health and happiness, sir," said Lady Glistonbury, attempting to rise, whilst some painful reminiscence altered her countenance.

"Pray do not stir, don't disturb yourself, Lady Glistonbury. I shall pay my respects to your ladyship again as soon as possible."

"And pray bring me good news of the election, and how the poll stands to-morrow, Mr. Vivian," added her ladyship, as he left the room.

CHAPTER XII

Vivian, who had felt oppressed and almost enslaved by his compassion, breathed more freely when he at last found himself in his carriage, driving away from Glistonbury. His own castle, and the preparations for his mother's arrival, and for the expected canvass, occupied him so much for the ensuing days, that he had scarcely time to think of Lady Julia or of Lady Sarah, of Russell or Selina: he could neither reflect on the past, nor anticipate the future; the present, the vulgar present, full of upholsterers, and paper-hangers, and butlers, and grooms, and tenants, and freeholders, and parasites, pressed upon his attention with importunate claims. The dissolution of parliament took place. Lady Mary Vivian arrived almost as soon as the newspaper that brought this intelligence: with her came a new set of thoughts, all centering in the notion of her son's consequence in the world, and of his happiness—ideas which were too firmly associated in her mind ever to be separated. She said that she had regretted his having made such a long stay in the country during the last session, because he had missed opportunities of distinguishing himself farther in parliament. The preceding session her ladyship had received gratifying compliments on her son's talents, and on the figure he had already made in public life; she felt her self-love as well as her affection interested in his continuing his political career with spirit and success. "As to the present election," she observed, "there could be little doubt that he would be re-elected with the assistance of the Glistonbury interest; and," added her ladyship, smiling significantly, "I fancy your interest is pretty strong in that quarter. The world has given you by turns to Lady Julia and Lady Sarah Lidhurst; and I am asked continually which of the Lady Lidhursts you are in love with. One of these ladies certainly must be my daughter-in-law; pray, if you know, empower me to say which." Lady Mary Vivian spoke but half in earnest, till the extraordinary commotion her words created in her son, convinced her that the report had not, now at least, been mistaken.

"Next to Miss Selina Sidney," continued Lady Mary, "who, after her positive and long persisted-in refusal, is quite out of the question, I have, my dear son, always wished to see you married to one of the Lady Lidhursts; and, of course, Lady Julia's talents, and beauty, and youth—"

Vivian interrupted and hastily told his mother that Lady Julia Lidhurst was as much out of the question as Miss Sidney could be; for that he had offered himself, and had been refused; and that he had every reason to believe that the determination of his second mistress against him would be at least as absolute and unconquerable as that of his first. His mother was in amazement. That her son could be refused by Lady Julia Lidhurst appeared a moral and political impossibility, especially when the desire for a connexion between the families had been so obvious on the side of the Glistonburys. What could be the meaning of this? Lady Julia was perhaps under an error, and fancied he was some way engaged to Miss Sidney; "or, perhaps," said Lady Mary, who had a ready wit for the invention of delicate distresses, "perhaps there is some difficulty about the eldest sister, Lady Sarah; for you know the first winter you were given to her.—Ay, that must be the case. I will go to Glistonbury to-morrow, and I will have Lady Julia to myself for five minutes: I think I have some penetration, and I will know the truth."

Lady Mary was again surprised, by hearing from her son that Lady Julia was not at Glistonbury—that she was gone with her brother into Devonshire. So there was a dead silence for some minutes, succeeded by an exclamation from Lady Mary, "There is some grand secret here—I must know it!" Her ladyship forthwith commenced a close and able cross-examination, which Vivian stopped at last by declaring that he was not at liberty to speak upon the subject: he knew, he said, that his mother was of too honourable and generous a temper to press him farther. His mother was perfectly honourable, but at the same time extremely curious; and though she continually repeated, "I will not ask you another question—I would not upon any account lead you to say a syllable that could betray any confidence reposed in you, my dear son;" yet she indulged herself in a variety of ingenious conjectures: "I know it is so;" or, "I am sure that I have guessed now, but I don't ask you to tell me.—You do right to deny it."—Amongst the variety of her conjectures, Lady Mary did not find out the truth; she was prepossessed by the idea that Russell was attached to Selina Sidney—a secret which her own penetration had discovered whilst her son was abroad with Mrs. Wharton, and which she thought no mortal living knew but herself. Pre-occupied with this notion, Russell was now omitted in all her combinations. His having quitted Glistonbury did not create any suspicion of the real cause of his sudden departure, because there was a sufficient reason for his going to the north to see his sick relation; and Lady Mary was too good a philosopher to assign two causes for the same event, when she had found one that was adequate to the production of the effect. She therefore quietly settled it in her imagination, that Lady Julia Lidhurst was going to be married immediately to a certain young nobleman, who had been lately at Glistonbury whilst they were acting plays. The next day she went with Vivian to Glistonbury Castle; for, waiving all the ceremonials of visiting, she was anxious to see poor Lady Glistonbury, of whose illness she had been apprised, in general terms, by her son. An impulse of curiosity, mixed perhaps with motives of regard for her good friend Lady Glistonbury, hastened this visit. They found Lady Glistonbury much better; she looked nearly as well as she had done before this stroke; and she had now recovered her memory, and the full use of her understanding. Vivian observed, that she and Lady Sarah were both convinced, by Lady Mary Vivian's curiosity, that he had given no hint of any thing which they did not wish to be known: and the pleasurable consciousness of his integrity disposed him to be pleased with them. Lord Glistonbury, on his side, was convinced that Vivian had behaved honourably with respect to his daughter Julia; so all parties were well satisfied with each other. His lordship answered Lady Mary Vivian's inquiries after his son and his daughter Julia by saying, that Miss Strictland had just returned to Glistonbury with rather more favourable accounts of Lord Lidhurst's health, and that Julia and he were now at his brother the Bishop of —'s. Between this brother and my Lord Glistonbury there had never been any great intimacy, their characters and their politics being very different. The moment Lady Mary Vivian heard Lord Glistonbury pronounce, with such unusual cordiality, the words, "my brother the bishop," she recollected that the bishop had a very amiable, accomplished, and remarkably handsome son; so she arranged directly in her imagination that this was the person to whom Lady Julia was engaged. Being now thoroughly convinced that this last conjecture was just, she thought no more about Lady Julia's affairs; but turned her attention to Lady Sarah, whose cold and guarded manners, however, resisted her utmost penetration. Disappointed in all her attempts to lead to sentiment or love, the conversation at last ran wholly upon the approaching election, upon the canvass, and the strength of the various interests of the county; on all which subjects Lady Sarah showed surprisingly exact information. Presently Lord Glistonbury took Vivian with him to his study to examine some poll-book, and then put into his hands a letter from Lady Julia Lidhurst, which had been enclosed in one to himself.

"I told you that I intended to rusticate Julia," said his lordship, "with a poor parson and his wife—relations, distant relations of ours in Devonshire; but this plan has been defeated by my foolish good brother the bishop. On their journey they passed close by his palace; I charged Miss Strictland to be incog.; but they stayed to rest in the town, for Lidhurst was fatigued; and some of the bishop's people found them out, and the bishop sent for them, and at last came himself. He was so sorry for Lidhurst's illness, and, as Miss Strictland says, so much charmed with Julia, whom he had not seen since she was a child, that he absolutely took possession of them; and Julia has made her party good with him, for he writes me word he cannot part with her; that I must allow her to remain with him; and that they will take all possible care of Lyndhurst's health. I believe I must yield this point to the bishop; for altogether it looks better that Julia should be at the palace than at the parsonage; and, though my poor brother has not the knowledge of the world one could wish, or that is necessary to bring this romantic girl back to reason, yet—But I keep you from reading your letter, and I see you are impatient—Hey?—very natural!—but, I am afraid, all in vain—I'll leave you in peace. At any rate," added Lord Glistonbury, "you know I have always stood your firm friend in this business; and you know I'm discreet."

Vivian never felt so grateful for any instance of his lordship's friendship and discretion as for that which he gave at this moment, by quitting the room, and leaving him in peace to read his letter.

CHAPTER XIII

"Before you open this letter, you will have heard, probably, that my uncle, the Bishop of —, has taken me under his protection. I cannot sufficiently regret that I was not a few years, a few months, sooner, blessed with such a Mentor. I never, till now, knew how much power kindness has to touch the mind in the moment of distress; nor did I ever, till now, feel how deeply the eloquence of true piety sinks into the heart. This excellent friend will, I hope, in time restore me to my better self. From the abstraction, the selfishness of passion, I think I am already somewhat recovered. After being wholly absorbed by one sentiment, I begin to feel again the influence of other motives, and to waken to the returning sense of social duty. Among the first objects to which, in recovering from this trance, or this fever of the soul, I have power to turn my attention, your happiness, sir, next to that of my own nearest relations, I find interests me most. After giving you this assurance, I trust you will believe that, to insure the felicity, or even to restore the health and preserve the life of any relation or friend I have upon earth, I should not think myself justified in attempting to influence your mind to any thing which I did not sincerely and firmly believe would be for your permanent advantage as well as for theirs. Under the solemn faith of this declaration, I hope that you will listen to me with patience and confidence. From all that I have myself seen, and from all that I have heard of your character, I am convinced that your wife should be a woman of a disposition precisely opposite, in many respects, to mine. Your character is liable to vary, according to the situations in which you are placed; and is subject to sudden but transient impressions from external circumstances. You have hitherto had a friend who has regulated the fluctuations of your passions; now that he is separated from you, how much will you feel the loss of his cool and steady judgment! Should you not, therefore, in that bosom friend, a wife, look for a certain firmness and stability of character, capable of resisting, rather than disposed to yield, to sudden impulse; a character, not of enthusiasm, but of duty; a mind, which, instead of increasing, by example and sympathy, any defects of your own—pardon the expression—should correct or compensate these by opposite qualities? And supposing that, with such sobriety and strength of character as I have described, there should be connected a certain slowness, formality, and coldness of manner, which might not at first be attractive to a man of your vivacity, let not this repel you: when once you have learned to consider this manner as the concomitant and indication of qualities essential to your happiness, it would, I am persuaded, become agreeable to you; especially as, on nearer observation, you would soon discover that, beneath that external coldness, under all that snow and ice, there is an accumulated and concentrated warmth of affection.

"Of this, sir, you must lately have seen an example in my own family. At the moment when my poor mother was struck with palsy, you saw my sister's energy; and her character, probably, then appeared to you in a new point of view. From this burst of latent affection for a parent, you may form some idea what the power of the passion of love would be in her soul; some idea, I say; for I am persuaded that none but those who know her as well as I do can form an adequate notion of the strength of attachment of which she is capable.

"You will be surprised, perhaps, sir, to hear me reason so coolly for others on a subject where I have acted so rashly for myself; and you may feel no inclination to listen to the advice of one who has shown so little prudence in her own affairs: therefore, having stated my reasons, and suggested my conclusions, I leave you to apply them as you think proper; and I shall only add, that the accomplishment of my wishes, on this subject, would give me peculiar satisfaction. It would relieve my mind from part of a weight of self-reproach. I have made both my parents unhappy. I have reason to fear that the shock my mother received, by my means, contributed much to her late illness. An event that would restore my whole family to happiness must, therefore, be to me the most desirable upon earth. I should feel immediate relief and delight, even in the hope of contributing to it by any influence I can have over your mind. And, independently of the pleasure and pride I should feel in securing my sister's happiness and yours, I should enjoy true satisfaction, sir, in that intimate friendship with you, which only the ties of such near relationship could permit or justify. You will accept of this assurance, instead of the trite and insulting, because unmeaning or unsafe, offer of friendship, which ladies sometimes make to those who have been their lovers.

"JULIA LIDHURST.

"— Palace:"

At the first reading of this letter, Vivian felt nothing but a renewal of regret for having lost all chance of obtaining the affections of the person by whom it was written: on a second perusal, he was moved by the earnest expression of her wishes for his happiness; and the desire to gratify her, on a point on which she was so anxious, influenced him much more than any of her arguments. Whatever good sense the letter contained was lost upon him; but all the sentiment operated with full force, yet not with sufficient power to conquer the repugnance he still felt to Lady Sarah's person and manners. Lord Glistonbury made no inquiries concerning the contents of his daughter Julia's letter; but, as far as politeness would permit, he examined Vivian's countenance when he returned to the drawing-room. Lady Glistonbury's manner was as calm as usual; but the slight shake of her head was a sufficient indication of her internal feelings. Lady Sarah looked pale, but so perfectly composed, that Vivian was convinced she, at least, knew nothing of her sister's letter. So great indeed was the outward composure, and so immoveable was Lady Sarah, that it provoked Lady Mary past endurance; and as they drove home in the evening, she exclaimed, "I never saw such a young woman as Lady Sarah Lidhurst! She is a stick, a stone, a statue—she has completely satisfied my mind on one point. I own that when I found Lady Julia was out of the question, I did begin to think and wish that Lady Sarah might be my daughter-in-law, because she has really been so carefully brought up, and the connexion with the Glistonbury family is so desirable: then I had a notion, before I saw her this morning, that the girl liked you, and might be really capable of attachment; but now, indeed, I am convinced of the folly of that notion. She has no feeling—none upon earth—scarcely common sense! She thinks of nothing but how she holds her elbows. The formality and importance with which she went on cutting off ends of worsted from that frightful tapestry work, whilst I talked of you, quite put me out of all manner of patience. She has no feeling—none upon earth!"

"Oh, ma'am," said Vivian, "you do her injustice: she certainly has feeling—for her mother."

"Ay, for her mother, may be! a kind of mechanical affection!"

"But, ma'am, if you had seen her at the time that her mother was struck with palsy!"

Much to his own surprise, Vivian found himself engaged in a defence, and almost in an eulogium upon Lady Sarah; but the injustice of his mother's attack, on this point, was, he knew, so great, that he could not join in Lady Mary's invective.

"Why, my dear Charles!" said she, "do you recollect, on this very road, as we were returning from Glistonbury Castle, this time two years, you called Lady Sarah a petrifaction?"

"Yes, ma'am; because I did not know her then."

"Well, my dear, I must have time to analyze her more carefully, and I suppose I shall discover, as you have done, that she is not a petrifaction. So, then, Lady Sarah really is to be the woman after all. I am content, but I absolutely cannot pretend to like her—I like the connexion, however; and the rest is your affair.—You haven't proposed yet?"

"Bless me! no, ma'am! God forbid! How fast your imagination goes, my dear mother!—Is there no difference between saying, that a woman is not a petrifaction, and being in love with her?"

"In love! I never said a word about being in love—I know that's impossible—I asked only if you had proposed for her?"

"Dear ma'am, no!"

Lady Mary expressed her satisfaction; and, perhaps, the injustice with which she continued, for some days, to asperse Lady Sarah Lidhurst, as being unfeeling, served her more, in Vivian's opinion, than any other mode in which she could have spoken of her ladyship. Still he felt glad that he had not yet proposed. He had not courage either to recede or advance; circumstances went on, and carried him along with them, without bringing him to any decision. The business of the election proceeded; every day Lord Glistonbury was with him, or he was at Glistonbury Castle; every hour he saw more plainly the expectations that were formed: sometimes he felt that he was inevitably doomed to fulfil these, and at other times he cherished the hope that Lady Julia would soon return home, and that, by some fortunate revolution, she might yet be his. He had not now the advantage of Russell's firmness to support him in this emergency. Russell's answer to his letter was so coolly determined, and he so absolutely declined interfering farther in his affairs, that Vivian saw no hopes of regaining his friendship, or of benefiting by his counsels. Thus was Vivian in all the helplessness and all the horrors of indecision, when an event took place, which materially changed the face of affairs in the Glistonbury family. Just at the time when the accounts of his health were the most favourable, and when his friends were deceived by the most sanguine hopes of his recovery, Lord Lidhurst died. His mother was the only person in the family who was prepared for this catastrophe: they dreaded to communicate the intelligence to her, lest it should bring on another attack of her dreadful malady; but to their astonishment, she heard it with calm resignation,—said she had long foreseen this calamity, and that she submitted to the will of Heaven. After pity for the parents who lost this amiable and promising young man, heir to this large fortune and to this splendid title, people began to consider what change would be made in the condition of the rest of the family. The Lady Lidhursts, from being very small fortunes, became heiresses to a large estate. The earldom of Glistonbury was to devolve to a nephew of Lord Glistonbury, in case the Lady Lidhursts should not marry, or should not have heirs male; but, in case they should marry, the title was to go to the first son. All these circumstances were of course soon known and talked of in the neighbourhood; and many congratulated Vivian upon the great accession of fortune, and upon the high expectations of the lady to whom they supposed him engaged.

On the first visit which Vivian and his mother paid after the death of Lord Lidhurst at Glistonbury Castle, they found there a young man very handsome, but of a dark, reserved countenance, whose physiognomy and manner immediately prepossessed them against him; on his part, he seemed to eye them with suspicion, and to be particularly uneasy whenever Vivian either mentioned the election or approached Lady Sarah. This young man was Mr. Lidhurst, Lord Glistonbury's nephew and heir-at-law. It was obvious, almost at first sight, that the uncle disliked the nephew; but it was not so easy to perceive that the nephew despised the uncle. Mr. Lidhurst, though young, was an excellent politician; and his feelings were always regulated by his interests. He had more abilities than Lord Glistonbury, less vanity, but infinitely more ambition. In Lord Glistonbury, ambition was rather affected, as an air suited to his rank, and proper to increase his consequence: Mr. Lidhurst's was an earnest, inordinate ambition, yet it was cold, silent, and calculating; his pride preyed upon him inwardly, but it never hurried him into saying or doing an extravagant thing. Those who were not actuated solely by ambition, he always looked upon as fools, and those who were, he considered, in general, as knaves: the one he marked as dupes, the other as rivals. He had been at the Bishop of —'s, during Lord Lidhurst's illness, and at the time of his death. Ever since Lady Julia's arrival at the bishop's, he had foreseen the probability of this event, and had, in consequence of the long-sightedness of his views, endeavoured to make himself agreeable to her. He found this impossible; but was, however, easily consoled by hearing that she had resolved never to marry; he only hoped that she would keep her resolution; and he was now at Glistonbury Castle, in the determination to propose for his other cousin, Lady Sarah, who would, perhaps, equally well secure to him his objects.

"Well! my dear Vivian," said Lord Glistonbury, drawing him aside, "how d'ye relish my nephew, Marmaduke Lidhurst? Need not be afraid to speak the truth, for I tell you at once that he is no particular favourite here; not en bonne odeur; but that's only between you and me. He thinks that I don't know that he considers me as a shallow fellow, because I haven't my head crammed with a parcel of statistical tables, all the fiscal and financiering stuff which he has at his calculating fingers' ends; but I trust that I am almost as good a politician as he is, and I'm free to believe, have rather more knowledge of the world—

'In men, not books, experienced was my lord'—

Hey? Hey, Vivian? and can see through him with half an eye, I can tell him.—Wants to get Lady Sarah—Yes, yes; but never came near us till we lost my poor boy—he won't win Lady Sarah either, or I'm much mistaken. Did you observe how jealous he was of you?—Right!—right!—he has penetration!—Stay, stay! you don't know Marmaduke yet—don't know half his schemes. How his brow clouded when we were talking of the election! I must hint to you, he has been sounding me upon that matter; he has a great mind to stand for this county—talks of starting at the first day of the poll. I told him it could not do, as I was engaged to you. He answered, that of course was only a conditional promise, in case none of my own relations stood. I fought shy, and he pressed confoundedly.—Gad! he would put me in a very awkward predicament, if he was really to stand! for you know what the world would say, if they saw me opposing my own nephew, a rising young man, and not for a relation either; and Marmaduke Lidhurst is just your deep fellow to plan such a thing and execute it, not caring at what or whose expense. I can tell him, however, I am not a man to be bullied out of my interest, or to be outwitted either.—Stand firm, Vivian, my good friend, and I'll stand by you; depend on me!—I only wish—" Here his lordship paused. "But I cannot say more to you now; for here is my precious heir-at-law coming to break up the confederacy. I'll ride over and see you to-morrow;—now, let us all be mute before Marmaduke, our master politician, as becomes us—Hey! Vivian? Hey?"

Notwithstanding this sort of jealousy of Marmaduke, and the bravadoing style in which Lord Glistonbury spoke of him, he spoke to him in a very different manner: it was apparent to Vivian that his lordship was under some awe of his nephew, and that, whilst he cherished this secret dislike, he dreaded coming to any open rupture with a man who was, as his lordship apprehended, so well able to make his own party good in the world. When Marmaduke did emerge from that depth of thought in which he generally seemed to be sunk, and when he did condescend to converse, or rather to speak, his theme was always of persons in power, or his sarcasms against those who never would obtain it; from any one thing he asserted, it could never be proved, but, from all he said, it might be inferred, that he valued human qualities and talents merely as they could, or could not, obtain a price in the political market. The power of speaking in public, as it is a means in England of acquiring all other species of power, he deemed the first of Heaven's gifts; and successful parliamentary speakers were the only persons of whom he expressed admiration. As Vivian had spoken, and had been listened to in the House of Commons, he was in this respect an object of Marmaduke Lidhurst's envy; but this envy was mitigated by contempt for our hero's want of perseverance in ambition.

"There is that Mr. Vivian of yours," said he to his uncle, whilst Vivian was gone to talk to the ladies—"you'll find he will be but a woman's man, after all!—Heavens! with his fluency in public, what I would have done by this time of day! This poor fellow has no consistency of ambition—no great views—no reach of mind. Put him in for a borough, and he would be just as well content as if he carried the county. You'll see he will, after another session or two, cut out, and retire without a pension, and settle down into a mere honest country gentleman. He would be no connexion to increase the consequence of your family. Lady Sarah Lidhurst would be quite lost with such a nobody! Her ladyship, I am convinced, has too much discrimination, and values herself too highly, to make such a missy match."

Lord Glistonbury coughed, and cleared his throat, and blew his nose, and seemed to suffer extremely, but chiefly under the repression of his usual loquacity. Nothing could be at once a greater proof of his respect for his nephew's abilities, and of his lordship's dislike to him, than this unnatural silence. Mr. Lidhurst's compliments on Lady Sarah's discrimination seemed, however, to be premature, and unmerited; for, during the course of this day, she treated all the vast efforts of her cousin Marmaduke's gallantry with haughty neglect, and showed, what she had never before suffered to be visible in her manner, a marked preference for Mr. Vivian's conversation. The sort of emulation which Mr. Lidhurst's rivalship produced increased the value of the object; she, for whom there was a contention, immediately became a prize. Vivian was both provoked and amused by the alternate contempt and jealousy which Mr. Lidhurst betrayed; this gentleman's desire to keep him out of the Glistonbury family, and to supplant him in Lady Sarah's favour, piqued him to prove his influence, and determined him to maintain his ground. Insensibly, Vivian's attentions to the lady became more vivacious; and he was vain of showing the ease, taste, and elegance of his gallantry; and he was flattered by the idea, that all the spectators perceived both its superiority and its success. Lady Sarah, whose manners had much improved since the departure of Miss Strictland, was so much embellished by our hero's attentions, that he thought her quite charming. He had been prepared to expect fire under the ice, but he was agreeably surprised by this sudden spring of flowers from beneath the snow. The carriage was at the door in the evening, and had waited half an hour, before he was aware that it was time to depart.

"You are right, my dear son!" Lady Mary began, the r moment they were seated in the carriage; "you are quite right, and I was quite wrong, about Lady Sarah Lidhurst: she has feeling, indeed—strong, generous feeling—and she shows it at the proper time: a fine, decided character! Her manners, to-day, so easy, and her countenance so animated, really she looked quite handsome, and I think her a charming woman.—What changes love can make!—Well, now I am satisfied: this is what I always wished—connexion, family, fortune, every thing; and the very sort of character you require in a wife,—the very person, of all others, that is suited to you!"

"If she were but a little more like her sister—or Selina Sidney even!" said Vivian, with a sigh.

"That very word even—your saying like Selina Sidney even—shows that you have not much cause for sighing: for you see how quickly the mere fancy in these matters changes—and you may love Lady Sarah presently, as much as you loved even Lady Julia."

"Impossible! ma'am."

"Impossible! Why, my dear Charles, you astonish me! for you cannot but see the views and expectations of all the family, and of the young lady herself; and your attentions to-day were such as could bear but one construction."

"Were they, ma'am? I was not aware of that at the time—that is, I did not mean to engage myself— Good Heavens! surely I am not engaged?—You know a man is not bound, like a woman, by a few foolish words; compliments and gallantry are not such serious things with us men. Men never consider themselves engaged to a woman till they make an absolute proposal."

"I know that is a common maxim with young men of the present day, but I consider it as dishonourable and base; and very sorry should I be to see it adopted by my son!" cried Lady Mary indignantly. "Ask your friend Mr. Russell's opinion on this point: he long ago told you—I know he did—that if you had not serious thoughts of Lady Sarah Lidhurst, you would do very wrong, after all the reports that have gone abroad, to continue your intimacy with the Glistonburys, and thus to deceive her and her whole family— I only appeal to Mr. Russell;—will you ask your friend Russell's opinion?"

Vivian sighed again deeply for the loss of his friend Russell; but as he could not, without touching upon Lady Julia's affairs, explain the cause of the coolness between him and his friend, he answered only, "that an appeal to Mr. Russell was unnecessary when he had his mother's opinion." Lady Mary's wish for the Glistonbury connexion fortified her morality at this moment, and she replied, "Then my decided opinion is, that it would be an immoral and dishonourable action to break such a tacit engagement as this, which you have voluntarily contracted, and which you absolutely could not break without destroying the peace and happiness of a whole family. Even that cold Lady Glistonbury grew quite warm to-day; and you must see the cause.—And in Lady Glistonbury's state of health, who could answer for the consequences of any disappointment about her favourite daughter, just after the loss of her son, too?"

"No more, mother, for Heaven's sake! I see it all—I feel it all—I must marry Lady Sarah, then.—By what fatality am I doomed, am I forced to marry a woman whom I cannot love, whose person and manners are peculiarly disagreeable to me, and when I'm half in love with another woman!"

"That would be a shocking thing, indeed," said Lady Mary, retracting, and alarmed; for now another train of associations was wakened, and she judged not by her worldly, but by her romantic system.—"I am sure I would not, upon any account, urge you to act against your feelings. I would not be responsible for such a marriage, if you are really in love with her sister, and if Lady Sarah's person and manners are peculiarly and absolutely disagreeable to you. I should do a very wicked action—should destroy my son's happiness and morals, perhaps, by insisting on such a marriage—Heaven forbid!" (A silence of a mile and a half long ensued.) "But, Charles, after all I saw to-day, how can I believe that Lady Sarah is so disagreeable to you?"

"Ma'am, she happened not to be absolutely disagreeable to me to-day."

"Oh! well! then she may not happen to be disagreeable to you to-morrow, or the next day, or ever again!—And, as to the fancy for her sister, when all hope is over, you know love soon dies of itself."

So ended the conversation.—The next morning, at an unusual hour, Lord Glistonbury made his appearance at Castle Vivian, with an air of great vexation and embarrassment: he endeavoured to speak of trivial topics; but, one after another, these subjects dropped. Then Lady Mary, who saw that he was anxious to speak to her son, soon took occasion to withdraw, not without feeling some curiosity, and forming many conjectures, as to the object his lordship might have in view in this conference.

Lord Glistonbury's countenance exhibited, in quick alternation, a look of absolute determination and of utter indecision. At length, with abrupt effort, he said, "Vivian, have you seen the papers to-day?"

"The newspapers?—yes!—no!—They are on the table—I did not look at them—Is there any thing extraordinary?"

"Yes, faith!—extraordinary, very extraordinary!—But it is not here—it is not there—this is not the right paper—it is not in your paper. That's extraordinary, too"—(then feeling in both pockets)—"I was a fool not to bring it with me—May be I have it—Yes, here it is!—Not public news, but private."

Vivian was all expectation, for he imagined that something about Lady Julia was coming. Lord Glistonbury, who, in his commerce with public men, had learned the art of paying in words, to gain time when in danger of a bankruptcy of ideas, went on, stringing sentences together, without much meaning, whilst he was collecting his thoughts and studying the countenance of his auditor.

"You recollect my suggestions the last time I had the honour of speaking to you on a particular subject. I confess, Mr. Lidhurst's conduct does not meet my ideas of propriety; but other persons are free to form what judgment they think fit upon the occasion. I shall submit the matter to you, Mr. Vivian, feeling myself called upon to come forward immediately to explain it to your satisfaction; and I do not fear to commit myself, by stating at once my sentiments, and the light in which it strikes me; for there must be some decision shown, somehow or other, and on some side or other.—Decision is all in all in public business, as the great Bacon or somebody says—and nobody knows that better than Marmaduke."

Here his lordship grew warm, and quitting his parliamentary cant, assumed his familiar style.

"Gad! he has stolen a march upon us—out-generalled us—but, in my private opinion, not in the handsomest style possible—Hey, Vivian?—Hey?"

"My dear lord, I have not heard the fact yet," said Vivian.

"Oh! the fact is simply—Look here, he has without my encouragement or concurrence—and, indeed, as he very well knew, contrary to my approbation and wishes—gone, and declared himself candidate for this county; and here's his fine flourishing, patriotic, damned advertisement in the paper—'To the gentlemen, clergy, and freeholders of the county.'—Gad! how it startled me this morning! When I first saw it I rubbed my eyes, and could hardly believe it was Marmaduke. Though I pique myself on knowing a man's style at the first line, yet I could not have believed it was his, unless I had seen his name at full length in these great abominable characters—'John Marmaduke Lidhurst.'—'Glastonbury Castle!' too— as if I had countenanced the thing, or had promised my support; when he knew, that but yesterday I was arguing the point with him in my study, and told him I was engaged to you. Such an ungentlemanlike trick!—for you know it reduces me to the dilemma of supporting a man who is only my friend, against my nearest relation by blood, which, of course, would have an odd and awkward appearance in the eyes of the world!"

Vivian expressed much concern for his lordship's difficulties; but observed that the world would be very unjust if it blamed him, and he was sure his lordship had too much decision of character.

"But, independently of the world," interrupted his lordship, "even in our own family, amongst all the Lidhursts and their remotest connexions, there would be quite a league formed against me; and these family quarrels are ugly affairs; for though our feudal times are done away, party clanships have succeeded to feudal clanships; and we chiefs of parties must keep our followers in good humour, or we are nothing in the field—I should say in the house—Ha! ha! ha!—I laugh, but it is a very serious business; for Marmaduke Lidhurst would be, in private or public, an impracticable enemy. Marmaduke's a fellow capable of inextinguishable hatred; and he is everywhere, and knows every body, of all the clubs, a rising young man, who is listened to, and who would make his story credited. And then, with one's nephew, one can't settle these things in an honourable way—these family quarrels must be arranged amicably, not honourably; and that's the difficulty: the laws of honour are dead letters in these cases, and the laws of the land do not reach these niceties of feeling.—But of the most important fact you are still to be apprised."

"Indeed!" cried Vivian.

"Yes, you have not yet heard Marmaduke's master-stroke of policy!"

"No!—What is it, my lord?—I am all attention—pray explain it to me."

"But there's the delicacy—there's the difficulty!—No, no, no.—Upon my soul, I cannot name it!" cried Lord Glistonbury. "It revolts my feelings—all my feelings—as a man, as a gentleman, as a father. Upon my honour, as a peer, I would speak if I could; but, for the soul of me, I cannot."

"You know, my dear lord," said Vivian, "there can be no delicacies or difficulties with me; your lordship has done me the honour to live always on such a footing of intimacy with me, that surely there is not any thing you cannot say to me!"

"Why, that's true," said Lord Glistonbury, quitting his affected air of distress, and endeavouring to throw off his real feeling of embarrassment: "you are right, my dear Vivian! we are certainly upon terms of such intimacy, that I ought not to be so scrupulous. But there are certain things, a well-born, well-bred man—in short, it would look so like—But, in fact, I am driven to the wall, and I must defend myself as well as I can against this nephew of mine—I know it will look like the most horrible thing upon earth, like what I would rather be decapitated than do—I know it will look, absolutely, as if I came here to ask you to marry my daughter,—which, you know, is a thing no gentleman could have the most remotely in his contemplation; but, since I am so pressed, I must tell you the exact truth, and explain to you, however difficult, Marmaduke's master-stroke—he has proposed for Lady Sarah; and has had the assurance to ask me whether there is or is not any truth in certain reports which he is pleased to affirm have gone abroad—Heaven knows how or why!—And he urges me—the deep dog! for his cousin's sake, to contradict those reports, in the only effectual manner, by a temporary cessation of the intimate intercourse between Castle Vivian and Glistonbury Castle, whilst Lady Sarah remains unmarried; or, if our master politician would speak plainly, till he has married her himself.—At any rate, I have spoken frankly, Vivian, hey? you'll allow; and I am entitled both to a candid interpretation of my motives, and to equal frankness of reply."

Whilst his lordship had been speaking, compassion, gratitude, vanity, rivalship, honour, Lady Mary Vivian's conversation, Lady Julia's letter, then again the connexion, the earldom in future, the present triumph or disappointment about the election, the insolent intrusion of Mr. Lidhurst, the cruelty of abandoning a lady who was in love with him, the dishonour, the impossibility of receding after certain reports; all these ideas, in rapid succession, pressed on Vivian's mind: and his decision was in consequence of the feelings and of the embarrassment of the moment. His reply to Lord Glistonbury was a proposal for Lady Sarah, followed by as many gallant protestations as his presence of mind could furnish. He did not very well know what he said, nor did Lord Glistonbury scrupulously examine whether he had the air and accent of a true lover, nor did his lordship inquire what had become of Vivian's late love for Lady Julia; but, quite content that the object should be altered, the desire the same, he relieved Vivian by exclaiming, "Come, come, all this sort of thing Lady Sarah herself must hear; and I've a notion—but I can keep a secret. You'll return with me directly to Glistonbury. Lady Glistonbury will be delighted to see you; and I shall be delighted to see Marmaduke's face, when I tell him you have actually proposed for Sarah—for now I must tell you all. Our politician calculated upon the probability that you would not decide, you see, to make a proposal at once, that would justify me to the world in supporting my son-in-law against my nephew. As to the choice of the son-in-law, Sarah settles that part of the business herself, you know; for, when two proposals are made, both almost equally advantageous, in the common acceptation of the word, I am too good a father not to leave the decision to my daughter. So you see we understand one another perfectly, and will make Marmaduke, too, understand us perfectly, contrary to his calculations, hey, hey?—Mr. Politician, your advertisement must be withdrawn, I opine, in the next paper—hey, Vivian? my dear Vivian!"

With similar loquacity, Lord Glistonbury continued, in the fulness of his heart, all the way they went together to Glistonbury Castle; which was agreeable to Vivian, at least by saving him from all necessity of speaking.

"So!" said Vivian to himself, "the die is cast, and I have actually proposed for Lady Sarah Lidhurst!—Who would have expected this two years ago?—I would not have believed it, if it had been foretold to me even two months ago. But it is a very—a very suitable match, and it will please the friends of both parties; and Lady Sarah is certainly very estimable, and capable of very strong attachment; and I like her, that is, I liked her yesterday very much—I really like her."

Upon those mixed motives, between convenience and affection, from which, Dr. Johnson says, most people marry, our hero commenced his courtship of the Lady Sarah Lidhurst. As the minds of both parties on the subject are pretty well known to our readers, it would be cruel to fatigue them with a protracted description of the formalities of courtship. It is sufficient to say, that my Lord Glistonbury had the satisfaction of seeing his nephew disappointed.

CHAPTER XIV

"And the marriage was solemnized with much pomp and magnificence, and every demonstration of joy."

Novelists and novel readers are usually satisfied when they arrive at this happy catastrophe; their interest and curiosity seldom go any farther: but, in real life, marriage is but the beginning of domestic happiness or misery.

Soon after the celebration of Vivian's nuptials, an event happened which interrupted all the festivities at Glistonbury, and which changed the bridal pomp to mourning. Lady Glistonbury, who had been much fatigued by the multitude of wedding-visits she was obliged to receive and return, had another stroke of the palsy, which, in a few hours, terminated fatally. Thus, the very event which Vivian had dreaded, as the probable consequence of his refusal to marry her daughter, was, in fact, accelerated by the full accomplishment of her wishes. After the loss of her mother, Lady Sarah Vivian's whole soul seemed to be engrossed by fondness for her husband. In public, and to all eyes but Vivian's, her ladyship seemed much the same person as formerly: but, in private, the affection she expressed for him was so great, that he frequently asked himself whether this could be the same woman, who, to the rest of the world, and in every other part of her life, appeared so cold and inanimate. On a very few occasions her character, before her marriage, had, "when much enforced, given out a hasty spark, and straight was cold again;" but now she permitted the steady flame to burn without restraint. Duty and passion had now the same object. Before marriage, her attachment had been suppressed, even at the hazard of her life; she had no idea that the private demonstrations of unbounded love from a married woman to her husband could be either blameable or dangerous: she believed it to be her duty to love her husband as much as she possibly could.—Was not he her husband? She had been taught that she should neither read, speak, nor think of love; and she had been so far too much restricted on this subject, that, absolutely ignorant and unconscious even of her danger, she now pursued her own course without chart or compass. Her injudicious tenderness soon imposed such restraint upon her husband, as scarcely any lover, much less any husband, could have patiently endured. She would hardly ever suffer him to leave her. Whenever he went out of the house, she exacted from him a promise that he would be back again at a certain hour; and if he were even a few minutes later than his appointment, he had to sustain her fond reproaches. Even though he stayed at home all day, she was uneasy if he quitted the room where she sat; and he, who by this time understood, through all her exterior calmness, the symptoms of her internal agitation, saw by her countenance that she was wretched if he seemed interested in the conversation of any other person, especially of any other woman.

One day when Vivian, after spending the morning tête-à-tête with Lady Sarah, signified to her his intention of dining abroad, she repeated her fond request that he would be sure to come home early, and that he would tell her at what o'clock exactly she might expect to see him again. He named an hour at hazard, to free himself from her importunate anxiety; but he could not help saying, "Pshaw!" as he ran down stairs; an exclamation which fortunately reached only the ears of a groom, who was thinking of nothing but the tops of his own boots. Vivian happened to meet some agreeable people where he dined: he was much pressed to stay to supper; he yielded to entreaty, but he had the good-natured attention to send home his servant, to beg that Lady Sarah and his mother would not sit up for him. When he returned, he found all the family in bed except Lady Sarah, who was sitting up waiting for him, with her watch in her hand. The moment he appeared, she assailed him with tender reproaches, to which he answered, "But why would you sit up when I begged you would not, my dear Lady Sarah?"

She replied by a continuity of fond reproach; and among other things she said, but without believing it to be true, "Ah! I am sure you would have been happier if you had married my sister Julia, or that Miss Sidney!"

Vivian sighed deeply; but the next instant, conscious that he had sighed, and afraid of giving his wife pain, he endeavoured to turn the course of her thoughts to some other subject. In vain. Poor Lady Sarah said no more, but felt this exquisitely, and with permanent anguish. Thus her imprudence reverted upon herself, and she suffered in proportion to her pride and to her fondness. By such slight circumstances is the human heart alienated from love! Struggling to be free, the restive little deity ruffles and impairs his plumage, and seldom recovers a disposition to tranquillity. Vivian's good-nature had induced him for some time to submit to restraint; but if, instead of weakly yielding to the fond importunity of his wife—

if, instead of tolerating the insipidity of her conversation and the narrowness of her views, he had with real energy employed her capacity upon suitable objects, he might have made her attachment the solace of his life. Whoever possesses the heart of a woman, who has common powers of intellect, may improve her understanding in twelve months more than could all the masters, and lectures, and courses of philosophy, and abridgments, and documenting in the universe. But Vivian had not sufficient resolution for such an undertaking: he thought only of avoiding to give or to feel present pain; and the consequences were, that the evils he dreaded every day increased.

Vivian's mother saw the progress of conjugal discontent with anguish and remorse.

"Alas!" said she to herself, "I was much to blame for pressing this match. My son told me he could never love Lady Sarah Lidhurst. It would have been better far to have broken off a marriage at the church-door than to have forced the completion of such an ill-assorted union. My poor son married chiefly from a principle of honour; his duty and respect for my opinion had also great weight in his decision; and I have sacrificed his happiness to my desire that he should make what the world calls a splendid alliance. I am the cause of all his misery; and Heaven only knows where all this will end!"

In her paroxysm of self-reproach, and her eagerness to set things to rights between her daughter-in-law and her son, she only made matters worse. She spoke with all the warmth and frankness of her own character to Lady Sarah, beseeching her to speak with equal openness, and to explain the cause of the alteration in Vivian.

"I do not know what you mean, madam, by alteration in Mr. Vivian!"

"Is not there some disagreement between you, my dear?"

"There is no disagreement whatever, madam, as far as I know, between Mr. Vivian and me—we agree perfectly," said Lady Sarah.

"Well, the misunderstanding!"

"I do not know of any misunderstanding, madam. Mr. Vivian and I understand one another perfectly."

"The coolness, then—Oh! what word shall I use!—Surely, my dear Lady Sarah, there is some coolness—something wrong?"

"I am sure, madam, I do not complain of any coolness on Mr. Vivian's part. Am I to understand that he complains to your ladyship of any thing wrong on mine? If he does, I shall think it my duty, when he points out the particulars, to make any alteration he may desire in my conduct and manners."

"Complain!—My son!—He makes no complaints, my dear. You misunderstand me. My son does not complain that any thing is wrong on your part."

"Then, madam, if no complaints are made on either side, all is as it should be, I presume, at present; and if in future I should fail in any point of duty, I shall hold myself obliged to your ladyship if you will then act as my monitor."

Hopeless of penetrating Lady Sarah's sevenfold fence of pride, the mother flew to her son, to try what could be done with his open and generous mind. He expressed a most earnest and sincere wish to make his wife happy. Conscious that he had given her exquisite pain, he endeavoured to make atonement by the sacrifices which he thought would be most grateful to her. He refrained often from company and conversation that was agreeable to him, and would resign himself for hours to her society. It was fortunate for Lady Julia Lidhurst that, by continuing with her good uncle the bishop, she did not see the consequences of the union which she had so strenuously advised. The advice of friends is often highly useful to prevent an imprudent match; but it seldom happens that marriages turn out happily which have been made from the opinion of others rather than from the judgment and inclinations of the parties concerned; for, let the general reasons on which the advice is grounded be ever so sensible, it is scarcely possible that the adviser can take in all the little circumstances of taste and temper, upon which so much of the happiness or misery of domestic life depends. Besides, people are much more apt to repent of having been guided by the judgment of another than of having followed their own; and this is most likely to be the case with the weakest minds. Strong minds can decide for themselves, not by the opinions but by the reasons that are laid before them: weak minds are influenced merely by opinions; and never, either before or after their decision, are firm in abiding by the preponderating reasons.

No letters, no intelligence from home, except a malicious hint now and then from her cousin Marmaduke, which she did not credit, gave her reason to suspect that the pair whom she had contributed to unite were not perfectly happy. So Lady Julia exulted in the success of her past counsels, and indulged her generous romantic disposition in schemes for forwarding a union between Russell and Selina, determining to divide her fortune amongst the children of her friends. She concluded one of her letters to Lady Sarah Vivian about this time with these words:—

"Could I but see one other person,—whom I must not name, rewarded for his virtues, as you are, by happy love, I should die content, and would write on my tomb:—

'Je ne fus point heureux, mais j'ai fait leur bonheur." 10

Far removed from all romance and all generosity of sentiment, Lord Glistonbury, in the mean time, went on very comfortably, without observing any thing that passed in his family. Whatever uneasiness obtruded upon his attention he attributed to one cause, anxiety relative to the question on which his present thoughts were exclusively fixed, viz. whether Lady Sarah's first child would be a boy or a girl. "Heaven grant a boy!" said his lordship; "for then, you know, there's an end of Marmaduke as heir-at-law!" Whenever his lordship saw a cloud on the brows of Lady Mary, of Lady Sarah, or of Vivian, he had one infallible charm for dispelling melancholy;—he stepped up close to the patient, and whispered, "It will be a boy!—My life upon it, it will be a boy!" Sometimes it happened that this universal remedy, applied at random, made the patient start or smile; and then his lordship never failed to add, with a nod of great sagacity, "Ah! you didn't know I knew what you were thinking of!—Well! well! you'll see we shall cut out Marmaduke yet."

With this hope of cutting out Marmaduke, Lord Glistonbury went on very happily, and every day grew fonder of the son-in-law, who was the enemy of his heir-at-law, or whom he considered as such. The easiness of Vivian's temper was peculiarly agreeable to his lordship, who enjoyed the daily pleasure of governing a man of talents which were far superior to his own. This easiness of temper in our hero was much increased by the want of motive and stimulus. He thought that he had now lost his chance of happiness; he cared little for the more or less pain of each succeeding day; and so passive was his listlessness, that to a superficial observer, like Lord Glistonbury, it looked like the good-nature of perfect content.—Poor Vivian!—In this wreck of his happiness, one saving chance, however, yet remained. He had still a public character; he was conscious of, having preserved unblemished integrity as a member of the senate; and this integrity, still more than his oratorical talents, raised him far above most of his competitors, and preserved him not only in the opinion of others, but in his own. When parliament met, he went to town, took a very handsome house for Lady Sarah, determining to do all he could to oblige and please the wife whom he could not love. Lady Sarah had complete power, at home and abroad, of her time and her expenses: her dress, her equipages, her servants, her whole establishment, were above Vivian's fortune, and equal to her ladyship's birth and rank. She was mistress of every thing but of his heart. The less he liked her, the more he endeavoured to compensate for this involuntary fault, by allowing her that absolute dominion, and that external splendour, which he thought would gratify, and perhaps fill her mind. As for himself, he took refuge in the House of Commons. There he forgot for a time domestic uneasiness, and was truly animated by what so many affect—zeal for the good of his country. He was proud to recollect, that the profligate Wharton had failed in the attempt to laugh him out of his public virtue; he was proud that Wharton's prophecies of his apostasy had never been accomplished; that, as a public! character at least, he had fulfilled the promise of his early youth, and was still worthy of himself, and of that friend whom he had lost. He clung to this idea, as to the only hope left him in life.

One night, in a debate on some question of importance, he made an excellent speech, which was particularly well received by the house, because it came from one who had an unblemished character. When Vivian went into the coffee-room to refresh himself, after he had done speaking, several of his acquaintance crowded round him, complimenting him upon his success—he broke from them all! for he saw, advancing towards him with a smile of approbation, the friend on whose approbation he set a higher value than he did even on the applauses of the house—the friend whose lost affection he had so long and so bitterly regretted. Russell stretched out his hand—Vivian eagerly seized it; and, before they had either of them spoken one word, they both understood each other perfectly, and their reconciliation was completely effected.

"Yes," said Russell, as they walked out arm in arm together, "yes, it is fit that I should forget all private resentment, in the pride and pleasure I feel, not merely in your public success, but in your public virtue. Talents, even the rare talent of oratory, you know, I hold cheap in comparison with that which is so far more rare, as well as more valuable—political integrity. The abhorrence and contempt of political profligacy, which you have just expressed, as a member of the senate, and the consistent conduct by which you have supported your principles, are worthy of you; and, allow me to say, of your education."

Vivian felt exalted in his own opinion by such praise, and by these the warmest expressions he had ever received of Russell's regard. He forgot even his domestic uneasiness; and this day, the first for many months he had spent happily, he passed with his friend. They supped together, and related mutually all that happened since their parting. Russell told Vivian that he had lately been agreeably surprised by the gift of a valuable living from the Bishop of —, Lady Julia Lidhurst's uncle; that the bishop, whom he had till then never seen, had written to him in the handsomest manner, saying that he knew the obligations his family owed to Mr. Russell; that it had been the dying request of his nephew, Lord Lidhurst, that some token of the family esteem and gratitude should be offered to him, to whom they owed so much; but the bishop added, that neither family gratitude nor private friendship could have induced him to bestow church preferments upon any but the person whose character best entitled him to such a distinction and such a trust.

This letter, as Vivian observed, was well calculated to satisfy Russell's conscience and his delicacy. The conversation next turned upon Lady Julia Lidhurst. Russell was not aware that Vivian knew more of her attachment to him than what had been discovered the day before he left Glistonbury; and Vivian could not help admiring the honourable and delicate manner in which his friend spoke of her, without any air of mystery, and with the greatest respect. He told Vivian he had heard that proposals had been lately made to her ladyship by a gentleman of great talents and of high character; but that she had positively declined his addresses, and had repeated her declaration that she would never marry. Her good uncle left her, on this point, entirely at liberty, and did not mention the proposal to Lord Glistonbury, lest she should be exposed to any fresh difficulties. Russell expressed much satisfaction at this part of the bishop's conduct, as being not only the most kind, but the most judicious, and the most likely to dispose his niece to change her determination. He repeated his opinion that, united to a man of sense and strength of mind, she would make a charming and excellent wife. Vivian agreed with him; yet observed, that he was convinced she would never marry—There he paused.—Could Lady Julia herself have overheard the conversation which afterwards passed between these two gentlemen, one of whom she had loved and the other of whom she had refused, not a word would have hurt her feelings: on the contrary, she would have been raised in her own opinion, and gratified by the strong interest they both showed for her happiness. They regretted only that a young woman of such talents, and of such a fine, generous disposition, had been so injudiciously educated.

"And now, my dear Russell," cried Vivian, "that we have finished the chapter of Lady Julia, let us talk of Miss Sidney."—Russell's change of countenance showed that it was not quite so easy for him to talk upon this subject.—To spare him the effort, Vivian resumed, "As you are a rich man now, my dear Russell, you will certainly marry; and I know," added he, smiling, "that Miss Sidney will be your wife. If ever man deserved such a prize, you do; and I shall be the first to wish you joy."

"Stay, my good friend," interrupted Russell; "your kindness for me, and your imagination, are too quick in this anticipation of my happiness."—Russell then told him, that he never had declared his attachment to Selina till Vivian's marriage had put an end to all probability of rivalship with his friend. She had expressed high esteem for Russell, but had told him, that she had suffered so much from a first unfortunate attachment, that she felt averse from any new engagements.

"Shall I assure you, as you assured me just now with regard to Lady Julia," said Vivian, "that Miss Sidney will he prevailed upon to alter her determination; and shall I add, that, though I should like Lady Julia the less, I should like Selina the better, for changing her mind?"—He went on, generously expressing sincere hopes, that his friend might obtain Selina Sidney's affections, and might enjoy that domestic happiness, which—Vivian was going to say, which he had himself forfeited; but checking this regret, he only said— "that domestic happiness, which I consider as the summit of human felicity, and which no man can deserve better than you do, my dear Russell."

Russell easily guessed that poor Vivian had not attained this summit of human felicity by his own marriage, but never adverted to any of the conversations they had held about Lady Sarah Lidhurst; never recalled any of Vivian's vehement declarations concerning the absolute impossibility of his making such a match; never evinced the least surprise at his marriage; nor inquired how he had conquered his passion for Lady Julia. With friendly forgetfulness, he seemed to have totally obliterated from his mind all that it could do no good to remember. Vivian was sensible of this delicacy, and grateful for it; but to imitate Russell's reserve and silence upon certain subjects required a force, a forbearance of which he was not capable. At first he had determined not to say one word to Russell of domestic uneasiness; but they had not been many hours together before Vivian poured forth all his complaints, and confessed how bitterly he repented his marriage: be declared that he had been persuaded, by the united efforts of her family and of his mother, against his own judgment, or, at least, against his taste and inclinations, to marry Lady Sarah.

"By whatever persuasions, or by whatever motives, your choice was decided," interrupted Russell, "reflect that it is decided for life; therefore abide by it, and justify it. Above all, make yourself happy with the means which are yet in your power, instead of wasting your mind in unavailing regret. You are united to a woman who has every estimable quality, as you candidly acknowledge: there are some particulars in which she does not please your taste; but withdraw your attention from these, and you will be happy with a wife who is so firmly attached to you. Consider, besides, that—romance apart— love, though a delightful passion, is not the only resource which a man of sense, virtue, and activity may find for happiness. Your public duties, your success, and your reputation as a public character, will—"

Russell was interrupted in this consolatory and invigorating speech, by the entrance of a servant of Lord Glistonbury's, who brought a note from his lordship to Mr. Vivian, requesting to see him as soon as he could make it convenient to come to Glistonbury House, as his lordship wanted to speak to him on particular business of the greatest importance. Vivian was provoked by being thus summoned away from his friend, to attend to one of what he called Lord Glistonbury's important mysteries about nothing. Russell was engaged to go into the country the ensuing day, to take possession of his new living; but he promised that he would see him again soon; and, with this hope, the two friends parted.

Vivian went to Lord Glistonbury's: he found his lordship in his study. "Where have you been, Vivian?" exclaimed he: "I have sent messenger after messenger to look for you, half over the town: I thought you were to have dined with us, but you ran away, and nobody could tell where, or with whom; and we have been waiting for you at our cabinet council here with the utmost impatience."—Vivian answered, that he had unexpectedly met with his friend Russell; and was proceeding to tell his lordship how handsomely the Bishop of—had provided for his friend; but Lord Glistonbury, like many other great men, having the habit of forgetting all the services of those from whom they have nothing more to expect, cut short Vivian's narration, by exclaiming, "True, true! well, well! that's all over now—Certainly, that Russell did his duty by my poor son; and acted as he ought to do—in all things; and I'm glad to hear my brother has given him a good living; and I hope, as you say, he will soon be married—so best—so best, you know, Vivian, for reasons of our own—Well! well! I'm glad he is provided for—not but what that living would have been of essential service, if it had been reserved for a friend of mine—but my brother the bishop never can enter into any political views—might as well not have a brother a bishop— But, however, Mr. Russell's a friend of yours—I am not regretting—not so rude to you to regret—on the contrary, rejoice, particularly as Mr. Russell is a man of so much merit—But all that's over now; and I want to talk to you upon quite another matter. You know I have always said I should, sooner or later, succeed in my grand object, hey, Vivian?"

"Your lordship's grand object?—I am not sure that I know it."

"Oh, surely, you know my grand object. You my son-in-law, and forget my grand object?—The marquisate, you know; the marquisate, the marquisate! Did not I always tell you that I would make government, sooner or later, change my earldom into a marquisate? Well! the thing is done—that is, as good as done; they have sent to treat with me upon my own terms."

"I give you joy, my dear lord!" said Vivian.

"Joy!—to be sure you do, my sober sir:—one would think you had no concern or interest in the business. Joy! to be sure you give me joy; but, I can tell you, you must give me something more than joy—you must give me support."

"How he looks!" continued Lord Glistonbury, "as if he did not know what is meant by support. Vivian, did you never hear of parliamentary support?"

"I hope, my dear lord," replied Vivian, gravely, "that you have not entered into any engagements, or made any promises for me, which I cannot have it in my power to perform."

Lord Glistonbury hesitated in some confusion; and then, forcing a look of effrontery, in an assured tone, replied, "No. I have not made any engagements or promises for you which you cannot perform, Vivian, I am clear; nor any which I have not a right to expect my son-in-law will confirm with alacrity."

"What have you engaged?—what have you promised for me, my lord?" said Vivian, earnestly.

"Only, my dear boy," said Lord Glistonbury, assuming a facetious tone, "only that you will be always one of us—And are not you one of us?—my son-in-law?—the deuce is in it if he is not one of us!—In short, you know, to be serious, a party must go together, that is, a family party must go together; and, if a ministry do my business, of course I do theirs. If I have my marquisate, they have my votes."

"But not my vote—pardon me, my lord—my vote cannot be bartered in this manner."

"But, you know, Mr. Vivian, you know it is for your interest as much as for mine; for, you know, the marquisate will probably descend, in due course of time, to your son. So your interest is full as much concerned as mine; and besides, let me tell you, I have not forgotten your immediate interest: I have stipulated that you should have the valuable place which Mr. C— was to have had."

All that Russell had said of public virtue was fresh in our hero's mind. "I thank you, my dear lord," said he; "for I am sure this was kindly intended; but I am not one of those persons, who in public affairs think only of their private interest—I am not thinking of my interest. But if a man maintains certain public measures one day, and the next, for valuable consideration, supports diametrically opposite opinions and measures, he will lose, and deserve to lose, all reputation for integrity."

"Integrity! political integrity!" said Lord Glistonbury; "fine words, which mean nothing. Behind the scenes, as we are now, Vivian, what use can there be in talking in that strain?—Between you and me, you know this is all nonsense. For who, of any party, now thinks, really and truly, of any thing but getting power or keeping it? Power, you know, stands for the measure of talent; and every thing else worth having is included in that word power. I speak plainly. And as honour is merely an affair of opinion, and opinion, again, an affair of numbers, and as there are numbers enough to keep one in countenance in these things; really, my dear Vivian, it is quite childish, quite boyish, smells of the lamp. To declaim about political integrity, and all that, is not the language of a man who knows any thing of business—any thing of the world.—But why do I say all this?" cried Lord Glistonbury, checking himself and assuming an air of more reserved displeasure.—"Mr. Vivian certainly knows all this as well as I do; I know how my nephew Marmaduke, who, with all his faults, is no fool, would interpret your present language: he would say, as I have often heard him say, that political integrity is only a civil put off."

"Political integrity only a civil put off!" repeated Vivian, with unfeigned astonishment. When he formerly heard similar sentiments from the avowed profligate and hackneyed politician Mr. Wharton, he was shocked; but to hear them repeated, as being coolly laid down by so young a man as Mr. Lidhurst, excited so much disgust and contempt in Vivian's mind, that he could hardly refrain from saying more than either prudence or politeness could justify.

"Now I am free to confess," pursued Lord Glistonbury, "that I should think it more candid and manly, and, I will add, more friendly, and more the natural, open conduct of a son-in-law to a father-in-law, instead of talking of political integrity, to have said, at once, I cannot oblige you in this instance."

"Surely, my lord, you cannot be in earnest?" said Vivian.

"I tell you, sir, I am in earnest," cried his lordship, turning suddenly in a rage, as he walked up and down the room; "I say, it would have been more candid, more manly, more every thing,—and much more like a son-in-law—much!—much!—I am sure, if I had known as much as I do now, sir, you never should have been my son-in-law—never! never!—seen Lady Sarah in her grave first!—I would!—I would!—yes, sir—I would!—And you are the last person upon earth I should have expected it from. But I have a nephew—I have a nephew, and now I know the difference. No man can distinguish his friends till he tries them."

Vivian in vain endeavoured to appease Lord Glistonbury by assurances that he would do any thing in his power to oblige him, except what he himself considered as dishonourable: his lordship reiterated, with divers passionate ejaculations, that if Vivian would not oblige him in this point, on which he had set his heart—where the great object of his life was at stake—he could never believe he had any regard for him; and that in short, it must come to an open rupture between them, for that he should never consider him more as his son. Having uttered this denunciation as distinctly as passion would permit, Lord Glistonbury retired to rest.

Vivian went immediately to his mother, to tell her what had passed, and he felt almost secure of her approbation; but though she praised him for his generous spirit of independence, yet it was evident the hopes that the title of marquis might descend to a grandson of her own weighed more with her than any patriotic considerations. She declared, that indeed she would not, for any title, or any thing upon earth, have her son act dishonourably; but what was asked of him, as far as she could understand, was only such a change of party, such compliances, as every public man in his place would make: and though she would not have him, like some she could name, a corrupt tool of government, yet, on the other hand, it was folly to expect that he alone could do any thing against the general tide of corruption—that it would be madness in him to sacrifice himself entirely, without the slightest possibility of doing any good to his country.

Vivian interrupted her, to represent that, if each public man argued in this manner, nothing could ever be accomplished for the public good: that, on the contrary, if every man hoped that something might be done, even by his individual exertion, and if he determined to sacrifice a portion of his private interest in the attempt, perhaps much might be effected.

"Very likely!" Lady Mary said. She confessed she knew little of politics: so from argument she went to persuasion and entreaties. She conjured him not to quarrel with the Glistonburys, and not to provoke Lord Glistonbury's displeasure. "I see all that artful Marmaduke's schemes," said she: "he knows his uncle's pertinacious temper; and he hopes that your notions of patriotism will prevent you from yielding on a point, on which his uncle has set his heart. Marmaduke will know how to take advantage of all this, believe me!"

Vivian was shaken in his resolution by his mother's entreaties—by the idea of all the family quarrels that would ensue, and of all the difficulties in which he might be involved, if he persisted in his generous determination.

"My dear son," resumed she, "it would be absolute madness to refuse the place that is now offered you: only consider the situation of your affairs—consider, I beseech you, the distress you will be in by and by, if you reject this offer—recollect the immense demands upon you; recollect that heap of bills for the election, and for the buildings, and all the poor workmen about the castle! and that coachmaker too! and remember, the purchase money of the house in town must be paid in three months. And the only possible means by which you can get out of debt, is by accepting this place, which would put you at ease at once, and enable you to continue in the style of life to which you have of late been accustomed."

"As to that, I could alter my style of life—I would do any thing," cried Vivian, "to pay my debts and preserve my independence. I will alter my mode of living, and retrench decidedly and vigorously."

"Well, my dear son, I admire your spirit, and, if you can do this, it will certainly be best; but I fear that when it comes to the trial, you will not be able to persevere."

"I shall—I shall! Believe me, mother, I have resolution enough for this—you do me injustice," said Vivian.

"No, my dear Charles, I do you justice; for I do not doubt your resolution, as far as your own privations are concerned; but, consider your wife—consider Lady Sarah—consider the luxury in which she has always been accustomed to live, and the high sphere in which her relations move! How her pride would be hurt by their looking down upon her! I have no doubt Lady Sarah would do her duty, and make any sacrifices for her husband; and if you were—I must now speak plainly—if you were passionately fond of her—an all-for-love husband—you could, with honour and propriety, accept of such sacrifices; but what would retirement be to poor Lady Sarah, and with Lady Sarah?"

Vivian told his mother that he would take a night to reconsider the matter coolly; and, satisfied with having gained so much, she suffered him to go home. As he was quitting his own dressing-room, he paused, to consider whether he should consult his wife, who was, as yet, in ignorance of the whole transaction, and who knew nothing of the deranged state of his affairs. He did her the justice to believe that she would be willing to live with him in retirement, and to forego all the luxuries and pride of her rank, for the sake of her duty and of her love. He was convinced that, in any opposition between her father's interests and her husband's honour, she would strongly abide by her husband. He recollected all Lady Julia had said of the advantage that her sister's firmness of mind might be in steadying his vacillating temper in any moment of trial. Here was the first great occasion, since his marriage, where his wife's strength of mind could be of essential service to him: yet he hesitated whether he should avail himself of this advantage; and every moment, as he approached nearer to her apartment, he hesitated more and more; He did not, in the first place, like to humble himself so far as to ask her counsel; then he had not courage to confess those debts and embarrassments which he had hitherto concealed. All that his mother had suggested about the indelicacy of requiring or accepting great sacrifices from a woman whom, though he esteemed, he could not love—the horror of retirement with such a companion—the long years tête-à-tête—all these ideas combined, but chiefly the apprehension of the immediate present pain of speaking to her on a disagreeable subject, and of being obliged to hear her speak with that formal deliberation which he detested; added to this, the dread of her surprise, if not of her reproaches, when all his affairs should be revealed, operated so irresistibly upon his weakness, that he decided on the common resource—concealment. His hand was upon the lock of his chamber-door, and he turned it cautiously and softly, lest, in entering his apartment, he should waken Lady Sarah: but she was not asleep.

"What can have kept you so late, Mr. Vivian?" said she.

"Business, my dear," answered he, with some embarrassment.

"May I ask what sort of business?"

"Oh!—only—political business."

"Political business!" She looked earnestly at her husband; but, as if repressing her curiosity, she afterwards added, "our sex have nothing to do with politics," and, turning away from the light, she composed herself to sleep.

"Very true, my dear," replied Vivian—not a word more did he say: content with this evasion of the difficulty, he thus, by his weakness, deprived himself of the real advantage of his wife's strength of mind. Whilst Lady Sarah, in total ignorance of the distress of her husband, slept in peace, he lay awake, revolving painful thoughts in the silence of the night. All that his mother had said about the pecuniary difficulties to which they must soon be reduced recurred with fresh force; the ideas of the unpaid election bills, all the masons', carpenters', painters', glaziers', and upholsterers' bills, with "thousands yet unnamed behind," rose, in dreadful array, before him, and the enthusiasm of his patriotism was appalled. With feverish reiteration, he ran over and over, in his mind, the same circle of difficulties, continually returning to the question, "Then what can be done?" Bitterly did he this night regret the foolish expenses into which he had early in life been led. If it were to do over again, he certainly would not turn his house into a castle; if he had foreseen how much the expense would surpass the estimates, assuredly nothing could have tempted him to such extravagance. The architect, the masons, the workmen, one and all, were knaves; but, one and all, they must be paid. Then what could he do?—And the debts incurred by the contested elections!—contested elections are cursed things, when the bills come to be paid; but, cursed or not, they must be paid. Then what could he do?—The distress in which he should involve his generous mother—the sacrifices he should require from his wife—the family quarrels—all that Lady Sarah would suffer from them—the situation of his wife. Then what could he do?—He MUST submit to Lord Glistonbury, and take the place that was offered to him.

Vivian sighed—and turned in his bed—and sighed—and thought—and turned—and sighed again—and the last sigh of expiring patriotism escaped him!—To this end, to this miserable end, must all patriotism come, which is not supported by the seemingly inferior virtues of prudence and economy.

Poor Vivian endeavoured to comfort himself by the reflection that he should not act from merely mercenary considerations, but that he was compelled to yield to the solicitations of his mother and of his father-in-law; that he was forced to sacrifice his own public opinions to secure domestic peace, and to prevent the distress of his mother, the misery, and perhaps danger, of his wife and child. Dereliction of principle, in these circumstances, was something like an amiable, a pardonable weakness. And then, see it in what light you will, as Lord Glistonbury observed, "there are so many who will keep a patriot in countenance now-a-days, for merely changing sides in politics. A man is not even thought to be a man of talents till he gets something by his talents. The bargain he makes—the price he gains—is, in most people's estimation, the value of the public man."

All this Vivian said to himself to quiet his conscience; and all this, he knew, would be abundantly satisfactory to the generality of people with whom he associated; therefore, from them he could fear neither reproach nor contempt: but he could not bear even to think of Russell—he felt all the pangs of remorse, and agony of shame, as the idea of such a friend came into his mind. Again he turned in his bed, and groaned aloud—so loud, that Lady Sarah wakened, and, starting up, asked what was the matter; but receiving no answer, she imagined that she had been in a dream, or that her husband had spoken in his sleep. He groaned no more, nor did he even sigh: but fatigued with thinking and with feeling, he at last fell into a sort of slumber, which lasted till it was time to rise. Before Vivian was dressed, Lord Glistonbury called upon him—he went into his dressing-room. His lordship came with his best address, and most courteous face of persuasion; he held out his hand, in a frank and cordial manner, as he entered, begging his dear son's pardon for the warmth and want of temper, he was free to confess, he had shown last night; but he was persuaded, he said, that Vivian knew his sincere regard for him, and convinced that, in short, they should never essentially differ: so that he was determined to come to talk the matter over with him when they were both cool; and that he felt assured that Vivian, after a night's reflection, would always act so as to justify his preference of his son-in-law to his nephew, hey, Vivian?—Lord Glistonbury paused for an answer—Vivian cut himself as he was shaving, and was glad of a moment's reprieve; instead of answering, he only exclaimed, "Cursed razor! cut myself!—My lord, won't you sit down? will you do me the honour to—"

Lord Glistonbury seated himself; and, in regular order, with his tiresome parade of expletives, went through all the arguments that could be adduced to prove the expediency of Vivian's taking this place, and assisting him, as he had taken it for granted his son-in-law would, on such an occasion. The letters of the great and little men who had negotiated the business of the marquisate were then produced, and an account given of all that had passed in confidence; and Lord Glistonbury finished by saying that the affair was absolutely concluded, he having passed his word and pledged his honour for Vivian; that he would not have spoken or acted for him if he had not felt that he was, when acting for his son-in-law, in fact acting for himself—his second self; that there had been no time to wait, no possibility of consulting Vivian; that the whole plan was suggested yesterday, in two hours after the house broke up, and was arranged in the evening; that search and inquiries had been made every where for Vivian; but, as he could not be found, Lord Glistonbury said he had ventured to decide for him, and, as he hoped, for his interest and for that of the family; and the thing, now done, could not be undone: his lordship's word was sacred, and could not be retracted.

Vivian, in a feeble, irresolute tone, asked if there was no possibility of his being allowed to decline the place that was offered him, and suggested that he could take a middle course; to avoid voting against his lordship's wishes, he could, and he believed that he would, accept of the Chiltern Hundreds, and go out of parliament for the session.

Lord Glistonbury remonstrated against what he termed the madness of the scheme.

"A man like you, my dear Vivian, who have distinguished yourself so much already in opposition, who will distinguish yourself so much more hereafter in place and in power—"

"No," said Vivian, rising as he finished shaving himself; "no, my lord, I shall never more distinguish myself, if I abandon the principles I believe to be just and true. What eloquence I have—if I have any—

has arisen from my being in earnest: I shall speak ill—I shall not be able to speak at all—when I get up against my conscience."

"Oh!" said Lord Glistonbury, laughing, "your romantic patriotism may be very nice in its feelings; but, believe me, it will not deprive you of the use of your speech. Look at every one of the fine orators of our times, and name me one, if you can, who has not spoken, and spoken equally well, on both sides of the house; ay, and on both sides of most political questions. Come, come, you'll find you will get on quite as well as they got on before you, hey?"

"You will find that I shall be of no use to you—that I shall be a dead weight on your hands."

"You a dead weight! you, who are formed to be—now, really, without flattery—you know there's no occasion for flattery between you and me—to be the soul, and, in time, the head of a party—Stay!—I know all you are going to say, but give me leave to judge—You know there's my own nephew, a very clever young man, no doubt, he is allowed to be; and yet, you see, I make no comparison between you. I assure you I am a judge in these matters, and you see the house has confirmed my judgment; and, what is more—for I can keep nothing from you—if it won't make you too vain, and make you set too high a price upon yourself, which will be very troublesome in the present case; but, I say, be that as it may, I will frankly own to you, that I believe you have been of essential service in procuring me this great favourite object of my life, the marquisate."

"I, my lord! impossible!—for I never took the slightest step toward procuring it."

"Pardon me, you took the most effectual step, without knowing it, perhaps. You spoke so well in opposition, that you made it the interest of ministry to muzzle you; and there was no way so effectual of getting at you as through me, I being your father-in-law and you my heir. You don't see the secret concatenation of these things with a glance as I do, who have been used to them so long. And there was no way of coming to the point with me without the marquisate—that was my sine qua non; and you see I gained my point—by your means, chiefly, I am free to allow—though Marmaduke would gladly persuade me it was by his negotiating. But I do you justice; I did you justice, too, in more than words, when I stipulated for that place for you, which, in fact, I knew you could not go on much longer without. So, my dear Vivian, all this explained to our mutual satisfaction, we have nothing more to do but to shake hands upon it and go down stairs; for I have engaged myself and Secretary—to breakfast with you, and he has full powers, and is to carry back our capitulation—and," continued Lord Glistonbury, looking out of the window, "here's our friend's carriage."

"Oh, my lord, it is not yet too late!" cried Vivian; "it may yet be arranged otherwise. Is there no way—no possibility—"

A loud knock at the house door.

"I wish to Heaven, my lord!—"

"So do I wish to Heaven, with all my soul, that you would finish this nonsense, my dear Vivian, and come down to breakfast. Come, come, come!—Hey, hey, hey!—This is absolutely too ridiculous, and I must go, if you don't. Only consider a political breakfast of this nature!"

Lord Glistonbury hurried down stairs:—reluctantly, and with a heavy heart and repugnant conscience, Vivian followed. At this instant, he wished for Russell, to prevent what he knew would be the consequence of this interview. But Russell was absent—the keeper of his conscience, the supporter of his resolution, was not at hand. Woe to him who is not the keeper of his own conscience—the supporter of his own resolution! The result of this political breakfast was just what every reader, who knows the world but half as well as Lord Glistonbury knew it, has probably long since anticipated. The capitulation of the patriots of the Glistonbury band, with Vivian at their head, was settled. Lord Glistonbury lost no character by this transaction, for he had none to lose—he was quite at his ease, or quite callous. But Vivian bartered, for a paltry accommodation of his pecuniary difficulties, a reputation which stood high in the public opinion—which was invaluable in his own—which was his last stake of happiness. He knew this—he felt it with all the anguish of exquisite but USELESS sensibility.

Lord Glistonbury and his new friend, Secretary —, who was a man of wit as well as a politician, rallied Vivian upon his gravity and upon his evident depression of spirits.

"Really, my dear Vivian," cried Lord Glistonbury, "my patience is now exhausted, and I must not let you expose yourself here, before our friend, as a novice—Hey! hey!—Why, will you never open your eyes, and see the world as it is! Why! what!—Did you never read the fable of the dog and his master's meat?—Well! it is come to that now in England; and he is a foolish dog, indeed, who, when he can't save the meat, won't secure his share—hey?"

His lordship and the secretary laughed in concert.

"Look, how Vivian preserves his solemnity!" continued Lord Glistonbury; "and he really looks as if he was surprised at us. My dear Vivian, it requires all my knowledge of your bonne foi to believe that you are in earnest, and not acting the part of a patriot of older times."

"Oh!" cried the secretary, with a facetious air, "Mr. Vivian assuredly knows, as well as we do, that—

'A patriot is a fool in ev'ry age, Whom all lord chamberlains allow the stage.'

But off the stage we lay aside heroics, or how should we ever get on?—Did you hear, my lord," continued the secretary, turning to Lord Glistonbury, "that there is another blue riband fallen in to us by the death of Lord G—?"

"I had a great regard for poor Lord G—. Many applications, I suppose, for the vacant riband?"

From the vacant riband they went on to talk over this man's pension and the other man's job; and considered who was to get such and such a place when such and such a person should resign or succeed to something better. Then all the miserable mysteries of ministerial craft were unveiled to Vivian's eyes. He had read, he had heard, he had believed, that public affairs were conducted in this manner; but he had never, till now, actually seen it: he was really novice enough still to feel surprise at finding that, after all the fine professions made on all sides, the main, the only object of these politicians, was to keep their own, or to get into the places of others. Vivian felt every moment his disgust and his melancholy increase. "And it is with these people I have consented to act! And am I to be hurried along by this stream of corruption to infamy and oblivion! Then Russell—"

Vivian resolved to retract the engagement he had just made with Lord Glistonbury and the secretary, and he waited only for a pause in their conversation to explain himself. But, before any pause occurred, more company came in,—the secretary hurried away, saying to Vivian, who would have stopped him at the door, "Oh, my dear sir, every thing is settled now, and you must be with us in the house to-night— and you will find the whole business will go on as smoothly as possible, if gentlemen will but act together, and strengthen the hands of government. I beg pardon for breaking away—but so many people are waiting for me—and any thing further we can settle when we meet in the house."

Lord Glistonbury also refused to listen to farther explanations—said that all was settled, and that it was impossible to make any recantations.

CHAPTER XV

The hour of going to the House of Commons at length arrived; Lord Glistonbury saw that Vivian was so much out of spirits, and in such confusion of mind, that he began to fear that our hero's own account of himself was just, and that he would not be able to command ideas, or even words, when he was to speak in opposition to what he called his principles and his conscience. "This son of mine, instead of being our great Apollo, will be a dead weight on our hands, unless we can contrive to raise his spirits."

So, to raise his spirits, Lord Glistonbury accompanied him to the coffee-room of the house, and insisted upon his taking some refreshment before he should attempt to speak. His lordship fortified him with bumper after bumper, till at last Vivian came up to the speaking point. He took his seat in his new place in the house, and, endeavouring to brave away the sense of shame, rose to speak. Notwithstanding the assistance of the wine, and the example of Mr. Marmaduke Lidhurst, who spoke before him with undaunted assurance, Vivian could scarcely get on with a hesitating, confused, inconsistent speech, uttered in so low and indistinct a voice, that the reporters in the gallery complained that they could not catch this honourable member's meaning, or that his words did not reach them. Conscious of his failure, and still more conscious of its cause, he retired again to the coffee-room as soon as he had finished speaking, and again Lord Glistonbury plied him with wine, saying that he would find he would do very well in reply presently. It happened that Lord Glistonbury was called away—Vivian remained. Mr. Wharton, with a party of his friends, entered the coffee-room. Wharton seemed much heated both with wine and anger—he was talking eagerly to the gentlemen with him, and he pronounced the words, "Infamous conduct!—Shabby!—Paltry fellow!" so loud, that all the coffee-room turned to listen. Colonel S—, a gentleman who was one of Wharton's party, but who had a good opinion of Vivian, at this moment took him by the arm, and, drawing him aside, whispered, in confidence, that he was persuaded there had been some mistake in the arrangements, which, as it was reported, Lord Glistonbury had just made with the ministry, for that Mr. Wharton and many of his lordship's former party, complained of having been shamefully deserted. "And to break our word and honour to our party, is a thing no gentleman can do. Wharton had a direct promise from his lordship, that he never would come in till he should come in along with him. And now it is confidently said, that Lord Glistonbury has made his bargain for his own marquisate, and provided only for himself, his nephew, and his son-in-law."

Thrown into the utmost consternation by the idea of this double forfeiture of honour, this breach both of public and private faith, Vivian, after thanking Colonel S— for his friendly manner of communicating this information, and declaring that the transaction was totally unknown to him, begged that the colonel would do him the favour and the justice to be present when he should require an explanation from Lord

Glistonbury. To this Colonel S— consented, and they hastened in search of his lordship: his lordship was not to be found; but Mr. Marmaduke Lidhurst was, however, in the coffee-room, and upon Vivian's referring to him, he could not deny the truth of the charge, though he used all his powers of circumlocution to evade giving a direct answer. The shame, the indignation, that rapidly succeeded to each other in Vivian's countenance, sufficiently convinced Colonel S— that he had no share in the private part of this disgraceful transaction; and he very handsomely assured Vivian, that he would set the matter in its true point of view with his friends. Marmaduke soon found a pretence to withdraw—some member was speaking in the house, whom he must hear, he said, and away he went.

At this moment Mr. Wharton, who was walking down the room with his friends, passed by Vivian, and, as he passed, said,

"That private vices are public benefits, we all know; but that public vices are private benefits, some of us, alas! have yet to learn. But I'd have that little, whiffling, most noble and puissant prince expectant, his majesty's right trusty and entirely beloved cousin elect, know, that plain Bob Wharton is not a man to be duped and deserted with impunity."

"Whom does he mean?—What does he mean?" whispered some of the bystanders. "What prince is he talking of?—Which of the princes?"

"Oh! none of the princes," replied another. "You know most noble and puissant prince is the title of a marquis, and our right trusty and entirely beloved cousin, the style in which the king writes to him."

"But who is this marquis expectant?"

"Don't you know?—Lord Glistonbury."

"But some of his lordship's friends ought to take it up, surely."

"Hush!—his son-in-law will hear you."

"Where?"

"There—don't look!"

Vivian was, with reason, so much exasperated by the treacherous duplicity of Lord Glistonbury's conduct, that he was ill inclined to undertake his lordship's defence, and determined to leave it to himself, or to his nephew; yet the whispers operated not a little upon his weakness. Wharton, who was walking with his set up and down the room, again came within Vivian's hearing, and, as he passed, exclaimed, "Public vice! and public virtue! precious, well-matched pair!"

"Who is public vice, and who is public virtue?" said one of Wharton's companions.

"Don't you know?" replied Wharton: "the heir-at-law and the son-in-law."

On hearing this speech, Vivian, who knew that he was one of the persons to whom it alluded, started forward to demand an explanation from Wharton: but Colonel S— held him back. "You are not called upon, by any means, to take notice of this," said the colonel: "Wharton did not address himself to you, and though he might mean what he said for you, yet he speaks under a false impression; and besides, he is not quite sober. Leave it to me, and I will settle it all to your satisfaction before to-morrow." Vivian listened unwillingly and uneasily to the friendly counsel: he was more hurt than he had ever before felt himself by any of Wharton's sarcasms, because there was now in them a mixture of truth; and a man seldom feels more irritable than when he is conscious that he is partly to blame, and apprehensive that others will think him more blameable than he really is. His irritability was increased by the whispers he had heard, and the looks he now perceived among the bystanders: the voice, the opinion of numbers, the fear of what others would think or say, operated against his better judgment.

"Come," said Colonel S—, "let us go and see what they are doing in the house."

Vivian refused to stir, saying that it would be leaving the field to Wharton. Wharton at this instant repassed; and still running the changes, with half-intoxicated wit, upon the same ideas, reiterated, "Public vice!—We all knew where that would end in these days—in public honours; but none of you would believe me, when I told you where public virtue would end—in private treachery!"

"That's neat!—that's strong!—faith, that's home!" whispered some one.

"Mr. Wharton!" cried Vivian, going up to him, "I could not help hearing what you said just now—did you intend it for me?"

"You heard it, it seems, sir, and that is sufficient," replied Wharton, in an insolent tone: "as to what I meant, I presume it is pretty evident; but, if you think it requires any explanation, I am as ready to give as you can be to ask it."

"The sooner the better, then, sir," said Vivian. The two gentlemen walked away together, whilst the spectators exclaimed, "Very spirited indeed!—very right!—very proper!—Vivian could do no less than call him out. But, after all, what was the quarrel about? Which of them was to blame?"

Long before these points were settled, the challenge was given and accepted. Colonel S—, who followed Vivian and Wharton, endeavoured to set things to rights, by explaining that Vivian had been deceived by Lord Glistonbury, and kept totally in the dark respecting the negotiation for the marquisate. But Wharton, aware that by taking up the matter immediately in such a spirited way he should do himself infinite honour with his party, and with that majority of the world who think that the greatest merit of a man is to stand to be shot at, was not at all willing to listen to these representations. Colonel S— declared that, were he in Mr. Wharton's place, he should, without hesitation, make an apology to Mr. Vivian, and publicly acknowledge that what he said in the coffee-room was spoken under a false impression, which a plain statement of facts had totally removed: but Wharton disdained all terms of accommodation; his policy, pride, and desire of revenge, all conspired to produce that air of insolent determination to fight, which, with some people, would obtain the glorious name of COURAGE. By this sort of courage can men of the most base and profligate characters often put themselves in a moment upon an equal footing with men of principle and virtue!

It was settled that Mr. Wharton and Vivian should meet, at eight o'clock the next morning, in a field near town. Colonel S— consented to be Vivian's second. Russell was not yet returned—not expected till ten the next day.

Left to his cool reflection, Vivian thought with horror of the misery into which the event of this duel might involve all with whom he was connected, and all who were attached to him. The affair was of course to be kept a secret from all at Glistonbury House, where Vivian was engaged to dine with a large ministerial party. He went home to dress, hoping to have a quarter of an hour to himself; but, on entering his own dressing-room, he, to his surprise and mortification, found his wife seated there, waiting for him with a face of anxious expectation; a case of newly-set diamonds on a table beside her. "I thought you were at your father's, my dear: are you not to be at Glistonbury House to-day?" said Vivian.

"No," replied Lady Sarah. "Surely, Mr. Vivian, you know that my father gives a political dinner, and I suppose you are to be there?"

"Oh, yes!" cried Vivian; "I did not know what I was saying—I am to be there, and must dress (looking at his watch), for I have no time to spare."

"Be that as it may, I must intrude upon your time for a few minutes," said Lady Sarah.

Vivian stood impatiently attentive, whilst Lady Sarah seemed to find it difficult to begin some speech which she had prepared.

"Women, I know, have nothing to do with politics," she began in a constrained voice; but, suddenly quitting her air and tone of constraint, she started up and exclaimed, "Oh, my dear, dear husband! what have you done?—No, no, I cannot, will not believe it, till I hear it from your OWN lips!"

"What is the matter, my dear Lady Sarah?—You astonish and almost alarm me!" said Vivian, endeavouring to preserve composure of countenance.

"I will not—Heaven forbid that I should alarm you as I have been alarmed!" said Lady Sarah, commanding her voice again to a tone of tranquillity. "I ought, and, if I were not weak, should be convinced that there is no reason for alarm. There has been some mistake, no doubt; and I have been to blame for listening to idle reports. Let me, however, state the facts. Half an hour ago, I was at Gray's the jeweller's, to call for my poor mother's diamonds, which, you know, he has reset—"

"Yes—Well!"

"And whilst I was in the shop, a party of gentlemen came in, all of them unknown to me, and, of course, I was equally unknown to them; for they began to speak of you in a manner in which none knowing me could venture in my presence. They said—I cannot bear to repeat or to think of what they said—you cannot have bartered your public reputation for a marquisate for my father!—You cannot have done that which is dishonourable—you cannot have deserted your party for a paltry place for yourself!—You turn pale.—I wish, if it pleased God, that I was this moment in my grave!"

"Heaven forbid, my dear Lady Sarah!" cried Vivian, forcing a smile, and endeavouring to speak in a tone of raillery. "Why should you wish to be in your grave, because your husband has just got a good warm place? Live! live!" said he, raising her powerless hand; "for consider—as I did—and this consideration was of no small weight with me—consider, my dear Sarah, how much better you will live for it!"

"And you did consider me? And that did weigh with you?"

"—Oh, this is what I dreaded most!" cried Lady Sarah.—"When will you know my real character? When will you have confidence in your wife, sir? When will you know the power, the unconquered, unconquerable power of her affection for you?"

Vivian, much struck by the strength of her expression as she uttered these words, was a moment silent in astonishment; and then could only, in an incoherent manner, protest, that he did know—that he had always done justice to her character—that he believed in her affection—and had the greatest confidence in its power.

"No, sir, no!—Do not say that which I cannot credit!—You have not confidence in the power of my affection, or you would never have done this thing to save me pain. What pain can be so great to me as the thought of my husband's reputation suffering abasement?—Do you think that, in comparison with this, I, your wife, could put the loss of a service of plate, or house in town, or equipage, or servants, or such baubles as these?" added she, her eyes glancing upon the diamonds; then, snatching them up, "Take them, take them!" cried she; "they were my mother's; and if her spirit could look down from heaven upon us she would approve my offer—she would command your acceptance. Then here on my knees I conjure you, my beloved husband, take them—sell them—sell plate, furniture, house, equipage, sell every thing rather than your honour!"

"It is sold," said Vivian, in a voice of despair.

"Redeem it, redeem it at any price!" cried Lady Sarah. "No! I will kneel here at your feet—you shall not raise me—till I have obtained this promise, this justice to me, to yourself!"

"It is too late," said Vivian, writhing in agony.

"Never too late," cried Lady Sarah. "Give up the place.—Never too late!—Give up the place—write this moment, and all will be well; for your honour will be saved, and the rest is as nothing in my eyes!"

"High-minded woman!" cried Vivian: "why did not I hear you sooner? Why did not I avail myself of your strength of soul?"

"Use it now—hear me now—let us waste no time in words—here is a pen and ink—write, my dearest husband! and be yourself again."

"You waste the energy of your mind on me," cried Vivian, breaking from Lady Sarah, and striking his forehead violently; "I am not worthy of such attachment! It is done—it cannot be undone: I am a weak, ruined, dishonoured wretch!—I tell you, it CANNOT be undone!"

Lady Sarah rose, and stood in despair. Then, looking up to heaven, she was silent for some moments. After which, approaching her husband, she said, in an altered, calm voice, "Since it cannot be undone, I will urge you no more. But, whether in glory or in shame, you are secure that your wife will abide by you."

Vivian embraced her with a tenderness which he had never before felt. "Excellent woman! in justice to myself, I must tell you," cried he, "that I was deceived into this situation. I CAN say no more!"

At this moment a servant knocked at the door, bringing a message from Lord Glistonbury, to say that all the company were assembled, and that dinner waited for Mr. Vivian.

"You are not in a fit state to go. Shall I send an apology to my father?"

"Oh, no! I must go," cried Vivian, starting up, "I must go, or it will be thought—or it will be suspected—I can't explain it to you, my dear; but I must go—I must appear to-day, and in spirits too, if possible."

He hurried away. A servant delivered to Lady Sarah a number of notes and cards. The notes were notes of congratulation, from many of her acquaintance, upon the report in circulation, that her father was immediately to be a marquis. The cards were from people who were to be at her assembly that night. This was one of her nights, which were usually crowded. Lady Sarah's first wish was to write apologies, and to say that she was not well enough to see company; but, recollecting that her husband had said, "he must appear, and in spirits, too, if possible," she thought that it might be more for their interest, and according to his wishes, that she should see company, and that no appearance of dejection should be discerned in his wife. She prepared herself accordingly, and, with a heavy heart, walked through her splendid apartments, to see whether the decorations had been properly executed.

In the mean time Vivian dined at Lord Glistonbury's, with a large ministerial party. As soon as he could, after dinner, Vivian got away; and Lord Glistonbury attributed his retiring early to the awkwardness he might feel in the company of men whom he had, till now, so violently opposed. This his lordship thought a foolish young man's feeling, which would soon wear away. Vivian returned home, anxious to escape from crowds, and to have some hours of leisure to pass alone; but, the moment he entered his own house, he saw the great staircase lined with roses and orange-trees; he found the rooms lighted up and prepared for company; and Lady Sarah dressed, for the first time, in all her mother's diamonds.

"Good Heavens!—Do you see company to-night?" cried he.

"Yes; for I thought, my dear, that you would wish it."

"I wish it!—Oh! if you knew how I wish to be alone!"

"Then, as no one is yet come, I can still shut my doors, and order them to say that I am not well enough to see company—I am sure it is true. Shall I?"

"No, my dear, it is too late," said Vivian: "I am afraid it is impossible for you to do that."

"Not impossible, if you wish it."

"Well, do as you please."

"Which is most for your interest? I have no other pleasure."

"You are too good to me, and I fear I shall never have it in my power to show you any gratitude—"

"But decide which is best to be done, my dear," said Lady Sarah.

"Why, my dear, I believe you judged rightly—see your friends, and make the best of it: but I can appear only for a moment; I have business of consequence—letters—papers—that must be finished to-night; and I must go now to my study."

"You shall not be interrupted," said Lady Sarah: "I will exert myself as much as possible."

A tremendous knock at the door.—Vivian passed through the saloon, and gained his study, where, after remaining for some time in painful reflection, he was roused by hearing the clock strike twelve. He recollected that he had several arrangements to make in his affairs this night; and that it was incumbent on him to sign and execute a will, which had been for some time in his possession, with certain blanks not yet filled up. His wife was, by his marriage settlements, amply provided for; but he inserted in his will some clauses which he thought would add to her peculiar comfort, and took care to word them so that his respect and esteem should be known hereafter to all the world; and that, if he died, he should leave her the consolation of knowing that his last feelings for her were those of gratitude and affection. To his mother he left all that was in his power to contribute to the ease of her declining years—often obliged to pause whilst he wrote, overcome by the thoughts of what her grief would be if he died. He left his friend Russell in remainder, to a considerable part of his estate; and he was just adding the bequest of certain books, which they had read together in his better days, when the door of the study suddenly opened, and his mother entered.

"What is all this?" cried she: "immersed in papers at such a time as this!"

"I so hate crowded assemblies," said Vivian, huddling his papers together, and advancing to meet his mother.

"So do I," said Lady Mary; "but I have been waiting with exemplary patience where I was stationed by Lady Sarah, at the card-table, every instant expecting your arrival, that I might have a few minutes' conversation with you, and inquire how matters went on at the house, and congratulate—"

Before she had finished the word congratulate, she stopped short; for she had, by this time, a full view of her son's countenance: and she knew that countenance so well, that it was impossible to disguise it so as to deceive her maternal penetration.

"My dear son!" said she, "something is going wrong: I conjure you, tell me what is the matter!"—Her eye glanced upon the parchments, and she saw that it was a will. Vivian forced a laugh; and asked her if she had the weakness some people felt, of disliking to see a will, or of fancying that a man was going to die if he made his will. Then, to quiet her apprehensions, and to put a stop to her farther inquiries, he threw aside his papers, and returned with her to the company, where he exerted himself to appear as gay as the occasion required. Lord Glistonbury, who had called in for a few moments, was now playing the great man, as well as his total want of dignity of mind and manners would permit; he was answering, in whispers, questions about his marquisate, and sustaining with all his might his new part of the friend of government. Every thing conspired to strike Vivian with melancholy—yet he constrained himself so far, that his charming spirits delighted all who were uninterested in observing any but the external signs of gaiety; but his mother saw that his vivacity was forced. She made inquiries from all the gentlemen of her acquaintance about what had passed the preceding day both at the House of Commons, and to-day at the dinner at Lord Glistonbury's: but those who had been at Lord Glistonbury's dinner assured her that every thing had been as amicable as could be; and his ministerial friends said that every thing had gone on as smoothly as possible at the house: of what had passed between Mr. Wharton and Vivian in the coffee-room nobody could give her an account. Baffled, but not satisfied, the anxious mother sent to the hotel where Mr. Russell lodged, to inquire whether he was returned to town, and to beg to see him immediately. From him, she thought, she should learn the truth; or, by his influence over her son, she hoped that, if there was any danger of a quarrel, it might be in time prevented. Her servant, however, brought word that Mr. Russell was not expected from the country till ten o'clock the next morning; but that her note would be given to him directly on his arrival. She applied herself next to the study of her daughter's countenance, whilst she asked two or three questions, calculated to discover whether Lady Sarah was under any anxiety about Vivian. But though Lady Sarah's countenance exhibited not the slightest variation under this trial, yet this tranquillity was by no means decisively satisfactory; because, whatever might be her internal agitation, she knew that Lady Sarah could maintain the same countenance. Lady Sarah, who plainly discerned her mother's anxious curiosity, thought it her duty to keep her husband's secrets; and, imagining that she knew the whole truth, was not farther alarmed by these hints, nor did they lead her to suspect the real state of the case.

Lady Mary was at length tolerably well satisfied, by a conversation with her son; during the course of which she settled in her imagination that he had only been inserting in his will a bequest to his friend Russell; and that the depression of his spirits arose from the struggle he had had in determining to vote against his patriotic ideas. She rose to depart; and Vivian, as he conducted her down stairs, and put her into her carriage, could scarcely repress his feelings; and he took so tender a leave of her, that all her apprehensions revived; but there was a cry of "Lady—somebody's carriage!" and Lady Mary's coachman drove on immediately, without giving her time for one word more. After his mother's departure, Vivian, instead of returning to the company, went to his study, and took this opportunity of finishing his will; but as the servants were all in attendance at supper he could not get any body to witness it; and for this he was obliged to wait till a very late hour, when all the company at last departed. The rattle of carriages at length died away; and when all was silence, just as he was about to ring for his witnesses, he heard Lady Sarah's step coming along the corridor towards the study: he went out immediately to meet her, drew her arm within his affectionately, and took two or three turns with her, up and down the empty saloon, whilst a servant was extinguishing the lights. Vivian's mind was so full that he could not speak; and he was scarcely conscious that he had not spoken, till Lady Sarah broke the silence by asking if he had finished his business.

"No, my dear, I have more to do yet; but you will oblige me if you will go to rest—you must be fatigued—mind and body."

"You seem fatigued almost to death," said Lady Sarah: "and cannot you finish the remainder of your business as well to-morrow?"

"No," replied Vivian; "it must be finished before to-morrow. I am bound in duty to finish it before to-morrow."

"If it is a point of duty, I have no more to say," replied Lady Sarah; "but," continued she, in a tone of proud humility, "but if I might so far intrude upon your confidence, as to inquire—"

"Make no inquiries, my dear; for I cannot answer any, even of yours," said Vivian. "And let me beg of you to go to rest; my mind will then be more at ease. I cannot command my thoughts whilst I am anxious about you; and I am anxious—more anxious than ever I was in my life—about you at this moment. You will oblige me if you will go to rest."

"I CANNOT rest, but I will leave you, since you desire it—I have no idle curiosity—Good night!"

"Good night! and thank you once more, my excellent wife, for all your kindness."

"There cannot be a better woman!" said Vivian to himself as she retired. "Why have I not loved her as she deserved to be loved? If I live, I will do my utmost to make her happy—if I live, I will yet repair all. And, if I die, she will have but little reason to deplore the loss of such a husband."

Vivian now executed his will—wrote several letters of business—burnt letters and arranged papers—regretted that Russell, who was to be his executor, was not near him—made many bitter reflections on the past, many good resolutions for the future, in case he should survive; then, overpowered with fatigue of mind, slept for some time, and was awakened by the clock striking seven. By eight o'clock he was at the place appointed—Mr. Wharton appeared a few minutes afterwards. Their seconds having measured out the distance, they took their ground. As Vivian had given the challenge, Wharton had the first fire. He fired—Vivian staggered some paces back, fired his pistol into the air, and fell. The seconds ran to his assistance, and raised him from the ground. The bullet had entered his chest. He stretched out his hand to Mr. Wharton in token of forgiveness, and, as soon as he could speak, desired the seconds to remember that it was he who gave the challenge, and that he thought he deserved to bear the blame of the quarrel. Wharton, callous as he was, seemed struck with pity and remorse: he asked what friends Vivian would wish to have apprised of his situation. A surgeon was in attendance. Vivian, faint from loss of blood, just pronounced Russell's name, and the name of the hotel where he was to be found, adding "nobody else." Wharton rode off, undertaking to find Mr. Russell; and Vivian was carried into a little public-house, by the orders of the surgeon, who thought that he could not bear the motion of a carriage. Wharton met Mr. Russell, who was coming from town. He had come to London earlier than he had intended, and, in consequence of Lady Mary Vivian's note, which he had received immediately on his arrival, had made such inquiries as convinced him that her apprehensions were just; and having discovered the place where the parties were to meet, he had hastened thither, in hopes of preventing the fatal event. The moment he saw Mr. Wharton he knew that he was too late. Without asking any other question than, "Is Vivian alive?" he pressed forwards. The surgeon, who was the next person he saw, gave him no hopes of his friend's recovery, but said he might last till night, or linger perhaps for a day or two. Vivian had by this time recovered his senses and his speech; but when Russell entered the room where he lay, he was so much struck by the grief in his countenance that he could not recollect any one of the many things he had to say. Russell, the firm Russell, was now quite overcome.

"Yes, my dear friend," said Vivian; "this is the end of all your care—of all your hopes of me!—Oh, my poor, poor mother! What will become of her! Where can we find consolation for her!—You and Selina Sidney! You know how fond my mother was of her—how fond she was of my mother—till I, the cause of evil to all my friends, separated them. You must reunite them. You must repair all. This hope—this hope of your happiness, my beloved friend, will soothe my last moments!—How much happier Selina will be with you than—"

Russell sobbed aloud.—"Yes, yield to your feelings, for I know how strong they are," said Vivian: "you, that have always felt more for me than I have ever felt for myself! But it is well for you that my life ends; for I have never been any thing but a torment and a disgrace to you!—And yet I had good dispositions!—but there is no time for regret about myself; I have others to think of, better worth thinking of."

Vivian called for pen, ink, and paper, had himself raised in his bed, and supported, whilst he wrote to Selina, and to his mother.

"Do not stop me," cried he to Russell; "it is the only act of friendship—the only thing I can do in this world now with pleasure, and let me do it."

His notes contained nearly what he had just said to Russell—he put them open into his friend's hand; then, good-natured to the last, Vivian took up his pen again, with no small difficulty, and wrote a few affectionate words to his wife. "She well deserves this from me," said he. "Be a friend to her, Russell— when I am gone, she will, I know, want consolation," After Russell had assured him that he would do all he desired, Vivian said, "I believe there is no one else in the world who will regret my death, except, perhaps, Lady Julia Lidhurst. How generous she was to forgive me!—Tell her, I remembered it when I was dying!—Weakness, weakness of mind!—the cause of all my errors!—Oh, Russell! how well you knew me from the first!—But all is over now!—My experience can be of no use to me—Every thing swims before my eyes.—One comfort is, I have not the blood of a fellow-creature to answer for. My greatest error was making that profligate man my friend—he was my ruin. I little thought, a few years ago, that I should die by his hand—but I forgive him, as I hope to be forgiven myself! Is the clergyman who was sent for come?—My dear Russell, this would be too severe a task for you.—He is come? Then let me see him."

Vivian was left for some time to his private devotions. The clergyman afterwards summoned Russell to return:—he found his friend calmed and resigned. Vivian stretched out his hand—thanked him once more—and expired!

"Oh! worthy of a better fate!" thought Russell.—"With such a heart!—With such talents!—And so young!—With only one fault of character!—Oh, my friend! is it all over?—and all in vain?"

Vivian's mother and widow arrived just at this moment; and Russell and Lord Glistonbury, who followed breathless, could not stop them from entering the apartment. The mother's grief bordered on distraction; but it found relief in tears and cries. Lady Sarah shed no tear, and uttered no exclamation; but advancing, insensible of all opposition, to the bed on which her dead husband lay, tried whether there was any pulse, any breath left; then knelt down beside him in silent devotion. Lord Glistonbury, striking his forehead continually, and striding up and down the room, repeated, "I killed him!—I killed him!—I was the cause of his death!—My victim!—My victim!—But take her away!—Take her away—I cannot.—For mercy's sake, force her away, Mr. Russell!"

"There is no need of force," said Lady Sarah, rising, as her father approached; "I am going to leave my husband for ever."—Then, turning to Mr. Russell, she inquired if his friend had left any message or letter for her—desired to see the letter—retired with it—still without shedding a tear—a few hours afterwards was taken ill, and, before night, was delivered of a dead son.

Lady Sarah survived, but has never since appeared in what is called the WORLD.

Maria Edgeworth was born at Black Bourton, Oxfordshire on January 1st 1768, the second child of Richard Lovell Edgeworth and Anna Maria Edgeworth (née Elers).

Her early years were with her mother's family in England. Sadly, her mother died when Maria was only five. When her father married his second wife, Honora Sneyd, in 1773, the family went to live at his estate, Edgeworthstown, in County Longford, Ireland.

Maria was later sent to Mrs. Lattafière's school in Derby after Honora fell ill in 1775. There she studied dancing, French and other subjects. After Honora died in 1780 Maria's father married Honora's sister, Elizabeth, causing much social disapproved.

Maria transferred to Mrs. Devis's school in Upper Wimpole Street, London. Her father began to focus more attention on Maria in 1781 when she nearly lost her sight to an eye infection.

She returned home to Ireland at 14, and took charge of her younger siblings. She herself was home-tutored by her father in Irish economics and politics, science, literature and law. Despite her youth literature was in her blood.

She became her father's assistant in managing the Edgeworthstown estate, which had become run-down during the family's absence. Maria would now live and write there for the rest of her life.

With her father she began a lifelong academic collaboration. She meticulously detailed daily Irish life; a valuable lodestone of references for later use in her novels. Maria mixed with the Anglo-Irish gentry, and her aunt, Margaret Ruxton of Blackcastle, supplied her with the novels of Anne Radcliffe and William Godwin and encouraged her ambition to write.

Edgeworth's first published work in 1795 was 'Letters for Literary Ladies'. That same year 'An Essay on the Noble Science of Self-Justification', written for a female audience, states that the fair sex is endowed with an art of self-justification and women should use their gifts to continually challenge the force and power of men, especially their husbands, with wit and intelligence.

In 1796 her first children's book, 'The Parent's Assistant', which included the much loved short story 'The Purple Jar' was published.

In 1798 her father married for the fourth and last time, this time to Frances Beaufort. Frances was a year younger than Maria and they quickly became close.

'Practical Education' (1798) is a progressive work on education that combines the ideas of Locke and Rousseau with scientific inquiry. Edgeworth believed that "learning should be a positive experience and that the discipline of education is more important during the formative years than the acquisition of knowledge." The ultimate goal of Edgeworth's system was to create an independent thinker who understands the consequences of his or her actions.

Her first novel, 'Castle Rackrent' (1800) was published anonymously without her father's knowledge. It was an immediate success and firmly established Maria's appeal to the public.

'Belinda' (1801), was her first full-length novel. It dealt with love, courtship, and marriage, and she examined these as conflicts within her "own personality and environment; conflicts between reason and feeling, restraint and individual freedom, and society and free spirit." Startingly, 'Belinda' also included a depiction of interracial marriage between an African servant and an English farm-girl. Later editions of the novel, in line with unforgiving times, removed these sections.

Frances also pushed the family to travel more first London (1800), the Midlands (1802) and later the continent; first to Brussels and then to France. They met all the notables, with Maria even receiving a proposal of marriage from a Swedish courtier.

'Tales of Fashionable Life' (1809 and 1812) is a 2-series collection of short stories that often had its focus on the life of women. The second series was so successful that she was now the most commercially successful novelist of her age and ranked alongside her contemporaries Jane Austen and Sir Walter Scott.

On a visit to London in 1813, she met many notables including Lord Byron. She entered into a long correspondence with Sir Walter Scott after the publication of 'Waverley' in 1814, in which he acknowledged her influence, and they formed a lasting friendship. She visited him in Scotland at Abbotsford House in 1823 and the following year he visited Edgeworthstown.

After debating the issue with the economist David Ricardo, Maria came to believe that better management and the further use of science in agriculture would raise food production and help to lower prices. They were both in favour of Catholic Emancipation, enfranchisement for Catholics without property restrictions, agricultural reform and increased educational opportunities for women.

She worked particularly hard to improve the living standards of the poor in Edgeworthstown and to provide schools for the local children whatever their denomination.

After her father's death in 1817 she edited his memoirs, and extended them with her biographical addenda. Her father had married 4 times and sired 22 children. At the height of her creative endeavours, Maria had written, "Seriously it was to please my Father I first exerted myself to write, to please him I continued."

Maria worked for the relief of the famine-stricken Irish peasants during the Irish Potato Famine. She wrote 'Orlandino' and gave the proceeds to the Relieve Fund. However, during the famine her 'business head' insisted that only those tenants who had paid their full rent would receive any relief. She also punished any tenants who voted against her Tory preferences.

'Helen' (1834) is Maria Edgeworth's final novel, the only one she wrote after her father's death. Here the focus was on characters and situation and not moral lessons.

William Rowan Hamilton was elected president of the Royal Irish Academy and Maria's advice was constantly sought especially regarding literature in Ireland. She suggested that women should be allowed to participate in Academy events. Hamilton made Maria an honorary member in 1837.

After a visit to see her relations Maria was struck with severe chest pains and died suddenly of a heart attack in Edgeworthstown on 22nd May 1849. She was 81.

Maria Edgeworth is buried in the family tomb at St. John's Church, Edgeworthstown, Longford, Ireland.

Letters for Literary Ladies (1795) Second Edition (1798)
An Essay on the Noble Science of Self-Justification (1795)
The Parent's Assistant (1796)
Practical Education (1798) (2 Vols; collaborated with her father and step-mother)
Castle Rackrent (1800) Novel
Early Lessons (1801)
Moral Tales (1801)
Belinda (1801) Novel
The Mental Thermometer (1801)
Essay on Irish Bulls (1802)
Popular Tales (1804)
The Modern Griselda (1804)
Moral Tales for Young People (1805) (6 Vols)
Leonora (1806)
Essays in Professional Education (1809)
Tales of Fashionable Life (1809)
Ennui (1809) Novel
The Absentee (1812) Novel
Patronage (1814) Novel
Harrington (1817) Novel
Ormond (1817) Novel
Comic Dramas (1817)
Memoirs of Richard Lovell Edgeworth (1820) Editor
Rosamond: A Sequel to Early Lessons (1821)
Frank: A Sequel to Frank in Early Lessons (1822)
Tomorrow (1823) Novel
Helen (1834) novel
Orlandino (1848) Temperance novel

www.ingramcontent.com/pod-product-compliance
Lightning Source LLC
Chambersburg PA
CBHW021927170626
46807CB00007B/3012